Strike!

Strike!

MARY HEATON VORSE

Introduction by
DEE GARRISON

UNIVERSITY OF ILLINOIS PRESS
Urbana and Chicago

This book is printed on acid-free paper.

Library of Congress Cataloging-in-Publication Data

Vorse, Mary Heaton, 1874-1966.
  Strike! / Mary Heaton Vorse : introduction by Dee Garrison.
    p. cm.
  Includes bibliographical references.
  ISBN 0-252-06217-5 (pb)
    1. Strikes and lockouts—Textile industry—North Carolina—
Gastonia—History—Fiction. I. Title.
PS3543.088S77 1991
  813'.54—dc20   91-61
                                                             CIP

Contents

PART III

PART IV

Introduction

DEE GARRISON

IN THE SPRING of 1929, the low hill country of the southern Piedmont, where the nation's cotton textile industry was concentrated, became a bloody union battleground. An uprising of female rayon workers began in Elizabethton, Tennessee, and spread within a few weeks through South Carolina and North Carolina. The most famous of these textile strikes occurred at the Loray Mill in Gastonia, North Carolina. Before the strike ended in a paroxysm of mob violence and the arrest of the strike leaders, the name of Gastonia had been trumpeted throughout the world as a symbol of Communist-led class struggle in a brutally hostile environment. Gastonia also survived as a literary event. Six novels published in the early thirties, of which Mary Heaton Vorse's *Strike!* was the first, were inspired by the strike, and the liberal and radical press gave the conflict thorough coverage.[1]

The fame of the Gastonia strike resulted largely from the compelling drama of actual events. The revolt of the textile workers came in a region that had been widely advertised as a refuge from unionism and restrictions on child labor. Beginning in the late nineteenth century, northern capital was drawn into the southern textile towns by the promise of docile laborers who were supposedly happy to escape tenant farms and mountain cabins for steady mill wages. Workers were allegedly content to endure fifty-five hour weeks, steadily increasing work loads, and pay so low that everyone in their families over sixteen normally was expected to enter the mills. Yet on April 1 a revolution was declared in the isolated mill villages near Gastonia. Eighteen hundred impoverished and resentful textile workers went on strike, led by a tiny band of young Communists who had been in town just a few weeks.

The millowners immediately won a court injunction prohibiting all strike activity. Governor Max Gardner rushed in the National Guard to prevent the overthrow of the U.S. government by the dangerous reds. The Gastonia *Daily Gazette* began its vitriolic campaign to incite violence; it warned of the challenge posed by Communist organizers to racial prejudice and Protestant theology—those key supports of the southern economic elite. An employer's handbill gloated: "Would you belong to a union which opposes White Supremacy?" Another circular proclaimed that "Communism will destroy the efforts of Christians of 2000 years."[2]

The ardent young Communist leaders in Gastonia were a hapless lot, forced to operate without adequate funds for strike publicity, relief work, or even food for themselves. They were isolated victims of a furious local elite and a factionalized party. In accord with new directions from Stalin, American Communists believed they were then entering a turbulent "Third Period" during which American workers would initiate a gigantic revolutionary uprising. Internal party affairs had reached a crisis in the spring of 1929, what with the Jay Lovestone and William Foster factions in Moscow fighting through all of April and May.

In mid-April the Gastonia union headquarters was destroyed by a masked mob led by local gentry and composed of townspeople. The National Guard "slept" through the noise of demolition but appeared in time to arrest nine strikers for destroying their own property. On April 20 the state militia was replaced by sheriff's deputies and a local force organized by the Loray Mill. Attacks on strikers intensified. Women pickets from the largely female strike force were beaten and dumped in jail. Because southern workers, unrestrained by state law, were often fully armed, many of the male strikers refused to function as helpless targets and would not picket without their weapons. This meant that women and children were usually the only strikers at Gastonia the organizers dared allow on the dangerous picket line.

Although the strike had virtually collapsed by early May, the mill-owners heightened their violence against the remaining workers who had not returned to the mills. Sixty-two families, including a child suffering from smallpox, were evicted from company-owned housing. On June 7 the local police invaded, without warrants, the tent colony set up by the union to house the evicted strikers. Two of the marauding officers, apparently drunk, had been involved in a shooting spree earlier that day. In the terror and confusion of the attack on the tent colony, both sides fired, the workers believing they were acting in self-defense. Four officers were wounded, including Gastonia's police chief, who died the next day. A mob of two thousand, led by a Gastonia attorney, razed the tent colony. Workers were chased down, threatened with lynching, beaten, and thrown in jail. The northern Communist strike leader, Fred Beal, and fourteen others were charged with conspiracy to incite murder.

The trial began in the presence of the largest press gathering ever in North Carolina, according to the *Nation*. Because state law required that names of prospective jurors be drawn at random by children too young to read or write, the wandering about the courtroom of the jailer's two barefoot children heightened many northern reporters' sense of being present in a weird and alien culture. After 408 challenges, a young, primarily working-class jury was selected. On the first day of the trial, the prosecutor rolled in a life-size mannequin dressed in the dead police chief's blood-stained uniform. With the jury reportedly sympathetic to the defendants, the defense was shattered on September 9 when the judge called a mistrial, the result of one juror's suddenly behaving as though he were insane (the breakdown allegedly induced by the grisly model of the dead police chief).

The mistrial declaration set off another orgy of mob terror. A pack composed of mill superintendents, businessmen, and lawyers for the prosecution, as well as local thugs, wrecked the union headquarters in Gastonia and nearby Bessemer City. The next morning the mob moved on to Charlotte. To the tune of "Praise God from Whom All Blessings Flow," they chased union sympathizers, kidnapped, stripped, and beat a union organizer, and attempted to lynch a union lawyer. Five days later another mob of armed men ambushed a truck full of strikers on their way to a union rally. Ella May Wiggins, a popular striker and an effective local organizer, was killed by a bullet through her chest. Wiggins, who was fated to be immortalized in American labor history, had not been singled out by chance. She was the bard of the Gastonia strikers, singing her mournful mountain ballads that described the workers' struggle. Her effort to organize black workers also made her a prime target for North Carolina justice. Although dozens of people witnessed the murder, her killers were acquitted.

The second trial of seven union leaders opened in the fall of 1929. The prosecution dropped charges against eight of the original defendants, including all the women, as a gesture of southern chivalry. Lessened charges enabled the selection of a jury that was less sympathetic to the defendants than at the first trial. The second trial became an examination of religious heresy when the judge ruled that atheistic-communist beliefs could impeach the credibility of witnesses for the defense. During his summation the prosecutor knelt, prayed, and wept. Holding the hand of the tearful widow of the police chief, he hinted at scenes of sexual debauchery at the strikers' headquarters. The jury returned in less than an hour with seven verdicts of guilty. Sentences ranged from five to twenty years in prison. The workers' desperate rebellion in Gastonia ended when the convicted unionists forfeited their bail, posted chiefly by the American Civil Liberties Union, and fled to the Soviet Union.

The artistic consciousness aroused by the drama of Gastonia led to the publication of six novels between 1930 and 1934.[3] While directly inspired by real-life events, the fictional outpouring was also influenced by wider literary and social currents. A revival of southern literature in the twenties and thirties was followed by a new interest in radical fiction as the misery of the Depression moved many American authors to the left. A debate on the definition and quality of "proletarian literature" flourished until the mid-thirties, especially among male intellectuals and writers in the New York City area. In a literary period characterized by the importance of realistic novels protesting social conditions under capitalism, the use of strikes in the fiction of the early thirties multiplied dramatically.

These strike novels often exhibit common qualities. The clash is described in lavish and often authentic detail. The strike is seen from the inside. The novelists take us into the workers' homes and union halls, into the jails, and on the picket lines. These struggles capture the natural rhythm of a strike: the first days of elation and the later moments of apathy, boredom, and despair, all leading to the climax of terror and defeat, although the workers retain the memory of their collective strength. The strike also functions as a symbolic microcosm of political revolution. The violent conflict advances the workers toward a higher form of class consciousness. In capitalist America, the bitter sadness of defeat forecasts the hope of a better future.

Strike fiction of the early thirties was also inspired by the dramatic tensions peculiar to the labor battles in southern textile mills. When the strikes began, one of the nation's most enduring folk figures, the southern poor white, was already well established in imaginative literature. Members of the southern white working class were pictured as lowland tenants or sharecroppers, or as sullen mountaineers. Forced by poverty to leave the land for work in the textile mills, they shared a common literary tradition. The stereotypical fictional portrayal of poor southern whites combined personal elements of individualism, violence, cunning, and absurdity with socially produced characteristics of religiosity and racism. The meeting of this presumed near-peasant with the northern urban revolutionary offered high literary promise as a provocative subject.

First among these intriguing literary possibilities was the clash of fatalistic theology with communism, of Christian mysticism with Marxist reason. Another was the tension between nature and industry. Many strike novels of this period compared the millhand's reverence for agrarian life and the rich beauty of the earth and hills to the worker's awed response to the new experience of an ordered industrial routine, powerful factory machinery, and the worldly pleasures offered by life in the textile towns. The complexity of race relations was a third common theme in American proletarian literature of the period. Poor southern whites were portrayed as alternating between clinging to the tiny advantages that race could offer and recognizing how racism functioned to bind white and black into a shared oppression. Sexual conflict is another important theme: the newly rebellious female—whether wife, striker, or union leader—is frequently presented as a threat to both capitalism and male supremacy in the South.

When Mary Heaton Vorse arrived in Gastonia in mid-April 1929, she was fifty-five, recovering from a major crisis in her life, and one of the most experienced labor reporters and popular writers of women's fiction in the country. She came in alone on the midnight train, drawn to Gastonia by the "grotesque savagery" that had led a local mob to demolish the union headquarters there a few nights earlier. "There is an element of the phantastic about the whole situation," she wrote in her journal that evening, thinking of her first glimpse of the southern textile strikers, many of them with missing or tobacco-stained teeth and wearing the most threadbare clothing she had ever seen on workers.[4] The new headquarters of the Communist-led National Textile Workers Union was a dimly lit store where she found strikers reading copies of the *Daily Worker*. The Communist newspaper carried wild exaggerations of the success of the strike, perverting reality in its desire to please its Soviet mentors.

Vorse met the union leader Fred Beal for the first time: "a nice boy, a weak boy, oppressed with the tremendous weight of the strike. He seemed to be at first touching and petulant . . . over-anxious." Her initial encounter with the three young female northern Communist leaders led her to judge the entire atmosphere as one of fright, disorganization, and factionalism, "the impressions of a first day which were all chiefly of deep criticism on the part of the women of the men," she wrote.

Beal was depressed "by the failure of the girls to acknowledge his leadership."[5] The three women leaders were resentful that Beal refused to join them and the striking women and children on the treacherous picket line. Everyone was panicky about money and highly critical of the lack of support from the distant New York party office. All the organizers desperately wanted to return to the North; yet they remained, riveted by courage, duty, and ideals.

It was natural that Vorse would have reached Gastonia just before the national press arrived in force. She had again and again demonstrated her uncanny ability to sense the moment and find the center of whatever action would likely occur. Since 1912 she had reported almost every major strike and international conflict, and she had appeared at crucial radical and women's meetings in Europe and the United States. "There was always an easy rule for locating her in time and space," Murray Kempton wrote in 1955. "Whenever you read across forty years about an event in which men stood in that single, desperate moment which brings all past, all present, and all future to one sharp point for them, you could assume that Mary Vorse had been there."[6]

Born into a wealthy New England family in 1874, Vorse had been expected to follow the traditional avenue into marriage and respectability. Instead, inspired by the social ideal of the New Woman of the time, she escaped to Paris and New York City as an art student in the 1890s. Widowed twice, in 1910 and 1915, Vorse was a single mother most of her life. Deprived of any inheritance by her disapproving mother, she never wavered in her resolve to support her three children through free-lance writing and reporting.

Vorse was happily situated in the bohemian center of Greenwich Village when the social revolution began there in 1912. As a founding editor of the *Masses,* a charter member of the Liberal Club, and a member of the group that formed the Provincetown Players, she was both a conduit for the younger men and women entering the world of the avant-garde and a core participant in the ongoing revolt. As an activist in the suffrage and women's peace movements, she also helped to found that Greenwich Village nursery of modern feminism—the remarkable Heterodoxy Club.

A whole-hearted commitment to labor's cause came late in Vorse's life. She was a thirty-eight-year-old mother of two and already a well-known author of women's fiction when she arrived in Lawrence, Massachusetts, to report on the famed textile strike of 1912. At Lawrence, the unity created among workers in struggle, their dedication and courage, her realization of the terrible human cost of profit making—

all these profoundly affected Vorse and altered the course of her life. "Some curious synthesis had taken place between my life and that of the workers," she wrote, "some peculiar change that would never again permit me to look with indifference on the fact that riches for the few were made by the misery of the many."[7] Until World War I, Vorse continued her important alliance begun at Lawrence with the radical union, the Industrial Workers of the World, or Wobblies, as they were known. She helped to organize the Wobblies' unemployment protest in New York City in 1914, and she reported on the Mesabi Range strike in 1916, where she served as a kind of coleader to her good friend, Elizabeth Gurley Flynn.

After a tour in the war zones, Vorse returned to the United States to serve as a publicist for the Great Steel Strike of 1919 and to organize women shirtmakers in Pennsylvania. Unlike most labor journalists, Vorse was often a strike participant. Her inside knowledge of union strategy, combined with her commitment to accurate reporting, brought uncommon depth and feeling to her work. Her measured, knowledgeable accounts found easy entry into major journals and the mainstream press, outlets usually closed to writers closely identified with the Left. But Vorse also wrote for radical magazines and for the workers themselves, in her dispatches for the union press. Perhaps her most significant contribution to the journalism as well as the fiction of her time, however, was her consistent attention to the role played by women. Through Vorse's eyes we see a wider span and we are offered a tantalizing glimpse of the contributions of women to labor's advance and to other world events.

While in Paris in 1919, Vorse fell in love with the egotistical and domineering Robert Minor, the famous American political cartoonist who one year later converted to communism. In early 1922 her affair with Minor ended disastrously. Four months pregnant with his child, she suffered a miscarriage following a fall and subsequently became addicted to morphine as a result of the medical treatment she received. Her despair intensified after she was rejected by Minor for a younger and more politically compliant woman.

In the 1920s, with the labor movement quieted, the feminist movement crushed, and a reactionary government in power, Vorse returned home to be a mother. Her massive depression centered on her previous "neglect" of her three children. For seven tortuous years during that dark decade she placed her work second to the presumed needs of her children. Sunk in maternal guilt, she wallowed, reached the brink of death, and found the courage to overcome her morphine addiction. In 1926, at the age of fifty-two, Vorse returned to labor work as the publicity director for the first major national strike led by Communists, in Passaic, New Jersey. The revolutionary publicity tactics she developed at Passaic would set the pattern for the successful techniques that marked the labor uprisings of the next decade. After a brief return to morphine use, followed by complete nervous collapse in 1928, Vorse finally confronted the obsessive self-sacrifice and role conflict that had shattered her life. Through the twenties she had performed a constant balancing act, suspended between societal expectations of femininity and the dreams of her own generation of achieving women. Her arrival in Gastonia therefore represented more to her than simply a chance to report on the great southern textile strikes in 1929. Rather, it marked her return to the adventurous life and her decision henceforth to devote her full energy to labor reporting and radical politics.[8]

Mary Heaton Vorse spent about six weeks in Gastonia, living in a boardinghouse with Vera Buch, one of the northern organizers. Vorse reported on Gastonia events for *Harper's* while she gathered notes for *Strike!*, which adheres closely to the events of the Loray strike: Fred Beal is Fer Deane; Ella May Wiggins is Mamie Lewes; Irma Rankin, the radical northern organizer, is a composite figure based on Vera Buch and the other women organizers Vorse met at Gastonia. Vorse describes her firsthand observations of working and living conditions, the wavering morale of the strikers, the mob spirit, eviction of the families, violence on the picket lines, and the erection of the tent colony.

At this point, Vorse made a brief trip to Elizabethton, Tennessee, to report on strike events there. During that trip Vorse became alarmed by something she had discovered, or at least sensed. On her way home, she made a special stop at Gastonia to warn Buch of the impending violence she foresaw and to urge Buch to leave Gastonia as soon as possible, a recommendation Buch did not choose to follow. Within a week the Gastonia police chief had been killed and Buch was in jail. In *Strike!* Vorse speaks of the "lynchy feeling" (138) she sensed building in Gastonia and of her premonition of coming trouble: "Something murderous was coming out of this. Some awful calamity was to happen. . . . It was like knowing by the clock when a catastrophe of nature was to occur. As though one could foretell earthquake. As though cyclone had a schedule. Only this was a cyclone of evil, and it was unclean" (198).

Vorse, who returned to Gastonia to report on the first trial and on the almost unbroken mob terror that followed the declaration of a mistrial, was near the open truck in which Ella May Wiggins was riding when she was killed. Vorse left Gastonia soon after for Marion, North

Carolina, to report on the massacre of six textile strikers, all shot in the back, by the Marion police force and mill deputies. The conclusion of *Strike!* is a description of the shooting and funeral at Marion; otherwise, the novel duplicates the chronology of actual events in Gastonia.

Strike! is told from the perspective of two northern journalists, Roger Hewlett and Ed Hoskins. Both men represent Vorse at various times in her life. Like Vorse at Lawrence in 1912, Hewlett came to report on his first strike believing that the only reason "good" people opposed the strike was because they lacked understanding of the facts. Hoskins is a cynical oldtimer in the labor movement who chides Hewlett: "There's no use being shocked about a thing that always happens. Whenever the workers make their initial revolt the instinctive action of the comfortable people is to put down the rebellion with violence—any violence, all violence" (15). Like Vorse, Hoskins makes a good living as a popular writer, "but let a strike come along . . . and there he'd be" (8), experiencing the workers' fight as the most exciting thing in the world. Hewlett slowly becomes radicalized by the events and people he observes in the course of the novel, and like Vorse he finally emerges as a Socialist committed to the workers' worldwide struggle: "He had lost his own class; he could never belong in their class of the workers. He was without country now, and yet wherever they went, whatever their destination might be, he had to go with them" (235-36).

Vorse's decision to reveal the process of her own intellectual passage through the story of two male journalists is significant. As a female labor reporter in a male profession, she realized that speaking through a male reporter would legitimize her views in a way that a woman character could not. Sex-role conflict followed her even into the symbol making central to the writer's work.

There is another kind of distance between self and subject that is apparent in Vorse's novel. Influenced by literary stereotypes of the South, as well as by her own class and geographical origins, Vorse presents the strikers as strangely foreign objects, especially in the view of the northern organizers. This is reflected most directly in the clumsy southern dialect and "colorful" phrases she imposes upon the speech of the Gastonia strikers. Significantly, when Vorse recorded in her earlier writings the words of recent immigrants to the North, her northern workers, despite their ethnic diversity, often spoke in the grandly structured grammar of educated New Englanders. However, sympathetic as she was to the political cause of the southern working class, she could not entirely escape conventional mythology about southern millfolk. In Gastonia, she remained an outlander in a distinctly different— sometimes even unintelligible or vaguely comic—environment.

Strike! is marked by its focus on women's courage and strength, a point that escaped the notice of reviewers. The women strikers, described as "pluckier than the men" (11), are beaten by thugs and deputies, pricked by bayonets, and evicted from their homes. The older women endure sacrifice for the future of their families, "so our chillen won't have to work like we done" (55). The younger strikers appear as gay and incautious: one grabs a pistol from a deputy; others go singing to jail or mock their accusers in the courtroom. Ella May Wiggins, about whom much of the action revolves, pays with her life for her heroism. In the novel, Vorse describes the real scene in Gastonia, where Vera Buch and the other female organizers resisted Fred Beal's demand that he be given command of a strike in which it was women who "manned" the hazardous picket lines.

Like other feminist authors of the strike novels of this period, Vorse gives little direct attention to what historian Jacquelyn Hall has termed the "erotic undercurrent" of the southern strikes.[9] Perhaps Vorse, like many contemporary supporters of the southern strike wave, wished to avoid any strengthening of the conservatives' claim that the young women workers were promiscuous and irreverent subversives defying respectable middle-class norms and masculine controls. Yet the sexual theme of *Strike!* emerges again and again. It appears when Vorse stresses the "bright eyes" and "repressed excitement" of gaily energetic young women workers who welcome the adventure, female unity, and independent thinking encouraged by strike events. These women "fraternize" with the National Guard in an effort to win the soldiers to the workers' side, and they scoff at the horrified response to their activity expressed by male union organizers and local elites. Vorse also emphasizes the conservatives' fear of the union as a center for "free love" doctrines. Despite her subtle presentation of sexuality as an aspect of female revolt, the role played by the disorderly women strikers of Gastonia is apparent.

Sexual antagonism between strikers, and between foremen and female millworkers, is mirrored in the animosity between the chief organizers. Powerful and arrogant Irma Rankin, a Communist with a taste for martyrdom, constantly derides Fer Deane, who she feels is lazy, unimaginative, and insufficiently ideological: "There was a continuous pull and strain between them of a man and woman fighting for supremacy over each other" (46). The battle between the sexes peaks when Fer assumes credit for the "incredible labor" expended by the women organizers to erect the tent colony. He smiles benignly upon the colony, as though he were responsible for creating the little settlement: "It was an attitude of his of which he was not conscious, but which infuriated the girls. They, and not Fer, had been responsible for the welfare of each baby and the safe transportation of each piece of furniture" (131). Vorse's emphasis upon sexual tensions at Gastonia highlights the contradiction between the masculinist orientation of American Communist leaders in the thirties and their often expressed belief in sexual equality.

Strike! negates the Communist formula for "proletarian realism" in several other important ways. Vorse was one of the first American radicals to recognize the nature of Soviet dictatorship. She had learned the failure of the Communist promise firsthand, especially through her 1922 tour in Moscow as a correspondent for the Hearst papers, her intimate knowledge of the national party leaders, and her experience at the Communist-led Passaic textile strike of 1926. In *Strike!* she gives little attention to Communist theory, except to portray red-baiting as a tactic used by conservatives to break the union. Thus the strikers frequently function as apathetic or befuddled political innocents, rather than as newly class-conscious militants. In addition, the workers' religiosity is shown sympathetically, not as an opiate of the people, but as a force used by the workers to strengthen human ties, build community solidarity, and encourage demands for justice. As a pioneer labor reporter, Vorse provides a fictional rendition of a strike that is devoid of propaganda yet allows a realistic portrayal of human complexity even the best journalism of the time did not permit.

The enemy in Vorse's book is not simply the few wealthy capitalists who control the means of production; her villains compose a much larger and more vicious group. The mob that threatens the union members is a collection of "comfortable people," the middle-class businessmen, professionals, and educated drones, including many middle-class women, whose psychological security and material privilege rest upon the continued exploitation of the millworkers. Just as the mob of comfortable folks was unconsciously manipulated by the very rich whom they never met, so did the mob use its own class inferiors, the "loyal workers" and "poor white trash" of the mill towns, to assault, terrorize, and sometimes kill the strikers. "Every one was mob who hated the Union. The minister's wife sitting in her safe and secluded parlor, the young girls who talked contemptuously about mill hands, [the rich wife] away in her fine house in Richmond, the editors of the papers, the ministers who tried to 'reason' with the poor, misguided people, the Governor of the State, so swift to call out troops, so slow to see that order was kept. . . . The community was responsible for Mamie Lewes' death. The whole community" (203).

The ideological dynamic of mass psychology — whether expressed in union spirit or mob terror—is a repeated theme in Vorse's tale of Gastonia: "Collectively human beings are at their best or their worst. They climb perilous heights of beauty and sacrifice together. And together they revert to the hunting pack, creatures aslaver for blood" (168). Her emphasis upon this dual image of the range of behavior possible at different times in the same class falls short of a simplistic allegory of class struggle and led the *New Masses* review of *Strike!* to note her neglect of the "logic that made the Carolina textile worker stand up in his proletarian dignity with a copy of the *Daily Worker* in his hand. . . . Had Mary Vorse [only] given us this . . . *Strike!* would glow with a revolutionary significance."[10]

When it was published in 1930, *Strike!* received wide attention. Liveright issued Vorse's fifteenth book with a detachable paper band that proclaimed Mike Gold's belief that "it was a burning and imperishable epic." This worried Sinclair Lewis, who voiced his fear in the *Nation* that an endorsement by the Communist Gold might prejudice readers against the book. Carl Haessler wrote to Vorse that Lewis was "praising you as the very best of all the writers on the textile strikes in the South."[11] The *New Republic* and the *New Yorker* reviewers were strongly positive; the *Saturday Review of Literature* and the *New York Times Book Review* offered mixed, but sympathetic, support. The book sold well, despite its bewildering number of characters and unwieldy presentation of the southern millhand's dialect. Vorse was pleased to learn that it would be published in German, Russian, and Japanese for distribution abroad.

As the author of a book that sympathetically portrays the workers' struggle, Vorse was pursued by Communist literary figures eager to build a coalition with non-Communist writers. However, she resisted their efforts to induce her to attend party-led literary meetings or to write for party publications. Through long contact with the Communist Left, she was more aware than most of the party quarrels and infighting then convoluting the party elite, as Earl Browder slowly gained a lead over William Foster in competition for the top position. The American Communist party, Vorse wrote in her journal in the early thirties, was headed by functionaries with "closed minds, so certain, so dull . . . miserable, pathetic, static. They *bore me, bore me, bore me.*"[12] More important, Vorse shunned the party because she had become deeply critical of the evolution of socialism in Russia. By the late 1920s, she was certain that Bolshevik-style socialism had become but another form of despotism.

Yet before and after the Gastonia strike, Vorse refused to publicly bait the Communist rank and file in the union trenches, for she knew that they often served justice with constancy and courage. She never confused the embattled labor activist, many of whom were women, with the Communist office functionary or the carping bystander, most of whom were men. She always understood the distinction between the immense club of official power and the tiny barb of the radical few. She was sure that the historic red hunt was not motivated by any actual threat of the Communist party to capitalist hegemony but was the prime means used by conservatives to discredit labor successes and progressive reform. She would not join that effort, not during the conservative retrenchment of the 1920s, nor during the cold war red scare of the 1950s, no matter what the consequences to her popular reputation or her publishing opportunities. This decision meant running the risk of being branded a Communist by the Right and even a "fellow-traveler" by non-Communist liberals and leftists, in spite of her early rejection of Bolshevik dictatorship. The FBI maintained a file on Vorse for almost forty years, until she was eighty-two, a distinction that may have earned her a place as some sort of record holder among targets of federal intelligence agencies.

After the Gastonia strike, Vorse went on to report on the labor war in Harlan County, Kentucky, in 1931; the unemployed workers' marches in 1932; the farmers' strikes in the Midwest; the trial of the Scottsboro Boys in 1933; the textile and mining strikes in the early New Deal period; and the fierce CIO struggles of the late thirties. During World War II, Vorse reported on the lives of American factory workers. She lived in semiretirement at her home in Provincetown, Massachusetts, during the fifties, though she continued to write—of Mafia union chiefs, textile workers, migratory labor, and civil rights work in the South. Her last big story to receive national attention was a 1952 exposé of crime in the waterfront unions, published in *Harper's* when she was seventy-eight. In her eighties and nineties, the scope of her battlefield shrank to Cape Cod, where she helped organize a Provincetown protest against offshore dumping of nuclear waste. At age ninety-one, one year before her death, Vorse began her last campaign: she backed Provincetown's Episcopalian minister who would be one of the first to march in protest of American involvement in Vietnam. From the Wobblies in Lawrence in 1912 to the young protestors of the 1960s, Mary Heaton Vorse was there.

Vorse's Gastonia novel is an early example of a lost genre in American literary history. The strike novel of the early thirties was written when the Left in the United States momentarily flourished. *Strike!* embodies the tension of the literary artist convinced by the suffering of the worker that the vision of liberal individualism must be replaced by an understanding of the class basis of reality. The efforts of Vorse and others to use the novel as an instrument for serious social analysis and as a guide to radical action treated the most serious social problems from an openly ideological but realistic perspective.

Strike! thus survives as much more than simply a historical document of the thirties or another illustration of the modern American intellectual's dissatisfaction with liberal verities. The larger questions it raises remain pertinent to an understanding of the thirties and beyond: What is the role of art, and the artist, in a political movement? What in American terms is the working class? How can a writer faithfully render the messy complexities of human ideals and behavior, while also imparting a vision of a better, more democratic and egalitarian American future?

Above all else, Vorse's book reveals the lost world of the mill family and the southern poor white woman. In contrast to the strongly masculinist cast of the cultural theory and practice of the Left in the thirties and later, feminist writers like Vorse chose to focus on the distinctly female experiences of the working class. Through her work we encounter two generations of poor and determined southern women — the haggard older mountain women, dressed in their long brown calico skirts, and the more vibrant "flappers," sporting their bright lipstick and rouge on the dangerous picket line or using their sexual charm to win the sympathy of the young soldiers in the National Guard. Vorse's concentration on the role of women as the vanguard of change in a period of great social conflict portends the growing importance of women in the national labor force and as active agents and critics in the public world.

NOTES

1. This history of Gastonia is discussed in Fred E. Beal, *Proletarian Journey: New England, Gastonia, Moscow* (New York: Hillman-Curl, 1947); Liston Pope, *Millhands and Preachers: A Study of Gastonia* (New Haven: Yale University Press, 1942); Theodore Draper, "Gastonia Revisited," *Social Research* 38 (1971): 3-29; Vera Buch Weisbord, *A Radical Life* (Bloomington: Indiana University Press, 1977); Jacquelyn Dowd Hall, James Leloudis, Robert Korstad, Mary Murphy, Lu Ann Jones, and Christopher B. Daly, *Like a Family: The Making of a Southern Cotton Mill World* (Chapel Hill: University of North Carolina Press, 1987); Dan McCurry and Carolyn Ashbaugh, "Gastonia, 1929: Strike at the Loray Mill," *Southern Exposure* (Winter 1973-74): 185-203. See also James A. Hodges, "Challenge to the New South: The Great Textile Strike in Elizabethton, Tennessee, 1929," *Tennessee Historical Quarterly* 23 (December 1964): 343-57;

Jacquelyn Dowd Hall, "Disorderly Women: Gender and Labor Militancy in the Appalachian South," *Journal of American History* 73 (1986): 354-82.

2. Cited in Weisbord, *Radical Life*, 183.

3. The other Gastonia novels are: Sherwood Anderson, *Beyond Desire* (New York: Horace Liveright, 1932); Grace Lumpkin, *To Make My Bread* (New York: Macauley, 1932); Dorothy Myra Page, *Gathering Storm: A Story of the Black Belt* (New York: International Publishers, 1932); William Rollins, *The Shadow Before* (New York: Robert M. McBride and Co., 1934); and Olive Tilford Dargan (Fielding Burke), *Call Home the Heart* (1932; New York: Feminist Press, 1983). For literary history and criticism, see the excellent study by Sylvia Jenkins Cook, *From Tobacco Road to Route 66* (Chapel Hill: University of North Carolina Press, 1976), as well as Daniel Aaron, *Writers on the Left: Episodes in American Literary Communism* (New York: Harcourt, Brace and World, 1961); David Madden, ed., *Proletarian Writers of the Thirties* (Carbondale: Southern Illinois University Press, 1968); Walter B. Rideout, *The Radical Novel in the United States, 1900-1954* (Cambridge: Harvard University Press, 1956); Fay M. Blake, *The Strike in the American Novel* (Metuchen, N.J.: Scarecrow Press, 1972); James Burkhart Gilbert, *Writers and Partisans: A History of Literary Radicalism in America* (New York: John Wiley and Sons, 1968).

4. Mary Heaton Vorse, "Strike Journal, Gastonia," box 155, Mary Heaton Vorse Papers, Walter Reuther Library, Wayne State University, Detroit, Michigan (hereafter cited as MHV-WSU).

5. Ibid.

6. Murray Kempton, *Part of Our Time: Some Ruins and Monuments of the Thirties* (New York: Simon and Schuster, 1955), 215.

7. Mary Heaton Vorse, *A Footnote to Folly: The Reminiscences of Mary Heaton Vorse* (New York: Farrar and Rinehart, 1935), 14.

8. See Dee Garrison, *Mary Heaton Vorse: The Life of an American Insurgent* (Philadelphia: Temple University Press, 1989), esp. "War in the South," 213-32.

9. Hall, "Disorderly Women," 356.

10. Walt Carmon, "Strike!" *The New Masses* 6-8 (November 1930): 18.

11. Sinclair Lewis, "A Novel for Mr. Hoover," *The Nation* 131 (October 29, 1930): 474; Haessler to Vorse, box 59, MHV-WSU.

12. Vorse, "Daily Notes," box 82, MHV-WSU.

Publisher's Note

In the course of resetting and proofreading this novel, which was originally published in 1930 and to our knowledge has not been changed since then, we encountered a number of errors. Most of them are minor, such as erratic capitalization and misplaced punctuation; but the fact that several characters experience name changes in the midst of the action is hard to ignore—for instance, Rob Trent and Dan Trent appear to be the same person, as do Will and Bill and Frank Gilfillin and also Mrs. Thorn and Mrs. Thomas. The decision was made not to violate the integrity of the original text, so we have not corrected these apparent errors.

PART

I

1

1

THERE WAS a strike in Stonerton. The employees of the Basil-Schenk Manufacturing Company had walked out. The strike was one of the explosions of textile strikes which in the spring of nineteen twenty-nine had so surprised the South and pleased the North. The North was pleased because for a long time now Piedmont, the high red earth district in North and South Carolina, had been steadily gaining the supremacy of the textile industry. Manufacturers were invited to come South where there were no labor troubles and an unfailing supply of a "hundred per cent loyal, docile American labor." But under the speed-up system, the "stretch-out" they called it in the South, the docile workers had struck. No sooner was one strike quelled or settled than another strike broke out somewhere else. They were almost leaderless. They had no unions, but they had had too much work and had been getting too little pay for too long. It was what one so rarely sees, a "spontaneous uprising of the people."

2

With a spirit of adventure Roger Hewlett got an assignment to do an article about the textile strike in Stonerton. The strike had been going on for two weeks, and had been in the papers from the first. There had been spectacular parades, many arrests, threats of violence against the strikers. Lynch law threatened the strike leaders. Mobs were formed, said to be fomented by prominent citizens.

Finally the strike leader, Ferdinand Deane, had been kidnapped, and railroaded out of the state.

He returned at once.

Roger Hewlett, who had done some labor reporting, hurried to Stonerton to be in time for the parade which the strikers were holding in honor of Deane's return, and at which it was believed there would be trouble.

Hewlett put his bag in the hotel and drove to the mill village, a distance of perhaps a mile. At the start the houses all had lawns; by the time the jitney stopped before strike headquarters, the street was lined with wooden shacks and mean brick stores, which cried aloud that here people bought but little. A huge and silent mill dominated the community. Around it was the mill village, running crazily up and down hill, every house like the other, bare wooden shacks standing in red mud on brick stilts. The little houses seemed like a flock of chicks beside a monstrous hen, as if the mill had hatched them from square wooden eggs. Well, in a way, it had, Roger reflected.

He found strike headquarters in a gloomy looking store. The windows had been broken in some affray and they were now boarded up. Inside, lanky men read papers. When Roger told them he was a newspaper man, they looked at him suspiciously and without goodwill. Experience had taught them. The local papers had attacked the Union. When Roger asked for Ferdinand Deane, one said laconically:

"Fer's speakin'." He was a young man with hollow cheeks and deep set eyes, who had the appearance of a solemn hound. One expected to see long ears flapping down the side of his face. Then he called out:

"Henry Tetherow!"

A red-headed boy appeared like a jack-in-the-box from beneath a counter. "Here, you take him to the speakin'," he directed, jerking a thumb at Roger.

They went down back alleys, across a railway track, and there, in an empty field, littered with trash and tin cans, a large crowd was gathered. They stood on the railway embankment while the boy gazed down at the speaker whose voice came to them, a carrying voice.

"That's Fer!" said the boy without turning to Roger, his eyes on the man who was talking. The two words which he dropped, "That's Fer," gave Roger a measure of the boy's adoration. He could not have said, "That's God!" with a more earnest simplicity of worship. The crowd was silent. There was no milling around on the outskirts of the assembly. No coming and going. The strikers stood stock-still, drinking in what Fer said. A curious sense flowed over Roger as though he were witnessing a happening of importance.

3

The Tetherow boy and Roger clambered down the embankment and as they approached, Fer's voice seemed scarcely louder. He spoke without any rhetorical tricks, conversationally. He was not above middle height, broad-shouldered, and over his forehead fell a wing of black hair which he perpetually tossed back with a gesture of his head like a spirited animal tossing a mane from its eyes. His dark hair glinted in the sun with reddish lights, and he had a smash of freckles across his face even though he was tanned a dark brown. His features were thin and aquiline—the dark Irishman. Now he told an anecdote about the sheriff, Dick Humphries.

"And Mumphries said—"and the way he pronounced his burlesque of the sheriff's name, one had a picture of the man,—a mumpy, jowlish creature. The audience rocked and roared. Now that he had them in good humor, he talked to them with rapid earnestness, always in this conversational tone that had in it no oratory and yet which carried extraordinarily.

"Now I'm going to end my sermon," he said. "It's the same old sermon. It's that I don't want no violence. Let the violence come from them, not us. You all keep cool. I talk it to you private and I talk it to you from the platform." And he gave them a lecture about the folly of talking about using guns. "I know it is natural for you from the mountains to reach for your guns, but this isn't a war and this isn't a feud,—this is a strike." He gave a picture of what would happen to them and to him if there was any shooting, and he wound up with something so earnest and yet so winning in his manner that Roger found himself liking Fer. He was a charmer, a great performer.

4

Other speakers followed. The crowd began to shift. Standing near Roger was a short curly haired woman dressed in poor clothes, but there was something about her that was alert and gay and extremely alive. She had an air of expectancy as if she were waiting for something interesting to happen. She looked at him once or twice, recognizing a stranger, and then looked away again, embarrassed.

"Do you belong to the Union?" he asked her. She shook her head with a quick pretty gesture.

"No," she said. "No, I ain't jined up yit, but I'm agoin' to. Where I live to Tesner, that's maybe eight miles from yere, they jist now have organized. Mr. Woods has organized it." The man Roger had seen in the gloom of the relief store said:

"Why, Mamie Lewes, ain't you jined yit?" He was tall, with deep set fanatical eyes. His face was red, and his dark hair stood up on his head. There was in him a fierce driving force.

"No, I never did git around to it, Wes," she answered.

"But yore strikin', ain't you? They's a strike to Tesner in Mill Number Two, where you is. You ain't scabbin' in, Mamie Lewes?" She laughed.

"No, I ain't scabbin' in o' course I ain't scabbin' in. You ain't no call to pounce on me so. Hit's agittin' time to come to headquarters, that's been akeepin' me back. I got to git my kids clothen straightened out. Workin' in the mill seems I never did git no time for they clothen noway." "How many children have you?" Roger asked.

"I got four now. An' it's awful hard taking keer o' them all alone, me gittin' only eight dollars and forty cents a week. I try and I try and I cain't seem to make no mo'n that."

"I don't see how you get along," said Roger, his voice sounding flat and inadequate.

"I don't git along," she said, a quiver of indignation in her voice as she raised her head. "I cain't even afford to git a house on the mill hill! The rent ain't much but I cain't afford even that. I live out o' town over a mile and a half with some kin o' mine in a shack. They got one room an' the kitchen hole and I got the other."

"Do you ever work nights?" Roger asked Mamie Lewes. Her face, till now gay and excited, grew pale. She looked at him with somber eyes.

"I couldn't git to work nights. I had eight children and they took sick with dipthery. I cried and begged for thet sup'intendent to let me work nights so's I could stay home and take keer o' the children daytimes but he wouldn't let me go. He's the sorriest man in the worl' I reckon." She paused, looked straight ahead of her, so did the tall boy called Wes. Then she said steadily, "Four o' my children died."

"Yore all alone now, ain't you, Mamie Lewes?" Wes asked gently.

"Yes. Will, thet's my husband, got kinda discouraged like, havin' the chillen die. Plum did take his ambition away. He went off to another town to git work and I never did yeah from him no mo'."

"I don't see how you get along," Roger said again stupidly.

"My little girl, she's eleven, and she heps me right smart. Don't none of my chillen git to school. How could they? I wouldn't have no one to leave the little ones with, and ef I could, how would I git clothen and shoes for 'em?"

5

The speaking was over. Mamie Lewes and Wes drifted away in the crowd. Roger Hewlett looked around for familiar faces and saw Dick

Durgan from the Baltimore *Planet* who had been reporting the strike. He hailed Roger.

"Come along," he said. "I'll have you meet Fer."

Fer was strolling toward them with a peculiar shouldering lunge that he had, as if he were perpetually plowing through a crowd.

"Gosh," he said to Dick, "how I want to get drunk!"

"Why don't you?" Dick asked. "There's plenty corn likker around here." Fer flushed darkly.

"I can't get drunk because I don't drink." He looked at them with a gaze that was so direct that it held the innocence of a child's stare "I don't drink," he explained further, "because I can't. It don't stay by me!" He spoke in all innocence. He didn't know he was explaining to a crowd of old newspaper men a vital deficiency.

He had no stomach.

There is something lacking in a man who has no stomach. A man ought to be able to drink if he wants to. If a labor leader doesn't drink it should be for the reason Bill Haywood didn't drink in his later days, which was because he made up his mind not to.

Ed Hoskins, the Affiliated Press man, said:

"What you so down in the mouth for, Fer? This is a swell strike."

"Yeah?" Fer said with an eloquent upward inflection.

"You said a mouthful when you said that 'Yeah'," Hoskins remonstrated. "What's the matter? Are they going to go kidnapping you again?"

"It's their damn guns. It's that damn parade tomorrow," Fer said. He shoved his hands down in his pockets and shouldered his way along through the invisible crowd. "This ain't a strike, Ed, like any other strike. This is a hell of a place. They're going to pop off one of their guns one of these days, then they'll get them,—and they'll get me."

"Who do you mean will get you?"

"The mob will, if the sheriff don't," said Fer. "I wisht I was North. I wisht I was leading a strike of fellers I was ust to."

6

They were walking along to a "Quick and Dirty." Behind them was a little group of newspaper men. Roger and Ed, somewhat privileged as they were labor reporters, were walking ahead with the organizers. Irma Rankin, a woman organizer, came up to consult with Fer about something. Ed Hoskins fell back with Hewlett.

Hoskins was an old time labor reporter. He had reported the Lawrence Textile strike in 1912. He had been up on the Mesaba range in

1916. There was no one in the labor movement he didn't know. He'd been a friend of Smitty, of the Structural Iron Workers, and the McNamaras. He knew Knockles and FitzPatrick of the Illinois Federation of Labor in their old fighting days. He'd reported strikes led by Haywood, Tresca, and Gurley Flynn.

He made a good living as a special writer for popular magazines, and would have been well off if he could have left the labor movement alone. He couldn't. He had to play in every radical camp. He'd swear off, but let a strike come along like this one in Stonerton, and there he'd be.

"What do you think of Fer?" he asked. Without waiting for an answer he went on. "Don't make the mistakes I did and think he's scared. First I thought about Fer, 'Why, the boy's scared.' He ain't. In circumstances like this the Wobblies were hell raisers. We don't seem to have any cussin' hell raisers in the labor movement any more. There isn't a one hard-loined son-of-a-gun among them all. They're little fellers, young fellers. You know radicals run kinda stringy in America. I guess because most of them come from cities while the Wobblies came out of woods and prairies and mines. I bet Fer has had another one of these blackhand letters he's always getting. They depress him. These folks are terribly isolated down here. There's a real terror here—"

"Worse than the Wobblies had?"

"Different," Hoskins answered. "Altogether different. The South's hard to understand. No one understands it, not even the Southerners. Fer doesn't understand it and he knows he doesn't understand it."

"Oh, Hos!" Fer called. "Listen to what Irma just told me." They changed partners.

Roger Hewlett was an old friend of Irma's from the Paterson strike.

"Well," she said, "what do you think?"

"About what?" he asked.

"About Fer's being sent down here to take charge of this Southern organization?"

"Well, he did pretty well in Paterson, didn't he? And in Lawrence?"

"Oh," she said, "he is not the kind to have *sent!* He is a nice fellow, he's a sweet fellow, but he hasn't the caliber to organize the *South!* They're trying to make a big leader of him. They're trying to shape him. You can't shape a piece of wood into a steel sword. You've got to consider what a man's capacities are."

"I thought you were Fer's girl!" Roger said bluntly. She threw back her head with its shock of pretty dark hair. He could see the clear line of her arrogant profile with its short upper lip, under which you could see very white teeth parted slightly in the middle. A queer girl in a mass movement, with her repressed, indifferent manner. Scornful, bookish, rude. When you talked to her you never knew whether she was listening to you or not except for her somewhat ironic sense of humor. Make her a joke and she would listen to you fast enough. Tell her something funny and you'd get a ripple of giggles. She swung along with her head up, with a nice breezy stride. It made Roger like her better than he ever had before.

"I know I have the reputation everywhere of being Fer's girl," she said with irritation.

"Well, aren't you?" She turned around and laughed, a sudden sound of gayety, youthful, quite different from her restrained manner and her repressed conventional bearing.

"I am and I'm not," she said. "What do you mean by his girl? We're used to each other. I'm enough his girl to know that I'm right when I say he's obstinate and he's lazy and he's no imagination. He has no *drive!*"

"What do you think," Roger asked, "about their wanting to lynch him? Do you think there's any danger of it?"

She reflected. "I think there's a fair chance of any organizer that comes from the North, getting either lynched or shot—or a long jail sentence." There was a certain undercurrent of exultation in her voice. She was the kind that expect martyrdom and are a little disappointed if they don't get it. Roger hadn't suspected her of being so romantic. She had seemed to him about as cold a proposition in girls as he'd ever known. He began to see something in her that had power, latent and unexpressed.

7

Fer dropped back to speak to Hewlett, and Irma joined Hoskins as they walked along; Fer shouldering along with his plunging gait, his head down, his pleasant mouth drawn into a straight line, he gave the air of some one driving through a storm. He was in fact breasting a sort of a storm. Men looked at Fer fiercely, people muttered at him as they passed him on the street. One man shouted,

"Goddam you, we'll run yah outa yere yet!"

There was hate in these people's faces. The three strikers following them closed in on them a little. A feeling of cold crept up Roger's spine. He had been in tense strike situations before. This hatred, these open threats of lynching, was like nothing he had ever known. This was Mob. These people swearing at them were like the isolated drops of a flood. They were what made Mob. Put them together and they would go roaring down the street on a manhunt.

They had gotten to the restaurant, and found a table as far removed from the screaming radio as possible.

"Do they always do that to you?" Ed Hoskins asked Fer.

"Yeah," said Fer. "They do it all the time." He looked up brightly. "It's a queer feeling just the same, that feeling of concentrated hate. I get letters every day, anonymous, telling me to get out,—if I don't I'll get lynched!"

"Oh, there's a terror here all right!" Irma corroborated with somber satisfaction.

"Gosh, I don't like it," said Fer. "It keeps you hopping."

"Do you carry a gun?" Roger asked.

"No," he said scornfully. "I wouldn't know how to use a gun. There's three of the boys follow me around and sleep in the room with me."

Three strikers had lounged along behind them. Two were of the long, rangy type, and one, Del Evans, was wide-shouldered and deep-chested, and the hair on his bullet head was red and cropped short so that it stood up like plush.

"When they came up to me to kidnap me, some way I wasn't scared. I had an idea those boys weren't going to lynch me."

"Drove you down to the station and put you on the train, didn't they?"

"Yeah," said Fer contemplatively. "Just put me on the train. Funny thing, I was in the hotel lobby. I promised to meet one of the newspaper boys. Then first thing I knew two fellers said they wanted to speak to me."

Irma turned her head quite far to one side as she spoke to Roger and he could see her little upper lip curve. "You feel it in the air. It is the queerest thing. You wouldn't believe you could feel an atmosphere."

"Yeah!" said Fer. "It's as though the way they hated you was something you could cut with a knife. Now you knew in Lawrence and in Paterson they were going to get you all right. You knew they would get you if they could, but it wasn't like this. Here they don't aim to get you. They aim to kill you!"

8

The Greek waiter came over and said in a conspiratorial voice, "Miss Rankin, you're wanted on the phone." The three watchful strikers sitting upon the mushroom seats in front of the counter turned their heads toward Fer. There was a curious feeling of apprehension as though they were expecting an explosion of some sort. It was Roger's first taste of this suspense and of an evil which was going to follow him through these next days and months. He saw the hate surrounding these young labor people as a tangible thing, as though the terror emanating from the community could be seen to rise like a poisonous vapor.

Irma came back. Her cheeks were flushed and her eyes were bright. "The dirty cowards!" she said. "The dirty cowards!"

"What's the matter?" asked Hoskins.

"Some one calling me up in the restaurant here to telephone me, to *telephone* me, mind you, to get out of town!"

"To get out of town!" he echoed.

"He swore at me over the phone and he told me to get out of town."

"What did you say?"

"I told him to come around here and tell me."

"What kind of a person did it sound like?" Fer asked.

"It sounded like a literate person with a kind of soft, drawly voice. I said, 'Come around here so I can see you.' He said, 'Oh, you'll see me all right, and a plenty mo' like me.'"

"You see, Hos," Fer explained, "they never let you forget that they're out itching to lynch you. They're just itching to lynch you."

"Yes," Irma said, "that's true enough. They send around all the time to the workers' houses and talk to the women and scare them."

"Yeah, and they knock on the window and boo and do silly scary tricks like that, keeping the women worked up."

"I think the women are pluckier than the men," said Irma. "They've got fighting stuff in them, these women."

They wrangled over this. There was an ancient animosity between them. Irma was trying to dominate Fer, to put something over on him. In a way, to diminish him. There was something arrogant and provocative in the way she met this menace coming over the telephone. Roger liked her less and respected her more.

9

"It gives you a queer jolt," said Ed, breaking into their wrangle, "to know that this town's got folks in it that would threaten a woman over a phone." It was as if a threat of violence had walked into the Quick and Dirty and sat down beside them. They were all a little self-conscious, all hurrying to chatter something to escape from the menace of hatred.

"How'd the strike start, Fer?"

Fer answered, "I was sent south by the Textile Workers Union to do some organizing. See, what they don't understand either here or in the North is that the folks down here have been organizing themselves. There've been spontaneous strikes in four or five different states. These fellows here had a little organization all by themselves. Two fellers,

Wes Elliott and Dan Marks, came over to where I was in Rockhill, so I came over here. We met around in houses. Then pretty soon the mill management found out about how we were meeting and they started firing some of the Union men and women. The workers elected a shop committee and had them go to the mill superintendent to make a request of reinstatement. Well, you know how it was, the management fired the whole lot of them. Then they all voted 'Strike' and they walked out. Gee, it was a swell sight. You know this is one of the queer things in the labor movement."

He leaned forward and spoke rapidly and eagerly, and with an enthusiasm that made one understand why the little Tetherow boys addressed him as though he were God.

"The movement seems dead and you think that there's nothing doing. Then all of a sudden it's alive again. It's never dead. When you find the willingness to fight among the workers, it's more exciting than anything else in the world. Well, they're awake in the South now."

"Didn't you help wake 'em?" Fer shook his head.

"There were things doing before I came. They'd do a lot better if they had a Southern feller for their leader. They like me but I don't belong to them."

"That's true," said Irma. "We're much more comfortable with the foreign workers, in the North. We understand them. We even understand their religious background better."

"Yes," said Fer. "The mill hill preachers are fundamentalists and half their salary is paid by the mill. And they think unionism in any form is the work of the devil."

They got up to go, Irma and Fer ahead, and the three strikers, Fer's guards, behind them, symbol of the menace of the mob.

Suddenly Roger saw the young leaders as terribly isolated and alone, undertaking a work of incredible difficulty, and burdened with the hatred of the comfortable people and equally burdened with the devotion of the mill workers, a load of love and hate too heavy for their shoulders.

2

1

THE TWO reporters left the restaurant together. Hewlett said:

"No wonder the North has paid so much attention to this strike."

"The North needn't be so snooty and self-righteous," said Hoskins. "There's not such a gap between the treatment of the Northern and Southern textile workers when they go on strike."

"They don't threaten to lynch the leaders in the North, though," said Roger.

"They've done plenty of their own threatening. There was just this bitterness in Lawrence in 1912 on the part of the respectable people. I collected editorials from conservative Boston papers which were incitements to violence, incitements to lynch, a whole series of them, and the Union brought them out in a folder. They had the State troops out. The town looked like an armed camp. All freedom of speech and assembly were taken from the workers. There was a woman doctor there who had statistics on infant mortality which have always been damning in the textile towns. She had a chart about the tuberculosis rate of the young people who had worked in mills from fourteen to twenty-four as compared with normal tuberculosis charts of Massachusetts.

"I was young then and innocent. I thought I could make a good article by using these facts and having some of the representative men, doctors and ministers, comment on this state of things. Every one I spoke to was furious against the Union leaders. They were so furious that you couldn't even get them to listen to the fact that hundreds of children died unnecessarily in Lawrence.

" 'What did they have in the Old Country?' one of the doctors roared at me. 'If they don't like conditions here let 'em go back to where they came from.' "

"Couldn't you find any one who was curious about why there was a strike—eight thousand people walking out of the mills?"

"Not a soul. They all thought they knew what was the matter. The matter was the leaders. The mill people had been a happy and contented lot, then came a half a dozen I.W.W.'s, Haywood, Ettor, Arturo Giovanitti, Gurley Flynn, Tresca. Well, these people in a few days stirred up the happy, contented mill people, misled them by their 'red' talk, and they walked out of the factory. So the comfortable people would have been glad to have seen these "outside agitators" hanged, then quartered. They would have liked to have 'em boiled in oil."

"That was the strike, wasn't it, when Vida Scudder, the professor in Wellesley, said that if the women of this country knew how the cloth was made in Lawrence and at what price of human life they would never buy another yard."

"Yes, that was the strike. And she was the great exception just as you'll find women through this state, probably more in North Carolina to-day than you would have found in Massachusetts in 1912, who realize that a strike is about life, and who really feel that life is more important than business. There is real liberal sentiment to-day in North Carolina. Men and women thinking about these problems and wishing to remedy them."

"You'd think everybody'd feel that."

"That's what you think when you're young. That's what I thought when I wanted to write my article in Lawrence. I went around saying 'This strike is about life. Here twenty per cent of the children under five years of age are dying, and the reason they die is their parents don't make enough and their mothers work too hard. Here, I can prove that hundreds of young people have got tuberculosis who needn't have it.' You'd think one minister in a town would be touched by such considerations. There wasn't one. No, the North doesn't need to be so high and mighty at what's happening down here. As soon as better labor conditions, shorter hours, slightly better wages made competition with the South difficult, Northern capital moved its mills right down here."

"Did people walk along the street and threaten the leaders in Northern cities?"

"Perhaps not, but they organized terror against them. Haywood always had to have a bunch of Italian boys follow him to guard him. He had to live in the workers' houses for protection, as they do here.

A. J. Muste was beaten. There's no use being shocked about a thing that always happens. Whenever the workers make their initial revolt the instinctive action of the comfortable people is to put down the rebellion with violence—any violence, all violence. Just go back in your history. Think what happened in the nineteenth century in England after the Enclosure Acts which dispossessed the farm laborers. After their mild uprising, scores were hanged, scores more deported."

"But in the end violence never works."

"No, violence doesn't stop them. The workers have been on the march for a long time. They'll be on the march some time more."

2

They went into the hotel lobby and sat down. A group of reporters joined them.

"What do you think of that speech of Fer's?" some one asked Hoskins. "Pretty violent lot, these Southern strikers."

"That's where you're all wrong," said Hoskins patiently, with the air of a man explaining something for the thousandth time. "Workers are mostly patient, frightfully patient, and these workers are as patient as other workers. And the leaders, like Fer did this afternoon, drill them in self-control. Think of the steel strike. There the State troopers broke up funerals, rode down school children, arrested men at their own front doors, broke into houses at night without warrants. There was no retaliation, no thought of doing anything, not even when they shot the woman organizer, Fanny Sellins, in the back while she was bending over two children to protect them."

"Well, Fer seemed to be afraid they were going to use their guns."

"Any man who has a gun on him may use it, of course. People carry guns much more in the South than in the North. It's legal here. One thing people don't understand in a strike is that in ninety-nine cases out of a hundred it's the police that start the trouble, especially among the textile people. They've always been peaceful; they haven't a militant tradition. It was a relief in New Bedford when those Portuguese women grabbed the police clubs from the police a few times and banged back. That's one of the few times I've seen the textile workers defend themselves. The miners defended themselves. The miners are militant. The building trades and the structural ironworkers. The needle trades have a fighting tradition. Not textiles. Get that into your head, if you want to report any strike, and get it into your head that the leaders want trouble even less. This small number of Northern people naturally don't want violence."

"How many Northerners are there," Durgan asked, "beside Fer and Miss Rankin and Doris Pond?"

"There's a fellow named Woods over in Tesner, organizing. That's six miles from here. There's a fellow who isn't here now, Summers, for the Workers' Defense. There's a third woman organizer, Elizabeth Black, in another town. There have been one or two men and one or two women in and out on relief or defense but not active in the Union."

"You mean that all this row in the papers about Northern agitators and reds is about three men and three girls, and one of the girls working only for relief? All this fear, all these editorials about a handful of kids?"

"Yes, that's it," said Hoskins. "But it's what's behind them they're scared of. Then, of course, there's been an immense amount of exaggeration. The local people are sure the place is honey-combed with Northern agitators."

"What kind of a demonstration are they going to have to-night at Jellico's meeting?"

"What meeting's that?" asked Roger.

"Oh, it's a meeting the Chamber of Commerce is giving. Didn't you hear about it? Got a speaker on from Chicago to talk on Americanism. They call him Old Heart Beats."

"They expect he'll attack the Union to bring back the workers to their senses."

"Weren't you there in time to hear Irma talk from the stand about the strikers attending his meeting?" asked Hoskins. "They are advised to attend en masse."

"The strikers are going to try to get a hearing, aren't they?"

"Yes, they are going to try, but I don't think they will."

<h2 style="text-align:center">3</h2>

Hoskins started to talk again on the labor movement, and what happened to labor leaders when there was any shooting. He was recalling how Ettor and Giovanitti had been kept in a cage for a year as accessories before the fact when a woman had been killed by a glancing bullet, in Lawrence in 1912. Then, on the Mesaba Range in 1916, Carlo Tresca and nine others were arrested as accessories before the fact when a deputy was killed in a scrimmage in a blind pig, in a scrap which had nothing to do with the strike. It was the inevitable history he was pointing out that any violence on the part of the workers would be used against the leaders.

Hoskins was apparently prepared to give a history of the entire labor movement. Roger had got to the point when he could listen no longer.

He recalled that he had friends in town. The Parkers, friends of his mother's, lived here. They spent the summers in Maine, where Roger's family went. He remembered Jean Parker as very pretty. He wanted to escape from any more talk of the strike and the labor movement and forget about it in the company of agreeable women who would ask him questions about his mother and prattle away pleasantly about inconsequential things. He felt that need of rest and of cheerful ordinary people sitting in comfortable rooms. He was conscious of having that stupidity which comes from having too many impressions at once.

How was he going to write his article? How was he going to give other people the impression he had received? How can you tell people who have never seen a strike what it means to the people who are striking? How can one indicate in the space of a few pages what makes people strike? How are you going to make other people feel terror?

Walking along the shaded streets in the very late afternoon, past rose gardens and pergolas, Roger still had the impression of walking along with Fer while people threatened him. He hadn't any of Hoskins' philosophy that such things always happened. He was new at the game and he had been shocked and disturbed by the terror.

4

It took him some time to find the Parkers' house. He had walked past it before he realized he had found it. The house was white and set far back from the street; it was surrounded by a lawn, and there were high shade trees over it. The street was lined with pleasant houses. There was a sense of good living about them.

The drawing room in which Roger waited was shady and cool and full of flowers. It seemed impossible that this world and the strike world should both exist in the same town. In a moment Jean Parker was calling:

"Mother, mother, who do you think is here? It's Roger Hewlett."

She was a tall girl with soft reddish hair and with the grace of manner that people identify with the South. Mrs. Parker was still beautiful with deep dark eyes and snow-white hair. Soon they were talking together as Roger imagined they would, and he was back in a familiar comprehensive world. Then Jean asked:

"What brought you down here, Roger?"

"I came to report the strike."

"That's fine," said Mrs. Parker. "You'll tell those people up North what's happening here. Mr. Schenk has left town now, I understand, and gone on back to Roanoke where he lives. But when he comes back

I'll have you meet him. He'll tell you how much he's done for these people who have turned on him now."

"It's all these Northern agitators," said Jean. "You have no idea how ignorant these mill hands are. My classmate, Marian Scott, teaches in one of the mill schools. You can't get anything through those ignorant women's heads, and so, of course, when a clever agitator, who is unscrupulous, like this Deane gets hold of them, why, he can do anything with such people."

"You've no idea how their conditions are bettered since they came down from the hills," said Mrs. Parker. "My father can remember mill hands so ignorant that they didn't even know what their last names were. They would say they were named John, son of David. They came from their mud-floored cabins and now they are getting nice houses with electric light free. And lots of them have baths."

"They never use the baths when they have them. They just use them to keep things in," said Jean.

"Where they didn't have a cent to bless themselves with before now they make more than professional men do. Take Jean's cousin. He's a young architect. He's been through college, studied architecture, studied abroad. Thousands of dollars have been spent on his education and all he's making is forty dollars a week. Take a family of four mountain people, each making eighteen-fifty a week, and that gives them an income of seventy-four dollars a week."

"Do they make that much," said Roger. "I thought the average wage was much lower than that."

"Oh, lots of them are making much more, my dear boy. Why, the time was when farmers with eggs and vegetables and chickens used to drive up to the house all the time to sell things. Now they never get past the mill village. The mill village buys up everything."

"They are awfully wasteful and extravagant buyers," said Jean. "You can't teach them to market properly. You know, Mother, how Marian tries and tries to teach them things, and how Miss Walters, the welfare worker, tries."

"It seems as if you could teach them devilment quickly enough," said Mrs. Parker. "Why, Roger, you'd hardly believe the things that have happened here. This fellow Deane preyed on their credulity and they came storming out of the mill like demons! And when the police stretched a rope across the street in front of the factory the strikers took hold of the rope and hauled it out of their hands so the chief of police fell right on his back. And then they barked at him like dogs."

"I understand the rope was put across a public road. Isn't it illegal to obstruct highways?"

"What would they do else? There those devils were calling, 'Scab! Scab!' and rioting and woofing and surging up on the mill, so naturally the police stretched a rope across to protect the mill."

"You write all these things, Roger. I understand there has been some adverse criticism in the Northern papers about them running that man Deane out of town. Why they didn't tar and feather him and ride him on a rail, I don't know. Men have no courage any more. They should have given him something to do that would have kept him out of here."

Mrs. Parker and Jean were both quivering with anger.

"You don't believe in kidnapping, do you?" Roger asked, his reporter's curiosity getting the better of his politeness.

"I believe in keeping the peace," said Mrs. Parker. "If the police and the law act too slowly, I believe in men showing their manhood."

"These people," repeated Jean, "these mill hands were all right before Deane came."

"We have never had any trouble with our workers," put in Mrs. Parker. "They are far better off than when they left the mountains, as I told you. Now these people are parading up and down with guns, setting off dynamite! No one's life is safe! Just because that Northern anarchist comes here and plays on their credulity! He's making any amount of money on them."

"Oh, certainly he is. What else is he here for?" said Jean. Into a moment's pause came Mrs. Parker's voice:

"I don't see why they haven't run him out of town. Why they should stop at such halfway measures I can't understand."

Roger shortly took his leave. Here was where the hate came from that he encountered on the street when he walked with Fer. Here was the home of the Mob. The comfortable people, the well-fixed people of Stonerton felt fury and outrage at the mill hands' revolt.

He thought of the little handful of organizers, Woods over in Tesner, Ferdinand Deane, Doris Pond working at relief, and Irma. They seemed to him incredibly isolated and remote.

3

1

A CROWD OF newspaper men were in the lobby of the hotel.

"Hey, Hewlett," some one called. "Saw you in the restaurant talking to Fer. Goin' to be trouble?"

"Looks like trouble, don't you think?" Durgan, the *Planet* man, called. "Sort of lynchy feeling in the air."

Three of the newspaper men were lean and dark, curiously of one type; they stood by Otis Bingham, a blond, inconspicuous little fellow with glasses. He was a local man, secretly sympathetic with the strikers. Suddenly some grotesque fancy made Roger see them as a pack of hunting dogs. There was gayety and alertness about them, you could fairly see their noses quiver at the scent of trouble, they wanted to go yapping down the wind together in the trail of disaster.

He went in to dinner by himself, seeing the world about him whirled into parable. There were the leaders, heavy with the love and hate about them. There was the mill village and the workers, a frail barrier between this handful of leaders and hate. And hate was the comfortable people. Hate and Mob were a multiplication of the Parkers. Roger meditated on what the basis was for their fury, which was as spontaneous as had been the workers' uprising. Well, that was the way things always were.

He came to no conclusion, but he had at that moment a picture, sharp and clear, of the cleavage in the community. It was as sharp as the feeling in a civil war.

2

A fat Chicago orator, Jellico, had been engaged at large expense by the Chamber of Commerce, to speak on "What Is Americanism?"

There was no hall large enough to hold the expected crowd, so by the courthouse and in the square in front, the streets had been roped off. A stand had been covered with American flags. It was dusk already, and the open spaces were filled with a crowd of working people which milled about gently and peacefully. Brown, lean people, poorly clad, dark-eyed, with long, rangy bodies. Groups of short-skirted young girls, with red-painted mouths. It was a crowd eager for anything that broke the routine monotony.

The people in the South will listen to more speaking than people anywhere else, though working people anywhere will come day after day and stand on their feet to listen to talk.

The high school band played. There was a little movement in the crowd. A delegation of strikers had asked, politely and timidly, to be allowed the stand some time during the speaking. The Mayor had replied that only the guest was to speak.

"There!" said Hoskins, who was standing beside Roger Hewlett. "Now there won't be any demonstration. The workers are so polite and timid. Those are the sorts of things that never get into the papers. Workers stand everything. They naturally shrink from initiative. They don't act until the breaking point. When we write about them in the papers, we always write about the moments of the breaking point, which gives the effect that the workers are always militant, looking for trouble."

"I know that's so, but how are we going to let the public know that it's so?" Roger asked.

"Take Fer; now there's a decent quiet chap, telling the workers to leave their guns at home; worried to death about a shooting. He's no fool; he's read the history of strikes. He knows what happens when anybody gets shot in a strike. The workers lose the strike, and the leaders go to jail. And do you suppose he could tell that to your friends the Parkers? They think Fer has hoofs and a tail."

"They believe that Fer, and Fer alone, has made the workers break out in a strike, and they believe a strike is a virulent disease like smallpox—catching." They talked while the music played. A tall bearded old man plowed past them. Hoskins told Roger:

"That's Oscar Williams, the preacher from the hills."

3

"Heart Beats," an enormous fat man, spoke. Everybody, including the Chamber of Commerce, expected him to attack the Union. Jellico was the type of man who weeps at the mention of a mother. He talked about his own mother and wept. He talked of brotherly love. He talked of this bright flowering spring time. This led him to a discussion of the flowers of all the different States, and that reminded him of all the war-ridden countries he had seen, and how much better was America, especially this beautiful, bright, flowering state of North Carolina. You could see a little stir in the crowd. A group of ex-service strikers who had planned to demonstrate and again ask for the floor, stirred restlessly. Irma came up to Hoskins and whispered:

"What's he talking about?"

For just at that moment, the fat orator started telling of the crowned heads of Europe and the generals he had met, with a childlike and engaging gusto. The Union leaders had expected a tremendous attack, a bitter denunciation of unionism. In place of this they were invited to consider the flowers of the States and how they grew. A fat, sentimental, good-natured man talking platitudes before these mill hands. An American flag before him, the principal men in the city on the platform beside him, all banded together against unionism, socialism, communism, anarchy. For in the minds of the important people assembled there beside Jellico, all these things were synonymous. Every one waited for the attack. There was none. Nothing but oozing sweetness. Every one was disappointed.

The people wove back and forth restlessly. Little bands were always passing and repassing. The crowd dribbled away.

"Well, Irma," said Hoskins, "you'd best have listened to Fer. What happened to the ex-service men and their demonstration? What you needed was a bunch of mothers and children with Mamie Lewes to sing one of her song ballads."

"The workers shouldn't be pathetic," she said dogmatically. "They should be militant!"

"We haven't been anything," said Fer in his matter-of-fact way. "We've just been a goose-egg, Irma." His reasonableness and absence of fanaticism was one of the reasons why Irma didn't consider him a leader.

4

"Where you staying, Hewlett?" he asked Roger.

"I'm at the hotel," said Roger.

"Oh, say!" Fer protested. "You oughtn't to be staying there. That's the scab hotel." He said it without enmity. "That's where I was kidnapped."

"Where do you stay?" Roger asked.

"I don't stay anywhere. I stay here some nights, and there some nights. Sometimes I stay at the Landors'. He's a carpenter. They've got a big house. Sometimes I go to Lafayette. Irma just lives around with the strikers, like I do. They're less apt to get me in a striker's house," he explained matter-of-factly. "Irma stays around the strikers because there isn't any regular money for salaries."

"I haven't been getting any regular salary," Irma threw in incidentally. "Sometimes I stay with Doris, she's got a room at Bispham's."

"Yeah, that's a good idea," said Fer. "Hewlett might stay at Bispham's. It's guarded nights. A good safe place to stay."

"Guarded?" Roger asked.

"Yeah, the boys wait up all night and take turns guarding. You know, so's the house won't get dynamited, and so no one will get kidnapped any more."

At this point young Hewlett, who had come to Stonerton in a light-hearted mood of adventure, found himself shoved violently out of his orbit and into the camp of the workers. The Parkers believed that all the trouble here in Stonerton was caused by Fer, and that it was their duty to "remove" him. Roger remembered Mrs. Parker's halo of white hair quivering as she assured him solemnly:

"If there is no law to remove this man and his associates, we will be compelled to take things into our own hands. We have a right to protect our lives and our property."

There was Fer sleeping around anywhere, without money and without privacy.

As a barometer of outside ignorance was old "Heart Beats," with his prattle about the crowned heads of Europe, American superiority, brotherly love and the State flowers.

5

Roger put his bags in a taxi and went down to Bispham's. The main street of Stonerton is as pretty a street as you would care to see. A river runs through the town, spanned by a suave and beautiful bridge. A simple shaft of a monument, commemorating the Veterans of the Spanish-American War, is at the end of the street. This street ends in a mountain, dark and beautiful. Opposite the monument is the court-house with a Colonial portico, flanked by a flight of white stone stairs.

On this street, further down, are the houses in which gentle people have lived, generation after generation. In the square before the courthouse is a tablet marking the fact that here was where the first settlers came seeking liberty and their own government. Piously, people pay tribute to their Revolutionary ancestors. They remember the pioneers, they remember the days of the Civil War. These same people who are always talking about patriotism and making Fourth of July speeches about liberty, were the same ones who had kidnapped Fer and visited such hate on striking workers that made the guarding of Bispham's necessary

6

Bispham's was a red brick house on the corner overlooking the square. Downstairs was a little restaurant, upstairs there was the rooming house. Next to Bispham's was a grocery store and next to that a filling station and garage. There was a gallery along the back of the house. And this, in turn, gave upon an open space which showed traces of once having been a garden. It was now littered with boxes and tin cans and other refuse from the grocery store.

Bispham was a heavy, silent man, broad-shouldered and stubby. Mrs. Bispham showed Roger a room which had a bed, a stand and a chair. The wide hall, lighted by a skylight, had a large sheet-iron stove and several chairs.

Max Harris and his wife lived here. He was a machinist in the mill and was well paid. He had struck with the others; and then one evening the bungalow which he had built had been blown up with dynamite. As she bustled about bringing fresh towels Mrs. Bispham informed Roger, "Wasn't pieces left large enough to pick your teeth with."

Doris Pond, the relief worker, a harassed, worried-looking girl, lived here, and Irma roomed with her from time to time. There was no water in the rooms, but at the end of the hall, near a window which looked out on the mountain, there was running water. Every one went out here to wash in the morning. It was simple and primitive and reasonably clean. He was glad to be here.

Presently four boys came in with guns. They were the same rangy mountain type that he had met before. One of them—a conspicuously good-looking lad—Del Cuthbert. They were conscious of their dignity. Two of them sat in the front room, where there was a piano, a suite of parlor furniture, of the kind that people buy on the installment plan, a bay window and two "store pictures." Two of them went out upon the back gallery. Mrs. Bispham called to Mrs. Harris:

"Law, Mis' Harris, it's thet back lot worries me. It's easy enough to slip in a piece of dynamite in thet thar back lot."

"It would be," Mrs. Harris agreed. She was a pretty, round-faced, dark-haired woman, and found pleasure in telling the story of hearing the explosion and coming home "never dreaming it was my house." Hoskins lived here too, and he sat talking to Fer and Bispham and Cuthbert, standing behind him and leaning upon his gun.

There was a sound of quick feet on the stairs. Mrs. Bispham called, "Howdy, Mis' Trent."

Mrs. Trent looked like a high school girl, with her short hair and very wide eyes.

"I jes' had to come up the street to-night and I thought I'd jes' come in and say howdy to youall. How is things?" She tried to be at ease but she kept twisting her hands nervously. Her eyes wouldn't leave Rob Trent's face. He had come in from the gallery. "How is things?" she repeated. "Is everything quiet? Is you lookin' for any trouble?"

"Everything's right quiet," said Mrs. Bispham, rocking.

"What's the matter, Lucy?" said Max Harris. "Is you skeered agin? You ain't any call for to be skeered."

"She ain't skeered," said young Trent. He leaned on his gun.

"No, I ain't skeered," she assured them. Presently she said good-night. The boys with guns went out on the gallery again.

"Pore little thing," said Mrs. Bispham. "Thet little Lucy Trent ain't been ma'ied but a couple of months and she's plum shore somethin's goin' to happen to her young husband. They ought to git one of the other boys to guard."

7

Roger waked up early in the morning. As he went out in the hall a woman was coming up the stairs carrying a heavy gray shawl. The guards were now sleeping in uncomfortable positions, one on the uncomfortable settee, one on the stiff sofa in the front room where they watched.

"I come to kiver up my boy. He's bin awatchin' all night. Come light they kin take a nap."

She moved quietly in where Cuthbert was lying. She looked very young to be the mother of so big a boy.

Soon the square began to fill with people. Trucks and cars came in from the mountains. The buzz of a crowd became loud. The police were already in evidence.

Trucks came adorned with red and white streamers. There were girls dressed in white, among the crowd, with blue ribbons and "Union" in red letters on a white band across their shoulders. Tall, large-featured old men shambled through the crowd. There were women from upland farms whose faces were tanned as though they were stained with butternut juice.

There were families of the workers in the new mill. These were workers newly drafted into the industry, mingling with the workers from the old mill village. They had come from far and near and some had been traveling before daylight. Their clothes told of how little they made. Their lined faces and their thin bodies told how hard they worked. It was the first time that Roger had seen a crowd of workers like this one, and he was unexpectedly moved. He wasn't ashamed to say as much to Hoskins.

"I know," he answered, "they get me too. I can't help remembering they're the docile one-hundred-per cent Americans. Look at them." Roger looked, and they made him feel mad inside.

"This makes me mad," he said. "They've been docile and one-hundred-per cent so long."

"I got mad seventeen years ago in Lawrence," Hoskins remarked without emphasis. "And I never did get over it."

8

The crowd in the square had grown. The police were uneasy and apprehensive. Harris, Wes Elliott, Irma, Doris Pond and other leaders were marshaling the workers in some sort of order. Roger had seen all kinds of workers' parades, and Hoskins had seen more. He had seen the beautiful parade which went from Passaic to Lodi where grave and impressive thousands walked unmolested and singing around the dye plant. Thousands on thousands of workers walking over the gray, wintry fields quiet and full of force and filled with hope.

But the parade of these North Carolina hill people would remain with him always as something more moving, in a way more significant, than any other demonstration he had seen.

They walked along with a good show of order, carrying their home-made signs. Men and women together, girls in groups, some riding in farm trucks and old Fords. They streamed forth with their banners of "WELCOME BACK FER!" demonstrating to whoever wanted to look—to the comfortable people, to the State of North Carolina, to America.

Here were people, men and women and children walking together, rank on rank of young mill workers walking along bearing banners that read "WE WANT SCHOOLS." Mill children's brigade.

There were smaller children with banners—"MUST WE GO TO THE MILL?" Here were men, women and children demonstrating by the means of marching through the streets with banners and a band that they wanted a little more pay and a few hours less work.

The Tesner workers had two trucks which had been lent them by neighboring farmers. Mamie Lewes was in one of the trucks. Her heart beat fast. She had lived alone and isolated. She made so little since her husband left that she couldn't even live on the mill hill. She knew few people. Now she was part of something—she was part of the parade. Yesterday she had joined the Union, as soon as she had gotten back to Tesner. And they had asked her if she would like to be in the parade. A band played. Banners waved. Mamie Lewes felt she would burst with excitement. Now Fer's car came along and every one was calling, "Fer! Fer! Fer!" at the top of his lungs. Mamie Lewes shouted.

She felt part of the crowd. They were all keeping time to one thing. They were all absorbed in something bigger than they were—something that brought them all together and merged them in something outside themselves. I reckon this is the solidarity that they's always talkin' about, thought Mamie Lewes, feeling she had made a valuable and novel discovery.

The windows were lined with comfortable people, people staring out with fear on the workers marching along. Police patrolled the streets. The newspaper men swept up and down in their cars, waiting for trouble.

There were two sides, mill workers and townspeople. It was almost a civil war. On the outside, a crowd of angry people, people buzzing like hornets when the nest has been disturbed. The workers with their ill-timed revolt had stopped the on-march of prosperity. Land values were booming, people coming into town, and just at this time the mill workers had to strike, and an unenviable publicity had resulted.

The river of workers flowed along, imposing. A menace in their numbers, a menace too, in their seriousness. Different from any other group of workers anywhere. Nothing like this had ever happened in these hills before. They had never looked upon each other, face to face, in a crowd like this.

It was heartening and inspiring. Little streamers, red, white and blue cheap paper ornaments. Everybody in his meager best. It was a strange thing to consider that all these people had come together because of Fer, a nice boy with a weak stomach. And Fer had been elected by what spin of the wheel of chance to lead them? Things like this skimming through Roger's mind while his heart beat fast to the tune of "Something's going to happen! Something's going to happen!"

Hoskins said: "It's dangerous, all right. Americans don't understand the philosophy of demonstration. European countries understand it—it's been their only right."

9

Just at this point it happened. No one knew exactly what.

Some one among the spectators made a cat-call. Some one had thrown something at the marchers.

The marching boys yelled back, "Kidnappers!"

Stones flew from the crowd on the sidewalk. The marchers broke ranks.

A fight started.

For a moment they wavered. It seemed hell was going to break loose. It seemed as if the parade would end in riot.

Just in time Dan Marks kept the workers in line. He was just in front of those who broke ranks, and called out:

"Keep marchin'!"

Other responsible workers took up the cry. "Keep marchin'!"

Just in time Harris and Old Man Trent and some of the Trent women drove up behind the fight and kept the rest in line.

The procession moved on, leaving a few people milling around in a fight.

There were some arrests. But the main part of the parade moved on.

Soon it was safe out of the town and headed for the mill village. Cars containing some of the older men and women bringing up the rear.

10

The departing parade left a crowd behind buzzing angrily in the streets.

"Ought've arrested them all."

"Ought've read the riot act to them."

"Guess they'll bring out the militia now."

"I expect they will, at that," said Hoskins.

The newspaper men were on their way to the telegraph station, there to write their stories from their various points of view. The *Times* man had just phoned the Governor. Dick Durgan had seen the Chief of Police. Some one else had an interview with Fer.

"Well," said Dick, "trouble all right. The Governor's sending the militia—be here to-night."

"Who started the row, did you see?"

"Some one threw rocks from the outside, then the fellows broke ranks."

Word sped out over the wires that there had been an attempt to break up the parade. These reports, not varying so greatly in substance, received their various interpretations, in the headlines of their papers. From the Press's "MILL THUGS ATTACK PARADE" to the local papers' "GOVERNOR CALLS TROOPS AS STRIKERS RIOT," which also that evening published the famous editorial, "How long is this fellow Deane to abuse our patience? How long are we to stand by and see mobs riot through the streets of our beautiful city?"

By the time the reporters were through, the parade was long over. People were dispersing. The feeling of tension did not abate. One still felt the imminence of violence.

At Bispham's Fer lay back in the stuffed armchair and fanned himself with his cap.

"That was a close call. Gee! Glad that's over." He took a deep breath. "I didn't want that parade. I didn't want it at all, but the strike committee wanted it and the workers wanted it. I want to get out of here, if it is only for the night."

One of the tall lantern-jawed men, followed by a big laughing girl, came in. The girl caught Fer's eye and smiled at him.

"Well, Fer," the man said, "I thought for a minute we was goin' to hev a war. Best come out to ma son's place for to-night. Youall come out and eat a bite with us." He included Hoskins and Roger. "The boys gotta car outside."

"Who'll hold the Union meeting?" Fer asked doubtfully. "There is a speakin' at the courthouse."

"They're getting everything ready to th' co'thouse," said the tall old man, Trent. "You speak firs', Fer, and weall be waitin' on you."

"Yeah," said Fer, "but what about the Union meeting?" Harris and some of the other boys had come in. Harris said, "It's best you shouldn't be raound town too much to-night. We'uns is techy and they'uns is techy t'night. You make yore talk shote, Fer, an' go off. We an' the other boys'll hold the meetin' 'thout you."

11

They drove up into the hills five miles. Fer and Roger and Trent and Hoskins and the girl in one rickety old car. A string of hair fell down beside her face; her cheeks, faintly pink, were covered with pale freckles. Her nose was exquisite, yet with a vague sensuality in its wide open nostrils. She was well built and plump and had a Rabelaisian quality in her laughter. She did not seem to fit into the severity of mountain life, yet she was an essential part of the whole scene.

A grandson of the tall old man was driving them. The girl was a daughter of the heavy middle-aged woman who received them. The house was a plain frame house, new. It was bought with money that the children had made in the mills. It had something of a frontier house about it, although it was in so old a community. Maybe the newness of it, or maybe the guns on the wall. Young men got up from everywhere as they came in. There were six boys, from fifteen to twenty-five. Only the eldest one was married, and lived at home with his wife.

Sitting against the wall was an older man with a kind, humorous face, whimsical lines around the mouth, and a well-shaped bald head. Beside him sat a very small, thin little girl. Her features were delicate and sharp with the finish of a woman. Her gray-green eyes at first seemed enormous. Roger later reflected that they looked so large only because her little face was so thin. She and her father held each other's hands.

Mrs. Trent said, "Fer, you know Mr. Jolas and Binney."

"Sure I do," said Fer, and he shook hands with them.

The women busied themselves in putting coffee and grits and hot biscuits, homemade jam and pickles, and fried salt pork on the table. The men talked together gravely. Binney Jolas and her father sat together in perfect contentment. From time to time she would look up at him with a swift birdlike look, from time to time he would look down at her. They were very poor, but at least they had each other. They had one thing no one could take from them. Binney had already worked over a year in the mill. It seemed impossible that she was fifteen.

The guests and the men all sat down at the table. The women waited on them. Presently Roger became aware of an atmosphere of affection among them. The young people really cared for one another. Here in the mountains kinship meant something. The boys' attitude toward their parents and toward each other, Binney and her father, together. Fer relaxed in this atmosphere of warmth and kindness.

After they had finished eating one of the boys brought out a fiddle. They started singing spirituals. They never sang popular music. They sang their own mountain ballads and hymns. When Hoskins and Roger drove away, Kate Trent had drawn her chair close to Fer. Her deep laughter seemed part of the warmth that was in the little frame house. They could hear this mingling with the singing as they drove down the hill.

4

1

THE MILITIA came in early in the morning. A company of boys in uniform tramped up from the railway station to the "scab hotel." There they spread over the small dining room as they had their breakfast. Tall boys for the most part, with accented features.

These boys were mountain boys too. They were kin to the boys and girls that they had come to guard. It happened in the Northern strikes Roger had seen, State troops had never been called out. In the North people take strikes with more philosophy. Here, where there had been practically no labor trouble, every one felt as though the end of the world was coming.

Roger watched the militia swinging smartly down the street with its young officers, one of whom fancied himself very much. He blustered along with a tear-gas bomb conspicuously at his belt. Presently they made a little encampment in front of the Basil Schenk Company's mill. Machine guns were planted on the top. There were only two companies, and yet the uniforms seemed everywhere.

The newspaper men talked to some of the boys. They didn't know what they had come for. They had heard of a dangerous young man, Fer. They heard he was stirring up folks and inciting riot. Roger thought of poor worried Fer back at Trent's, wishing to God he could stay there for a few days and look at the trees.

Ma Gilfillin and old Mis' Whenck came up to the boys while the newspaper men stood there.

"Boy," said Ma Gilfillin, "what youall reckon yore goin' to do yere? Yore goin' to guard the mill agin me, boy?"

The boys shuffled uneasily, and one of them said, "Why, no, Ma, I don' reckon we're agoin' to do no guardin' agin youall."

"Her an' me is strikers, son, and if yore aguardin' yore guardin' agin me. Look out you don' run no baynit into no old lady."

"Oh, no, ma'am," said the boy, "don' you worry, Ma."

"Thar's a good boy," said Mis' Gilfillin. "Reckon youall don' know what fer we're strikin', do you?"

"I never did yere much about it," the boy said.

Then one said, "We wuz just give word las' night to come. Heared they was a riot or somethin'."

"They wasn't no such thing," said Mis' Gilfillin. "We wuz aparadin' an' there was some thugs started to throwin' things, and they was a little mixup and when the shurf come they was a little woofin'. We don' need youall. They is all good quiet folks, jes like me."

The boys laughed uneasily. Girls came down the street grinning. The troops looked a little sheepish. They hadn't expected old ladies and girls. They had come for mobs and riots. The old ladies with their butternut-color faces, like their own women in the mountain villages, called out:

"Now you be good boys, an' be keerful with yore baynits."

2

Roger had had too many impressions in too short a time and he felt tired. The peculiar enervating feeling of terror. Trying to express to himself what their especial flavor was and how they differed from other people. A nagging persistence of something different in them, something very good, something at once complete and limited. The hate of the Parkers. The parade, at once beautiful, inspiring and nerve-racking.

Then there was the question of Fer. Roger saw one person, and Irma saw another. Fer appeared as the very anti-Christ to the Parkers and as a Messiah to the workers. And he was all these things. Actually this burdened anxious boy was all these many different things.

Roger decided to rest by driving around and diverting himself with a look at things and see what sort of story the stones and bricks would have to tell him. They never lie to you. They will, if you let them, tell you all the aspirations of the people. They will name their rulers and their gods and tell you of their defeats and their victories. The story was this.

Stonerton Old Town had been the county seat, which it yet was. You could see the trace of an old Southern village, sleepy and yet with its own proud dignities. The Taliaferros and the Cuthberts had years before started a boom here. At that time a handsome boulevard had been cut. The suave bridge had been built on which now was cut the name of Taliaferro, who built it.

Then came the cotton mill boom, and the new town of Stonerton had reared its head. Stonerton Old Town had only one mill village, the Basil Schenk Company, which employed over a thousand people. This mill village clustered around the mill in the valley and then ran crazily up and down hill. Forlorn wooden houses perched in red mud on brick legs. The hyphen of a street that connected the mill village to Stonerton had a few plaintive, down-at-the-heel stores. The workers on their small wages did not make enough for them to need more. Everything in the mill village was slack and depressing.

New Stonerton, two miles away, was as though in a different world. It lacked the mellow-faced Colonial courthouse, and the beautiful little stream flowing under its gently arched bridge. It had a humming, youthful vitality. There were two parallel business streets, crossed by two more parallel business streets. These were full of modern shops. It had been no more than a crossroad thirty years before. Now it could almost boast of being the center of Piedmont textile industry. There were fine new public buildings everywhere, mostly of a light brick and designed by competent architects on good Colonial models. The town had everything: hospitals, schools and, what was unusual for a Southern town, a handsome library building with grounds around it.

How dignified and pleasant was the "residence section." Beautiful grounds, lawns, rose-gardens, and shade trees. Out of town, where the pretty river had been coaxed to give water for a swimming pool and an artificial lake, was the country club. Boys in flannels, girls in white dresses were flashing around the tennis court. The wide grounds of the country club were a pleasant mixture of wildness and landscape gardening.

Meantime, encircling the town were the mills. One mill after another, each with its mill village clustered about it. Some of the older mill villages had shade trees and gardens and plants. For the most part there were ugly monotonous frame houses growing out of red mud. The whole spectacle was, for a Northerner, as astounding as America is to an Englishman. Within a generation, hundreds of mills had been built. Millions on millions had been invested. A whole new order had come to pass. The plate-glass and brick mills were all new. Very different from the forbidding gray and brick barracks of Fall River and New Bedford, or of Passaic and Paterson.

The people who had made this prosperity, and the workers who had made possible this prosperity, were all Americans. No foreigners here. Northern capital had poured in, but the initiative of all this had been of the South. Here was an industry as new and as powerful as anything the West could show in the new automobile towns—and now the workers had checked this progress with their demands.

The answer had been Fury and Terror.

3

When Roger got back he found Dick Durgan and Hoskins talking with Fer in the little restaurant underneath Bispham's.

"Hey! Listen to this," Dick called to him.

"You know how the picketing's done here?" Fer said. "The boys and girls go out in cars, sometimes twenty or thirty miles, and try and block the roads that lead into Stonerton County. They are bringing strike breakers from Gaston and Carrabus and other places."

"How many are out?"

"Over eighty per cent," said Fer, "easy."

"The mills say they got workers enough."

"They always say that. That's their regular song. What they mean," said Fer, "is they could get scabs enough—if we'd let 'em come in. But it would take them awhile to get any production." He looked refreshed and young. His skin was clear and his eyes were clear. The shadow of the Terror was lifted from him for the moment.

"Who's the picket committee?" Ed asked.

"Oh, there are a lot of the boys. They all get together at Union meetings and make up their plans. There come a lot of the fellows now."

A lot of young men came in calling, "Hey, Fer, Fer! We want to speak to you!" Behind them a crowd of young girls. There was life about them; a young initiative. A lack of sullenness. Lusty young people, close to the soil and conscious of their own unspoiled power.

"These kids," said Hoskins, "are individualists. Up in the mountains they scarcely know what the machine age is. They think they have political power to run things. They haven't the slightest idea what they are bucking, for back of these manufacturers is the Textile Manufacturers Association and back of that are all the organized employers of the South."

"You don't think they got a chance, do you?" asked Dick Durgan.

"Gosh, boys," said Hoskins, "I don't say who's got a chance, when I think of Rome and the early Christians, and I remember the Catacombs and what happened to Rome. Then I remember that, after all, the Roman Empire won out and the Christian statuary became as expensive as Caesar's!"

4

Roger was awakened before dawn by Dan Trent, Old Man Trent's boy, knocking on his door. Cautiously he put his head inside the door and said in a low tone:

"Youall want to get out on the picket line?"

He had a gracious and pleasant voice. There was an old touring car in front and Roger piled in with a crowd of strikers. Dawn was breaking clear and pure among the lovely hills. They turned off without going into New Stonerton. The emptiness made the streets of Old Stonerton seem wide. They turned into a dirt road which followed a winding creek up a narrow mountain gorge. They heard two cars honking ahead of them. A crowd of young strikers out on the picket line.

"They's lots of them boys been tearin' up an' down these hills all night. They's them that says that when they work all night for the bosses they can work all night for the Union," Dan said.

He was a big boy with rusty brown hair and brown eyes of a warm red color like all the Trents, and with a supply of freckles with his deep tan.

The road was winding always upward. Once in a while they passed a neat-looking farmhouse. Throughout this country the growing prosperity had done away with the old-time log cabins and blackened frame houses. New farmhouses had been built, small but neat and painted.

Soon above the motor they heard shouts and "woofing." This was a sound that Roger had heard in no other place. He had heard "booing" and there is dread in it, he had heard cat-calls, and there is malice in cat-calls. But the woofing of Stonerton had in it something gay and taunting and dangerous. The barking of a dog and yet not the barking of a dog. On the clear morning breeze came the high yapping of girls—

"Woof! Woof! Woof!" taunting and insistent and provocative.

"That's them," said Dan.

They turned a corner and stopped with a sudden jolt. They were at the end of a long line of cars and trucks.

Mamie Lewes and four other strikers from Tesner were on the picket line. They had come in an old Ford. Woods, the Tesner organizer, had suggested that Tesner send a car of pickets to show the solidarity of the Tesner workers.

Williams had said, "I want you should come, Sister Mamie Lewes. Kin yo' git to leave the chillen?"

"I nat'chally jist had to leave 'em when I was aworkin'. Sense we struck I ben with 'em more'n ever I could. I reckon ef I kin leave 'em to work I kin leave 'em to picket."

She was a little frightened and a little defiant. Ef they touch me I'll fight 'em, she thought, and then she saw the scabs and forgot everything else in her opposition to them. She set herself against them as though she alone could keep them out of the mills. Excitement mounted in her. She saw a young soldier who looked like kin of hers and shouted to him:

"Youall oughta be fightin' fer us instead of agin us." He flushed and his embarrassment gave her courage. "Youall oughta be ahepen' us instead of ahinderin' us," she cried.

Some one near Mamie Lewes started the cry of "Woof! Woof! Woof!" and she, not conscious of what she did, took up the cry of:

"Woof! Woof! Woof!" in her high, clear voice.

Boys and girls had gotten out and were strung along the road. Opposite them, terribly uncomfortable, a little bristling, a little truculent, were the State troops. There was something in their bearing at once insolent and apologetic.

The opposing sides were all young. Few older men and women came out on this distant picket line. They were not only all of the same State, but of the same blood. There was something between them defiant and glittering and dangerous. Anything could happen.

Everybody was walking like dogs tiptoeing about to pounce. Everybody had been moving with terrible gentleness. Old men said to one another:

"We don't want a war, but ef we have to have a war, if they bring a war to us, why, we are bound to fight."

5

There was the sound of wheels from both directions. A truck load of scabs, with the National Guardsmen riding on the radiator, came around the curve in the dirt road. Behind them was a car full of the newspaper boys.

The strikers made a dash forward. The "Woof! Woof! Woof!" grew to a formidable howl, shrill girls' voices barked, "Scab! Scab! Scab!" The truculent young lieutenant called out:

"Get back every one of you!"

Rocks flew through the air.

A girl stood in the middle of the road her arms out-stretched, a little laughing girl with curly hair, whom they later came to know was Cactus Kate, snatched a pistol from the hand of an astonished deputy and stood brandishing it in midroad. An absurd and melodramatic little figure.

There was the sound of more wheels and another truck load of scabs approached. A cry went up from the workers; they moved forward. The girls, gay, the younger ones as though they were acting before a movie camera.

"There always are girls like that who keep in the limelight in every strike," Hoskins growled. "And they do a lot of harm."

The strikers moved forward. Roger's sense of what happened afterwards was like something on a slow-motion screen. Both sides seemed tentative and uncertain.

6

The second truck tried to move out. Strikers were in front of it. The boys of the National Guard grasped their guns ready for an order. Roger had the impression of something terribly insecure; something that had in it all the elements of both farce and frightful tragedy. For a moment all action seemed to stop, all action seemed poised like the moment before water flows over a dam.

A peculiar split second moment of division between probability of what may happen and action. The strikers and the scabs were swearing at each other and shouting nervously. The young lieutenant, still nervous and truculent, gave an order. A tear gas bomb was thrown. Everybody was hiding his eyes now. The strikers drew back.

An order was given by the soldier who sat with the driver of the truck. He plowed through the crowd, scattering them before him.

There were screams. As the truck went strikers, their hands over their eyes, staggered forward to pick up a girl. Another girl rose up in the road, her face a mass of blood. A third screamed.

"I'm killed! I'm killed! It ran over my body."

The little girl in red, who had brandished the deputy's gun, gave little staccato yelps. "Ow! Ow! Ow! They ran over Annie! Ow! Ow! Ow!"

"Hey, help me with this one. Goddamn them bastards, they ran over the girl!"

"Did you hear them give the order, 'Step on it! Clean 'em up, boys'?"

Some one said, "Put them under arrest. Come on." The deputies and police sprang forward.

A girl's voice, loud, "Come on. Save them the trouble, boys. They're arrestin' us."

A few were still wiping their eyes, but most of them had now recovered their spirit. Defiant and gay they made for the trucks. They were rounding up as many as they could of the crowd of two hundred strikers. Nearly a hundred were arrested or arrested themselves. As they clambered into the trucks they were saying, "I done as much as he done. Ef you're goin' to arrest him, arrest me."

"Arrest us all. We was all in it together."

Trouble had passed over in a moment like the shadow of a cloud. The boys in uniform were grinning again. A little angry, a little peevish and infinitely relieved. Strikers were growling among themselves.

"Did you see 'em run us down?"

"Yeah, run us down like dawgs."

Roger's car led that procession back to town out of the narrow road. After them, singing Union songs, shouting and woofing, came the arrested strikers in their trucks.

7

The arrested strikers were confined in the courtroom pending the trial. The courtroom was upstairs, led to by the handsome white marble steps. They were shut up in the courtroom because the jail was already full of other arrested strikers. The brick courthouse with its two lofty pillars looked like a stage setting. The militia with rifles and bayonets were lounging around at the pillar base. They deployed themselves picturesquely the length of the flight of steps. The girl strikers leaned out of the window singing:

> "Listen you scabs ef you want to hear
> The story of a cruel millionaire.
> Basil Schenk is that millionaire's name.
> He bought the law with his money and his frame
> But he can't buy the Union with his money and frame!"

More guards around the courthouse, more of them around the mill. The boys and girls who were arrested had refused to give their names or had given fantastic ones. Stories were being sent out by some of the reporters: "PICKETS BATTLE MILITIA!" Hoskins was picking away for the Affiliated a story that read:

> "A hundred boys and girls, striking textile workers, were shut up in the courtroom awaiting trial. Are the hospitals of Stonerton full of wounded scabs? Are the local police walking around tied up in bandages and adhesive tape? Not at all. The only blood that has flowed has been that of the strikers. Why then this lavish display of armed forces? What of the machine guns and guards around the mills? Why are the militia men strung all over the courtyard as though they were 'The Army of Occupation'? Well, the striking workers picket the entire county. They object to the importing of

scabs from other counties. They cover the roads to the mountains and those leading to Virginia and Tennessee."

Hoskins was having a swell time with his story. Crowds of boys and girls were buzzing around Bispham's rooming house or sitting around downstairs getting a cup of coffee. From far and near, people were coming in to the trial. The square around the monument again was filled with rangy, gentle-voiced farmers; more old women this time coming in to see the young people tried.

8

Trials and camp-meetings are some of the natural forms of amusements in the Southern mountains. There was a tremendous contrast between the brown women and their long, gray calico skirts, some of them still wearing old-fashioned sunbonnets and the kids of the picket line with their jauntily swinging skirts and their lip-sticks.

"They may not have time to brush their hair before they go on the picket line, but every mother's daughter paints her cupid's bow before she gets out," observed Hoskins.

It got to be time for the trial. Roger walked up the steps and encountered six soldiers with crossed bayonets who asked him his business. The trial was already on. Ty Burdette, the strikers' lawyer, was cross-questioning one of the deputies. A lot of people were in the courtroom in spite of the amount of questioning they were subjected to. A row of the militia men was strung along in front of the rail which divides the court from the audience.

The young "Looie" who looked like a stern-lipped movie actor, strolled up the aisle followed by his men at arms. The "Looie" showing a little tear gas bomb at his belt. The whole, the inside and out, was like a stage set: the audience, farmers and strikers. The hundred defendants, excited, full of their own importance. The scene here, like the parade, like the picket line, was full of danger, now at the moment full of laughter. Burdette, gray, hook-nosed, with sixty murder trials to his credit, was heckling Thomas A. Dixon, a deputized lawyer.

"Didn't you know that it was against the law for a lawyer to be deputized?" Burdette snarled. Dixon's answer was inaudible, then louder he told the story of the run-in with one of the strikers.

"Did she injure you; hit you or inflict a wound upon you?" Burdette barked with insulting sarcasm.

"She swore at me and called me all kinds of a son—you know what kind of a son she said I was!"

"I can surmise," said Burdette dryly. The courtroom of strikers roared.

The judge, enormous, with a face the color of a purple plum, pounded with an empty pop bottle.

"This is not a show, but a court of law," he proclaimed. It was so much more like a show than any court of law. Every one too typical. Long, lean farmers, country women, the red-faced judge who looked as if he liked his liquor; the keen, gray-haired lawyer with his delicate parchment-colored face and his sharp, pouncing manner; all far too typical. All as though cast for type, and yet there it was really happening.

"Which is the little girl you say intimidated you?" said Burdette. The small, curly-haired little girl in the red coat—Cactus Kate—stood up smiling. There was a shout of laughter again and tramping.

The young "Looie" gave an order to the sergeant, who started to put a man out. He protested.

Suddenly the courtroom was in an uproar.

A moan swept over it.

The judge hammered with his pop bottle.

In the back of the room Fer got to his feet. His voice came out extremely clear, dominating the menacing tumult.

"Everybody keep their seats, it's all right." They sank down quietly. Fer stood among them, his shoulders forward, looking a little heavy as though he were about to lunge; and then he dropped back in his seat.

5

1

THAT NIGHT they all sat talking in the hall with the skylight,
around the cold cast iron stove in Bispham's. They congregated here
rather than in the stuffy and uncomfortable sitting room. Mrs. Bispham,
fat and unpretentious, sat with her hands on her knees. Irma was full
of excitement. She and Hoskins wrangled about Cactus Kate. Irma said
she was a militant worker. Hoskins said she was a limelight artist and
had seen hundreds like her, always getting into trouble. Doris Pond
sat on the uncomfortable settee, her head in her hand, and a stream
of hair hanging down.

"Tired, Doris?" Irma asked.

"Uh-huh," she said. "I expect every last mother of all the girls that
are arrested have been around headquarters asking about them."

"This ought to help the relief," said Irma practically.

"Something's got to," said Doris.

"Aren't you getting help from the farmers?" Hoskins asked.

"This is an awful bad time for the farmers," said Doris. She was in
a bad humor, and life looked dark to her. In a strike a frightful weight
falls on any one who is directly responsible for the relief work. It falls,
of course, on the strike leader, but with his problems of strike leadership,
bolstering morale and his daily meetings, the actual administration of
relief does not fall on him. The collection of local funds and the
administration of the funds collected by the Workers' Aid from labor
union and sympathizers is left to some head relief worker and to the
relief committee.

Here in Stonerton Doris was responsible. Each day saw her gutted, and days like this a flood of human beings poured over her. She was scooped out, crouching over; while Irma sat on the edge of her chair, gushing a little. Roger heard her say:

"Such militancy! Such militancy!"

"You won't be satisfied until every last one of you are in jail, will you?" said Hoskins.

Irma said in an aggravated tone, "I don't wish to go to jail, but I expect to."

"If you let folks like this Cactus Kate caper around, your expectations are going to be fulfilled," said Hoskins. "Where's Fer to-night?"

"How should I know?" said Irma, flushing a little. Kate Trent had been waiting around to get a sight of Fer, but Fer had been too involved in the morning's arrests to notice anything else. Roger had an idea Irma was thinking of this. She had been walking with him when he noticed Kate Trent. Kate was that earthy type of woman who, as a possible rival, infuriates a girl of Irma's intellectual pretensions. Irma wasn't in love with Fer, but he was enough hers to make her resentful of a girl like Kate.

The core of the strike, its fighting machine, had very little time for romance or even sex; but always beating up around the outskirts of it were a tribe of pretty little girls, excited about the strike leaders, using the strike and the excitement of the strike to attract the boys.

Days in a strike that began with almost the excitement of war, danger, girls hurt, cars crashing through crowds, arrests, courts, end with a depression of fatigue. They sat and stared at one another. Doris was too tired to go to bed. The stout Bisphams seemed rooted to their chairs. The Harrises, and various other boys were standing around. Bits of the morning's events drifted through their talk. Presently the guards came in. They clanked their guns, loaded them, while the rest drifted off to bed. Roger didn't go to sleep right away. He wondered where Fer was. That set him off on a train of thought as to the extravagant absurdity of settling an industrial dispute with near war.

2

It seemed to Roger that he hadn't been asleep at all when he was awakened by an explosion. The crash came so loud, it seemed that it was in the back yard. He jumped out of bed thinking, "They've dynamited us." Every one appeared at the doors of their rooms, simultaneously, like people in a bedroom farce — the chunky Bisphams, the Harrises, Irma and Doris, Hoskins, together with some of the other boys.

"What was that, it seemed near by?"

"Wes, did you see any one?"

"No, I didn't see a thing."

"I thought I seen a couple of fellows pass a while ago."

"Where was it, do you suppose?" Every one of them was sure that some worker's house had been dynamited.

Every one of the comfortable people who were awakened by the blast were sure that it was the strikers.

They sat there for over an hour tensely waiting for something to happen. Twice footsteps came down the deserted street. A few cars passed. Otherwise silence. Then further away came another explosion. It seemed to rip through them like shell fire. It was almost more nerve-racking than bombardment, sitting waiting like this. They sat staring at each other.

There came an alarm of fire. That was something to do. They dressed and streamed out into the street. Before they started they could see the flames streaming up from one of the hills. People flocked from all parts of town. Excited faces silhouetted around the fire.

It turned out to be the chicken houses and outhouses of a man in no way connected with the strike. The fire was exasperating and mean-ingless.

"What were the explosions?" Roger asked some of the newspaper men who had been down to police headquarters.

"They don't know where it was. They haven't located it. They blew up the old water wheel down in the creek. It belongs to Trent's brother." There was a disconcerting aimlessness about both fire and explosions. One had the feeling of mischief being afoot, indirect, spookish, un-accountable.

3

Roger slept late. He was awakened by rapping on his door. Irma's voice, urgent, worried, awoke him. He threw a bath robe on and she came in.

"Dress quickly, will you? Fer hasn't come in yet. A woman's been arrested, Liza Robertson, a lame woman. On the picket line this morning they arrested two other women. Woods is gone and Doris is off on some relief work."

He got into his clothes while he could hear her walking up and down in the hall outside.

"Woods is gone?"

"He left for New York," said Irma briefly. "I want you to go over with me to Burdette's over to Lafayette. I haven't been able to get him on the phone."

4

Burdette's office was in an adjoining town twenty miles away. Lafayette is older and larger than Stonerton. It has existed quite a long
time as a city. It was there that Burdette had his headquarters. One of
the strikers drove them over in an old Ford; they paid for the gas. It
was the first time Roger had driven through Piedmont. It was exciting
landscape. Piedmont is red. Some fields were a tender rose color, and
again there was a purple bloom over the earth. They rolled along a
plateau fringed by beautiful hills.

There was beauty here to make the fortune of a European princi-
pality. The road wound sharply upward toward a narrow gorge. Everywhere the hillsides were clothed in rhododendrons. The laurel, white
and pink, flung its lovely branches through the woods and everywhere
was the flash of orange azalea. The road was magnificent. The houses
along the road were new, the farms looked prosperous. Where was the
slow and sleepy South of which we read so much? Tucked away perhaps
in places of Virginia and South Carolina. Not here in Piedmont. They
drove past rows of handsome houses surrounded by gardens. Wealth
had poured into this city. Here peoples' houses were even better than
the good and substantial houses in Stonerton. A few were old, the
most of them were comparatively new, built after models Colonial of
the eighteenth century, each with its porte-cochère.

They turned into a shabby quarter of the town, overhung with dusty
trees. The yards were shabby and ill kept. It would have been hard
to find an equal contrast in a New England town. The houses would
have at least been painted and the yards kept clean and the fences in
repair. In this slack part of the town they stopped. A pleasant faced
woman in a neat starched wash dress came to the door. Irma asked
before she could speak:

"Is Fer here?"

"Fer's asleep, Irma," she answered. "He's awful tired."

"Oh, he is here then?"

"Wherever did you think he was?"

"I didn't know," said Irma. Roger had a sudden flash that she might
have imagined that he had gone. All the way over she hadn't spoken
nor had she seemed to hear Roger when he spoke to her. Sunk in her
own thoughts she had not made the slightest response to his occasional
comments. She was as unconscious of her rudeness as she was of
Roger. Fer came out yawning. He looked tired and white.

"Hello, Irma!" he said. "Hello, Roger. What's up?" He let himself
down on a chair inert and heavy, like one unrested.

"What are you doing over here?" Irma said. "Why haven't you showed up after the arrests yesterday, after everything. What's happened? Why do you stay off like this?"

"Gosh, Irma, I was up late last night with the strike committee. I was up till three and then I had to drive over here. Burdette told me not to sleep in Stonerton last night. Not for anything. He said they were laying for me."

"Well, Woods is gone," Irma threw at him. He stared at her point-blank.

"Woods gone! Where?"

"Gone to New York. That's where he's gone. Gone North, anyhow."

"Gone and left that strike situation over in Tesner! Gone and left his workers!" said Fer.

"That's what he's done. You know they threatened to run him out. He said that he had told you already, that he wasn't going to be any martyr stuff for you, that you could stay down here and be a martyr if you wanted to but he wasn't. That's what you get, getting a fellow like that, just in the labor movement for the fun he has in it."

"But, gosh, Irma," he said, "there's a strike situation in Tesner. Things just coming to a head."

"He said he told you he was going."

"I told him not to go," said Fer.

"Oh, you told him not to go," said Irma insultingly, "and that was going to settle it, was it?"

"I told him not to go until I could get some one else." He looked at Irma with a certain air of grimness that Roger hadn't seen before. "God Almighty," he said, "I'd like to wring his neck."

"You don't need to blame anybody but yourself, Fer. Did you go over and do anything about it? No, you didn't! You knew he was going to leave. What did you do? Go over to Trent's and play a fiddle, running around with Kate Trent!"

"Shut your trap!" said Fer shortly. "You haven't any right coming to talk to me like this, Irma, trying to crow over me the way you do all the time. You try to get in my way in the running of this strike. The next thing you know you'll be out, too."

"My having to come here," cried Irma, "to tell you Woods was gone! Pull you out of bed, hold down the strike committee and relief committee this morning and none of your men showing up at a critical moment!"

Fer looked at her with forbidding contempt. "We all know you're perfect, Irma," he said. "Come on, Roger, I'm going to throw some coffee into myself and I've got to go up and see Burdette."

5

They had coffee. Fer and Irma didn't speak again except when he threw her an abrupt question concerning Woods, and she threw her answer back with a brevity as insulting as his. There was friction between them and yet it wasn't warfare. Underneath their mutual irritation there was something deep between them of understanding.

They seemed more like married people bickering because the stuff of which their understanding was made was durable, rather than like young people who were sweethearts. There was a continuous pull and strain between them of a man and woman fighting for supremacy over each other.

Burdette was waiting in his office. His face was more parchment-like than ever. The bold hook of his nose, his overhanging fine white brows made him resemble an eagle more. He was having a swell time. He was a true fighter. If he had been in Fer's place he would have had no dark moments of doubt nor of anxiety. He had fought for the lives of over sixty men. He was one of the most noted criminal lawyers in the county, or in the State, for that matter. More than once in the old days he had been shot at. He had never known what fear was, only an itching to get at the enemy, and he was full of fine, round Southern oratory about the sufferings of the workmen.

"At no time and in no State, suh, have the liberties and rights of a sovereign people been so trampled underfoot. At no time and at no place has the murderous cupidity of a few men dared to trample underfoot a people's just demand for their betterment. Have these workers asked a fraction more money? What are they getting, from $6.90 to $14 a week, suh, fo' eleven hours' work a day.

"What is their crime? Why are the jails full? Have they kidnapped any one? Have they dynamited houses? Have they set fires? Have they assaulted persons or threatened them with murderous weapons? No one pretends they have. They have exercised their constitutional rights and for that the military forces of the country are illegally being used against them. Machine guns, tear gas, bayonets, intimidations, threats, dynamitings. The terror that walks by night and the terror that brazenly parades the streets of our peaceful town by day."

He might have been pleading a case before the Supreme Court of the United States. His eyes snapped, and for all his oratory he was sincere. A good Jeffersonian Democrat who believed in the constitutional rights and in such things as liberty and democracy. One still finds such people who are not cynical when they voice beliefs of this kind. He heard Irma's account of the fracas this morning with the lame woman.

"Fer," he said, "what about getting her affidavit for me?"

"Roger," Fer said, turning to him, "here's that chance you've been wanting, to get in touch with the workers. You could get this affidavit and some others. You can hang around the relief store and ask the folks as they come in for their statements."

6

The relief store was gloomy. On account of the windows being boarded up it was always in a half light. It had been a real store once, and now its empty shelves seemed to spread themselves with a sort of taunting symbolism. The store was always full of people, women with babies, children playing under foot, groups of men talking in corners. Women waiting for the moment to come when food would be distributed.

"Wait in the relief store for a day and you will see American prosperity pass before your eyes," said Irma. Here, by the shoes on their feet and by the faded, skimpy dresses you could learn the condition of these American workers, for they had nothing. The church and the State can investigate the textile industry, North and South, but for the average person all they need to know is that the mothers of small children have to work at night to keep their families in food and necessities.

Here were old and toothless women who yet had delicate and fine features. In one corner sat a listless man with his face the peculiar yellow by which in wartime one recognizes prisoners. He sat emaciated and staring at nothing almost with a certain expression of idiocy.

"What's the matter with him?" Roger asked Doris, who was standing beside him.

"Pellagra," she answered briefly. "It's all through the mills here. It's caused by their diet."

"Why don't they eat more cabbage and green things?" he asked. "Can't they get them?"

"Give them more money," she said, "and they'll eat better. All they have money for now is fatback and flour and grits." The crowd shuffled aimlessly to and fro. They had the patient air of people existing in a vacuum with nothing to do. The older men and women were almost all lean and meager.

Nowhere does one see the blooming peonies of women which one will inevitably see in any group of Italian or Portuguese or Hungarian workers. Yet now and then there were men and women, too, of striking physical beauty. Something at once unspoiled and potent and complete. Even though they now drifted back and forth slackened there was an undercurrent of excitement. Even in this place that had something about it of a waiting room where trains never left, there was an undercurrent of hope.

7

A stout woman in her thirties limped into the room. One would notice her because she had a little weight.

"Hello, jail bird," they called to her, "when did you get out? Huccum you got arrested?" It was Liza Robertson. "Huccum they 'rested you, Liza?"

"Well, I was astandin' over near the mill offices watchin' the military line up, yestiddy. A military guard, he come out and he says to me, 'You git along crost the street.'

"I says, 'You ain't in no call to sass me like that.'

" 'Dam quick git along crost the street,' he says.

" 'Quit you cussin', you ain't got no call to sass me like that.' He cussed at me ag'in, tol' me to git to hell out ef I didn't want to git arrested. Well, I went on crost the street. I didn't go fast enough to suit him. When I got most two feet from the curb up comes a military boy and don't he start cussin' at me, too.

" 'Goddamn you,' he says to me. 'You git a move on you. I've a mind to arrest you, crawlin' along like that to be aggrivatin'.'

"I said, 'I'm not goin' to move no faster than I'm amovin' now. I couldn't go no faster, you fool,' I says to him. 'Cain't you see I'm a cripple?'

"I been a cripple since I was five years old. Youall know I had a fall when I was five years old and got a hip out and I cain't walk no faster. That's how come I'm fat because I cain't move like folks.

"Well, he jis put his gun and baynit there acrost his breast and hung onto it and he shoved me. I was mad, and I took my two arms and I came up against him and I shoved him and he took his gun and shoved me clean acrost the sidewalk and I most fell, but I was so mad that I came for him and shoved him and then the police came arunnin' up and that low down Murck and that there Zober they lay hold of each one of my arms and they twisted my arms and I gave a holler.

" 'Shet you mouth,' they said, 'you goddam son-of-a—.' And they threw me into the police wagon. I mean they tuck and threw me. Three or four of them lifted me right up and threw me into the car.

"Then on the way to the jail they started in and they called me all the vile names they is. They called me a big fat you know what, and I says, 'Leave me alone,' and they kept on atwisten' and I said, 'You ain't got no manhood, you low down trash,' and that Murck leaned forward and slapped me in the face five times and he says, 'Goddam you to hell, we're goin' to twist your big fat arms most off you.' And they most did."

The people stood around, listening solemnly to this recital. Their world had been turned upside down by the strike. The sheriff, whom they had helped to elect, had turned against them. The policemen — the "laws" — twisted the arms of respectable women like Liza Robertson, and slapped them.

8

The Northern mill workers, composed almost entirely of foreign-born, have a strike tradition. They know what to expect. They know the police are going to be against them. They can meet brutality without the fury that possessed these Southerners.

The next few days were quiet. The interest focused in the courthouse where Burdette furnished a free show to the people. Mill workers and farmers crowded the courthouse to capacity every day. The guard had been dispensed with. As Burdette pointed out, the police had been sufficient to preserve order in the county up to now, and the people were much more likely to listen to their own sheriff than to some eighteen-year-old whippersnapper. Burdette made a monkey of the prosecution. The enormous, red-faced judge shook silently as the old lawyer lashed with sarcasm, ridiculed, turned their testimony inside out.

Meanwhile, there was a curious shift in the temper of the workers. The first day or so that the military came in, they had been full of suspicion. Roger was walking along the street with Irma and Fer a day or two after this, and Irma said sharply:

"Look at that!"

He followed her eyes across the street. There was Cactus Kate and two other girls, each arm-in-arm with guards. The boys in uniform were half-sheepish, half-pleased.

"I'd think you'd stop that," Irma said.

Fer grinned.

"They're fraternizing," he said. "I told them to."

"You told them to?"

"Sure," said Fer. "They're the same folks, the same blood. There's no reason why they shouldn't understand what this is about. Make 'em good and ashamed of being put on this kind of guard duty."

"You are confusing the minds of these workers," said Irma. "The police and soldiers are their natural enemies, and they ought to be taught to consider them so."

"You read that in a book," said Fer. "You'd better go and read another book, Irma, that will tell you about winning over the military."

They had bickered about this for a long time. Irma had a way of trying to ride over Fer, of trying to undermine his dignity, and to pluck from him his confidence in himself. But he resisted her stubbornly.

"Irma," he said in the end, "you're a good girl, but you don't know everything. This fraternizing business is going to be carried out."

6

1

THE CROWD milled around the speaking stand. A row of men sat on the railway embankment. On the outskirts of the crowd were little families—a man and a woman and several babies playing around. They sat down on the ground. Ma Gilfillin and Ole Mis' Whenck cruised through the crowd, stopping everywhere to ask:

"Ain't Fer acomin'? You seen Miss Irma?"

They were both dressed in long, gray calico dresses, patched and worn but clean. They had no teeth, but they chewed vigorously and spat. They had never had anything as exciting as this come into their experience before.

A heady feeling ran through the crowd, a vibration of excitement. Every one was full of expectation. Talk drifted around of exciting events.

"The boss came to my house. 'When you comin' back to work?' he said—"

" 'You git along quicker or I'll arrest you,' he tole me. I said, 'Arrest me! I don't keer if you do arrest me!' "

"Did you yere how Mamie Pratt went back to work—"

"They's scabs livin' alongside o' me—"

"Whar you reckon Fer is? You reckon he's been kidnapped again?—" Dan Marks said to Max Harris,

"Reckon we'd best begin this yere meetin'. Reckon somethin's holdin' up Fer." They gave each other a significant look. They were men in their late twenties and early thirties, powerful, well built, able. They had none of the indirection which assails some crowds of workers when they have no leadership. The two men who had organized the workers in the beginning could carry on meetings and picket lines.

Dan called the meeting to order.

"Our speakers is a little late, friends," he said, "so we may's well begin. An' we cain't begin enny better than to let Brother Williams lead us in prayer."

Brother Williams, whose long hair hung down under his wide hat and mingled with his long gray beard, closed his eyes tightly, raised his head to Heaven, spread his arms out in the form of a cross, and began:

"*Oh*, how these people have suffered, Lord!

"*Oh*, Lord, hear them in their struggle!

"*Oh*, Lord, *oh*, soften the hearts of their employers!

"*Oh*, I never heard anything like how they treat these folks!

"*Oh*, I come from the mountains where folks is free to breathe God's free air!

"*Oh*, I seen women and little, little children aworkin' in the mills whar they wasn't meant to!

"*Oh*, the Lord sent the children of Israel out of bondage!

"*Oh*, the Lord softened Pharaoh's heart!

"*Oh*, ain't Basil Schenk's heart goin' to be softened?

"*Oh*, this ole man ain't never seen nothin' like these milishy with their tear-gas bombs and their baynits!

"*Oh*, they're aprancin' all over the town!

"*Oh*, they're arrestin' girls and wimmin."

He went on with his chant, staccato, exciting, until the meeting swayed in unison with his cry; until there was a low sigh of "Oh," throughout the audience. The old women stood with their eyes tightly closed. The young men and young women watched him intently. The prayer had knit them together and focused their emotion into a flame.

2

Dan said, "We may as well go on and hold our meetin' till Fer and the others git here. Now, here's a sister that's made up song-ballits. She's writ 'em herself. Youall mought o' heard her asingin' of 'em up to the relief store some days. Now, I have got Mamie Lewes to sing out loud before all of you folks, though she says she's ashamed to do it."

Old Ma Gilfillin called out:

"Mamie Lewes, don't you be 'shamed. Weall admires fer to hear you sing your song-ballits."

Mamie Lewes was helped on the stand. She had her air of expectancy as though wishing for something pleasant and exciting to happen. She threw her head back and sang easily and without effort. She had a natural voice, untrained but very sweet.

"We leave our homes in the morning,
We kiss our children good-by,
While we slave for the bosses,
Our children scream and cry.

"And when we draw our money
Our grocery bills to pay,
Not a cent to spend for clothing,
Not a cent to lay away.

"How it grieves the heart of a mother
You every one must know,
But we can't buy for our children
Our wages are too low.

"It is for our little children
That seems to us so dear,
But for us nor them, oh, workers,
The bosses do not keer."

They listened to this with moist eyes. It was their own story, put in incredibly simple terms. Every one had lived through this. There was no piece of sentiment; it was the history of every one there put into song.

3

The policemen were there—the "laws" had come. Usually but one policeman stood on the outskirts of the crowd. To-day there were several; prowling through the strikers and seeing nothing especial going on, they started to go away.

Old Ma Gilfillin climbed up on the stand. "I got somethin' to say," she proclaimed. "I seen the laws awalkin' round yere. We didn't ask 'em to come, with their bloody han's thet's been punchin' us an' arrestin' us, to our meetin'. Their hearts is too hard to be softened even ef they yere Brother Williams aprayin'. An' I want to tell Mister Policeman Zober that the only part of him I keers fer to see is the hind sides of him agoin' away from me like they's adoin' now!"

A roar of laughter went up. They were rocking together. Something alive and quick emanated from them. They felt a sense of companionship and power. The crowd had its own powerful vitality. It had a beauty which was also a little dangerous. These people, individually so poor and so weak, were strong. The eyes of the young girls and the young men were bright. They were ready for anything. Danger beckoned them.

While the laughter was still booming and echoing through the crowd and the scarlet-faced policeman was making his way back to the street, Fer came plunging along. Shouts greeted him.

"Fer!" they shouted. "Fer! Fer!"

He took the platform. He felt the weight of their faith, and his own smallness and inadequacy.

4

A big girl, one of Ma Gilfillin's daughters, came up to Mamie Lewes.

"You do sing beautiful, Mamie Lewes," she said.

"Yore abraggin' on me."

"No, I ain't abraggin' on you. It's the truth. You live a piece from yere?"

"Yeah, quite a piece."

"Ma sez come over to our house and rest you and eat a bite." She was bigger and stronger than Mamie Lewes, and looked older. "Is yore husband left you too, Mamie Lewes?" she asked.

"He didn't rightly leave me. He jist went to git work and didn't come back. I wasn't 'spectin' him to leave me."

"Thet's how they do. My husband and I, I kinda suspicioned he was leavin' me. He says to me, 'Daisy, you take the baby over to Ma's while I'm gittin' work, and git you a job in the Nuren factory ef you kin, and I'll be ascoutin' fer a good place.' Then I never did yere from him no more."

"Yes, my Will was like that."

"I don't think they aim fer to leave us always. They's lots of 'em on the mill hill, they husbands goes, and they don't come back."

"They git discouraged. My husband los' his ambition when the chillen died with diptherey."

"Well, wouldn't you think they would lose their ambition? 'Spect it seems good to be able to use all your wages on yourself. Joe West made fourteen dollars and forty cents—I known him to make up to eighteen, then when I was workin' too, we was right smart well off for a spell, but don't seem like luck lasts long."

"No, luck don't seem never to last long with us mill hands. You only got one chil', Mis' West?"

"I hed four. I los' three. How long you been workin' in the mills, Mamie Lewes?"

"I'm jist workin' sence I was ma'ied. I was ma'ied eleven years ago. I'm twenty-nine now."

"So! you was real ole when you begun. How come you was so ole?"

"We was mountain folks, an' come a man from the mills atalkin' how much folks made. Me an' Will thought th' money grew on trees down yere ahearin' his talk, so when we got ma'ied we come down. Seems like they's been nothing but trouble sence. How long you been aworkin'?"

"Huh, me? I was ten when I began workin' in the mill. I'm twenty-six now, and I worked sixteen years. When I begun I worked twelve hours a day for seventy-five cents a week."

"Lawd! that was awful young! Up with us in the mountains we don't have much but they's fresh air. Seems like you could breathe. I got awful homesick for to go back to the hills. We lived beyon' Asheville."

"Why don't you go? What all's keepin' you yere ef you got kin up there?"

"Oh, I got kin. I got Ma and my Pappy, but however would I get money nuff to go? Fer me an' my four chillen 'twould cost me all o' eighteen dollars." Daisy West shook her head. They both looked at the impossibility of getting eighteen dollars.

"Ennyhow, I want to stay and help win this strike. I want to see this Union grow so our chillen won't have to work like we done. It's jist about all the things I'll be able to git my chillen. I can't git 'em no school, no clothen, no shoes, but maybe I'll leave 'em a Union."

"Ennyhow they'll be treated better'n what I was when I was in the mill. I was treated like a dawg down there in South Ca'olina. Many and many a time I been stretched on the flo' 'cause I didn't clean up fast nough. We kids wuz knocked around and slapped around. Why, time and ag'in bosses put me over their knee and spanked me sore and didn't no one dare say nothin'. They would take and strap us kids good. They don't do that so much now. They cain't git 'em quite so young. They's supposed to go to school."

"You moved a lot, didn't you?"

"Oh, Lawsy, I say, moved an' moved. Maw was always amovin' and I moved after I was ma'ied. Shore hev los' count o' all the mills I worked in. Changin' and changin' all the time. Hopin' to find somethin' better. They was all the same. Ain't you moved some?"

"Yeah, my husband and me, I reckon we mus' 'av' worked in ten or twelve mills, eight or nine, ennyway."

"They wuz all the same, wa'n' they?"

"Yeah, they wuz all the same everywhere, cursin' bosses, an' stinkin' toilets an' poor pay."

"Everythin' so full of dus' you cain't breathe. All the same in all them mills I worked fer."

5

They had got to the house which was placed sharply on a side of the hill. The red ground around it was beaten hard, but there was one tree in back and some flowers at one side.

They went in the house, which had four rooms. Ma Gilfillin, Flora, her youngest girl, Daisy and her child slept in one room, and they rented the two others. One to a married couple with a child. Four boys lived in the front room, Will Gilfillin, who was a boy of eighteen with strong and delicate features, Dewey Bryson, and two other boys who hadn't been there long. The three boys boarded with them, paying five dollars a week a piece for room and board which was a dollar less than they would have had to pay in a regular boarding house. The married couple did their own cooking and were planning on having a house of their own presently when they could pay the installment on their furniture. They were very young. They looked like a high-school boy and girl.

"Every one o' 'em," said Ma Gilfillin, "has jined the Union. Jones didn't want to jine, but I didn't give him no indulgence to scab in. I says 'Jine or git,' so he jined. I reckon he was afeerd that my boy or Wes would bus' his hed fer him ef he didn't."

"I wisht I could live in a nice house like this. You got 'lectric lights, ain't you?"

"Yeah, we git lights."

"Is they water?"

"No, they ain't water, weall got to go out to the facet for our water. They say they's going to let in water but they ain't done hit."

"My, how nice to live in a house where they was water runnin', jist go to your sink and turn on yore water! That mus' be wonderful, and havin' a separate kitchen."

6

"However do you come to think up yore ballits, Mamie Lewes?" Ma Gilfillin asked.

Mamie Lewes clasped her hands around her knees and looked with her clear, alert stare. She was puzzled about the matter herself.

"I cain't rightly tell yo'. I was jist ahummin' thet ole ballit to myself and first I know I was singin' the firs' two lines out loud. I was singin':

> 'We leave our house in the mornin',
> We kiss our chillen good-by,'

an' I sung it over an' over, an' the last two lines come and I sung and then I wint and I writ 'em down. I was glad I knew how to write then."

"You went to school, Mamie Lewes?"

"Yeah. We warn't so fur from a school. I went through up to th' fifth grade an' I would 'a' gone more ef Ma hadn't tuk sick with the misery in her back."

"An' huccum you thought the rest of thet ballit, Mamie Lewes? Did it jist come into yore head?"

"Yeah, jist seems like it comes into my haid. They's other ballits that I'm aponderin' on. Seems like I'll git a line then like it'll slide off from me, most like it was somethin' alive tryin' to git away."

Wes Elliott came in.

"Why, howdy, Mis' Mamie Lewes," he said. "How did youall git yere?"

"Mis' West, she ast me. I didn't know youall lived yere. 'Twas Wes yere got me to jine up with the Union."

"Yeah, Wes is a great one to bring youall into the Union. If he don't git 'em in by kind words he'll see ef a lump on the hed won't git 'em." Ma Gilfillin laughed, a high, eerie laugh. They sat together, curiously united in their beliefs in the Union. They all of them belonged to the floating populations of mill workers which drift slackily back and forth, to and fro, from one mill hill to another. Like the Gilfillins they change yearly. Sometimes oftener.

Now a new mill starting up offers inducements such as the free moving of their furniture, such few sticks as they have. They own nothing else. Ma Gilfillin had had eight children. Three of them were still with her. One daughter was married and was a mill worker; she worked in the Full Fashioned Hosiery Mills in Marion. A son had disappeared, and two more had died. She owned four double beds, some chairs, a table, two dressers, some framed pictures, a second-hand sewing machine, several linoleum rugs, and a clock. She also had a coal stove.

A hall went down the middle of the house. There were two rooms on each side. Three of the rooms had small, shallow fireplaces. The house, like all the rest of the houses on the mill hill and most other mill hills, was a frame dwelling through which the wind swept. When there was a wind storm, the wind howled under the house and poured up cracks and knot holes. There was a front porch with a swing on it. Ma Gilfillin had lost sight of the number of times which she had loaded her beds, her two dressers and her table and rockers on a cart and moved. The moving van backed up in the mill villages on Mondays and Fridays, and people went on their pilgrimages again. They scarcely took notice of the different towns in which they lived. Though for the last many years, the Gilfillins had always lived near some fairly big town like Greenville, or Spartanburg, or Gastonia or Stonerton.

Twice they had been caught out in unincorporated towns, and being always a little in debt, it had taken them two years before they could get away. Ma Gilfillin liked the minister here and she liked to be where on Saturday afternoons one could go to the five and ten cent store.

The mill population never becomes part of the town. The mill operators remain "mill hands," separated forever from the city's population of comfortable people. They marry among themselves and live and die among themselves. Since the passage of school bills in various Southern States make it necessary for children to attend school until they are fourteen, fine, modern school houses have appeared all over the land. The children attend the mill schools, waiting the day to come when they may go to the mill and earn money, too. This is their natural destiny and they do not question it.

That anything could be done about it, it hadn't occurred to them until the "stretch-out" came. Pay had been cut and work increased and they began to organize. They had for the first time begun to realize one another. Up to this time they had all lived each to themselves. The old and worn phrases of solidarity, "An injury to one is an injury to all," "The mass power of the workers," which they were hearing from the speaking stand, came like a revelation.

A strike was dangerous adventure. New and exciting as warfare. They sat in front of Ma Gilfillin's coal stove, while the grits were cooking, and talked about the time when the strike would be won.

7

"What youall got such a scratch on yo' neck?" Mamie Lewes asked Elliott.

"Wes, he hed some trouble on the picket line the time the military come."

"Was lots of folks had trouble when the military come."

"Yeah, they was right savage. That day seems they was jist tryin' to sca' us all."

"What was it happened to you, Wes?"

"I was astandin' by the mill gate when they come in, jist awatchin'. They had run to git the crowd out of the way, and the crowd was fallin' back. I seen two girls in there I knowed an' I went into the crowd to keep 'em from bein' hurt."

"Yeah, I seed you in the crowd an' I seed you go furrad, thin I seed the police grab you an' put you in a police-druv automobile."

"Yeah, they threw me in the automobile and two dep'ties they beat me and thin they took me in the jail an' they beat me with a bunch o' keys an' blackjacks. They was akickin' me an' callin' me names."

"Didn't they choke you?" Ma Gilfillin prompted.

"Yeah, they choked me unconscious. I never did know when they put me in my cell."

"Was you afightin' back at 'em?"

"Well, I was awrastlin' with 'em like, when they was puttin' me in the automobile. I was shore surprised when they grabbed me an' they started abeatin' of me in the automobile. Thar wasn't no use, they took an' twisted me an' I kicked back a little so they let me have it, when they got me in the jail. But they didn't have no call to choke me unconscious."

7

1

THE FRATERNIZING went on. Boys in uniform walked down the street, a girl striker on each arm, grinning shamefacedly. Ma Gilfillin and old Mrs. Whenck were always around wherever there were three or four boys gathered.

"Boys, whut you doin' yere? Boys, don' you think we ought to git enough for to live on?"

"Shore, Ma."

"Whatall do yo' think yore adoin' with thet big baynit aguardin' the mill? We ain't bad folks. We is all jist like youall." Sheepish grins. Boys talked among themselves.

"I aim fer to do my duty, but I didn' know I was agoin' to be makin' a war on old women an' kids. They got a right to strike. Hit's constitutional."

"They ain't no call to riot."

"Who's been ariotin'? They ain't no call to kidnap that thar leader, either."

"We wasn't called out when they was akidnappin' an' adynamitin'."

"Who was adynamitin'?" "The strikers done the dynamitin'."

"How you know the strikers done the dynamitin'? I know they didn't do no dynamitin'. They'd 'a' arrested the strikers if they'd 'a' done it."

"I didn't jine no State guard to make war on old women. They got a right to peaceful picketin'."

It went on all the time.

2

There were rumors of something going to happen. Everybody felt it. The air of the town was oppressive like the air before a storm. People going in and out of Bispham's. Old Mr. Trent sitting around talking to Bispham and Jolas.

" 'Pears like they's fixin' to do somethin'. "

"Yeah, seems like they was fixin' fer some mischief."

"Reckon they's goina be some dynamitin'?"

"I never kin tell. I always am kinda worried about that thar yard. It's kinda unpertected-like."

"Did you yere shootin' las' night?"

"Yeah, I heeard guns agoin' off somewhar. They's always guns agoin' off. Every night seems like they's somethin' in the air."

"I yere they's more o' the boss's men bein' deputized."

"They sez the Mill's aformin' a Committee of a Hundred."

"Say, Fer, did you yere about this Committee of a Hundred?"

"Yeah, I heard about it."

"Whatever all is hit?"

"It looks to me like 'twas a committee o' men to git th' leaders an' smash the Union."

"Whoall's in it, Fer?"

"Well, there's a lot of the mill bosses and some stool pigeons and clerks in stores. Say, you know what these mill people are like." He sat down and stretched his legs out, and smiled at them engagingly. Harris came out of his room, and a half dozen strikers had come up the stairs. "You know I had a friend once. He belonged to the Barbers' Union and he was sure if the Barbers' Union could only get into Russia and do its duty Bolshevism would vanish off the face of the earth. Well, that's the way with these folks here. They think that if they can lock me up and get rid of all the leaders, the Union's going to vanish." A shout of laughter came from the men. Then a pause. They all looked at Fer. Wes Elliott asked:

"You reckon, Fer, they're afixin' to do ennything to you? Thet they're afixin' to do somethin'?"

3

Boys stood on the street corners talking together. Young men out looking for trouble. "Something ought to be done about this Union. If the laws and the military couldn't do it somebuddy else ought to."

"Say, did yuh ever hunt a nigger?"

"Naw, there ain't many niggers yere to hunt, ain't many niggers *to* Stonerton."

"It shore would be fun to hunt a nigger."

"Yeah, it shore would be fun to hunt a nigger."

"They say they's goin' to hunt this yere strike leader out o' town."

"They ought to tar and feather him an' ride 'im out on a rail."

"They ought to hunt 'im outa the State. Did youall yere they was makin' a Committee of a Hundred?"

"Whatall is it fer, this Committee of a Hundred?"

"It's fer pertectin' the people. It's fer stoppin' these yere Union leaders tearin' up our city an' makin' incitements to riot."

4

Mrs. Parker sat in her cool, spacious sitting room.

"I hear they're getting ready a Committee of a Hundred to do something about this strike leader."

"It's high time," said Jean.

"My heart bleeds for these poor misguided people. Did you see the paper to-day, Jean?"

"Yes, there was a fine editorial."

"If the citizens did their duty the way it suggests, we'd soon be through with this."

"I hear that a newspaper reporter was knocked unconscious by a policeman on the picket line. They ought to be more careful."

"Oh, my dear, don't waste any sympathy on him, he's been seen carrying the strike leaders to Lafayette in his car."

"Oh, well, no wonder they arrested *him*. I think something will have to happen soon."

"Oh, sure, something must happen." Everybody felt in the mill hill, and in the comfortable residences that something must happen. Every one except some of the comfortable people who chose to ignore the strike. They would say:

"We don't know that there is a strike. They say the workers are going back every day. The strike's practically over."

5

"Whar you goin', Wes?"

"It's my turn to guard the relief store, Ma."

"Take good keer o' yoreself."

"Oh, we'll be all right. No one won't want to kidnap one of us."

"Somebuddy might want to steal our supplies, jes fer meanness."

"Yeah, thar's some so ornery they'd steal our supplies."

The six boys in the relief store stretched themselves out on chairs and counters. Three of them played cards for a little while and three of them shot craps, but none of them had any money and it wasn't much fun.

"Say, Wes, did you bring yore gun?"

"No, I lef' mine with some o' the boys over t' the boardin' house. They heard how they was agoin' to raid the boardin' house. D'ya believe it?"

"Seems lak they's going to raid somethin' with all the talk they is. 'Twon't be the fault of th' newspaper ef they ain't somethin' happens. They shore bear down pow'ful."

"I been up every night sence the strike on picket duty."

"Well, you worked every night in the mill, didn't you?"

They all settled down to sleep but Wes. They watched turn and turn about. Often when he sat on guard, Wes would be half asleep. Just awake enough to see he was awake. To-night he was stark staring awake. His small eyes shone in their deep-set sockets. His fair hair stood up around his head, a young fanatic waiting for what, he didn't know.

Waiting for something coming out of the dark. Something hidden ready to spring. The other boys snored and lay asleep in chairs and on the counter. He heard something far off. Something was coming around the back of the store. He sprang up and went to the door and listened. Sounds, stealthy.

His gun, he looked around for it. It wasn't there. They were none of them armed. Some one's coming. People, many people. The dim electric light made funny shadows. Wes had the feeling as though his hair was rising on the back of his head.

Now he knew he had heard it. People stealing around the store.

He called out. Twelve masked men broke in. Flashlights and guns were put in the faces of the sleeping boys.

"Git out. Git along outa yere!" The little band of guards were herded across the street. The street now boiled with masked men. Masked men everywhere. Some seemed to have stockings pulled over their faces with holes cut in them for eyes. One man had a green mask.

They started in tearing down the little building with fury, chopping it with axes, pulling its timbers with grab-hooks. And now they started throwing the flour out in the street.

Wes made a movement. A masked man cocked his gun at him. Wes knew who he was. He was Will Fallon, a mill guard. This was the mill's Committee of One Hundred.

6

The little band of strikers guarded by masked men with guns stood in the middle of the road watching the fantastic sight and talking in low tones.

"Look yere, they's achoppin' down the whole buildin'."

"Yeah, they's bustin' everything."

"They's achoppin' the underpinnin's."

"Listen to the windows go."

"They's throwin' the supplies in the street."

"They's haulin' out the bags o' meal."

"Wes, look! See the fellas under the arc light throwing the meal and traumpin' it."

"Wonder where the militia is?"

"Wonder the militia wouldn't hear this row."

"Look, Wes, look! Thar comes Major Furness and some of the militia."

The major of the State guard with a small band of soldiers was coming down the street. Police were with him. The man in the green mask, who seemed to be the leader, now cried:

"Fifty in the back!"

This was evidently a signal of some kind, for the masked men ran back of the wrecked building into the vacant lot. One of the men guarding the strikers ran down the alley and came back unmasked. He was Olsen, another mill guard.

All the boys recognized him.

A masked man passed close to the major and his militia. The boys stared. He had gone right past, close enough for them to put out a hand and touch him, yet they had not arrested him. They stood there murmuring:

"Gee, did you see that?"

"Gee, they didn't arrest him."

The major approached the little huddle of strikers.

"What are youall doing here?" he inquired. He turned to the police. "Arrest these fellows."

"We wasn't doin' nothin'."

"They stuck us up, Major."

"We were sleepin' in the headquarters and guardin' it. They came and wrecked it."

"Get along," said the policeman. "Tell that to the Judge to-morrow."

Strikers attracted by the noise were now being hustled along the street. Strikers who had been awakened by the noise and had come out to see what it was were arrested on the supposition that the strikers had destroyed their own headquarters. Irma and Doris were arrested. The masked men had disappeared. Not one of them was arrested.

PART
II

8

1

THE WINDOWS of the relief store had been boarded up again. The headquarters Relief Committee had cleared up the wreckage. The masked raiders had torn up the literature they had found; they had chopped and hewed and broken with the wanton destructiveness of a crazy child.

In front of the relief store in the road were spots of white where flour sacks had been emptied into the mud and spots of yellow where cornmeal had been strewn around. The result of this was as though an electric shock had run through the strikers.

Masked men knocking down their headquarters! Straw bosses and foremen haulin' stockens over their faces and cuttin' holes for eyes!

Think they didn't know what 'twas? Well, they know well enough who 'twas. Hedn't the boys rekonized enuf of them? They shore had.

The Grand Jury sat at once. Scores of people were examined. The boys who had recognized the mill men gave their testimony. There were no arrests. Days dragged on and there were no arrests at all.

A shout had gone up all over the country from the newspapers. Every one throughout the South clamored for arrests. It gave the South a bad name, that it was possible for a company of over a hundred masked men to wreck a building and destroy food intended for women and children without any one having to suffer for it.

Reporters poured into town. Stonerton was becoming a national issue. The Stonerton *Times* spoke vaguely that "people from out of town" had come to knock down buildings and hinted that probably the strikers themselves had committed the outrage.

2

Meantime the fraternizing went on more than ever. The strikers formed little groups around national guardsmen.

"What made 'em arrest our boys? Funny youall couldn't hev got youah han's on none of them masked men."

"Don't blame us. We cain't do no 'restin' onles' we's ordered. We gotta follow our ordehs."

"Funny ordehs you all got. Yere's Wes tells how them fellows with they stockens pulled down oveh they face walked right pas' th' Major and he cums up and 'rests our boys en takes 'em off to jail."

Presently it was decided that the National Guard was no longer required,—the situation had calmed down. It had calmed down. Black-hand letters were less frequent. People had stopped threatening Fer on the street.

It was as though this demonstration of irrational hate and of mob violence had appeased the community. This eruption of fury had been like the lancing of a boil. The community was a little afraid of itself. The comfortable people were disposed to shift the responsibility of the outrage—maybe the strikers had done it, as the papers hinted. The Northern papers made a great deal of the throwing out of food and supplies for women and children. Stonerton did not want to admit its responsibility.

Now presently the soldiers were going. They were not needed any more,—but people hinted that they had become ineffective. Fer was sure this was so—his policy of fraternizing had been successful. This was the first time strikers had ever gotten the sympathy of a National Guard.

"It's natural they should,—ain't they our kin? It's foolish fer them to be called out to guard mills 'gainst wimmen and children who's strikin' 'gainst hevin' to work twelve hours en twenty minutes a day, besides takin' a five per cent wage cut."

The troops had been withdrawn, but the deputies had been added to. They had been armed with rifles and bayonets. The strikers grumbled about the composition of the deputies.

" 'Skinflint,'—why he's jes' outen the chain gang."

"Tom Farris, everybody knows he gits drunk en beats his wife en goes with wimmen."

"Murck and Zober is bad enuf but these new deputies is jes' onery, low down trash."

3

A city ordinance had been made against "parades." The lawyer, Burdette, was questioning the validity of this injunction in the courts. Picket lines, he contended, were not parades. The local authorities contended picket lines were *parades* and broke them up and arrested the strikers. The largest picket line occurred in the afternoon before the changing of the day shift to the night shift. There was no more picketing on the roads. Scabs were no longer brought in by trucks.

"We've got to have larger picket lines than we've had before to show them deputies," the picket captains had agreed.

The national guardsmen had left on Saturday night. Sunday the mills were closed but the new deputies with their long bayonets had swaggered in front of the mills.

The picket line formed on the speaking ground after the meeting was over.

Two little girls in overalls headed the picket line. They were followed by Ma Gilfillin and old Mrs. Whenck. The two little girls were chewing gum for they felt their responsibility, while the older women chewed their snuff-sticks.

"What's the matter with you men?" asked Irma. "Why do you let the women and kids go like this?" The men held back a little, their dignity was wounded that little girls dressed in overalls and with painted lips should be given the honor of leading the parade. The young Northern organizers had not understood this.

Down here men still ruled life,—no matter how poor a man might be, he still was the head of his household and kept his dignity. He didn't like to see his natural place usurped by little girls.

The picket captains ran around among them and they began to fall in line—men, women, boys and girls—they streamed out in an orderly fashion.

Irma led them. It had been considered policy not to let Fer go on the picket line as it made it too easy to arrest him and thus remove him out of the strike area for a few days by demanding excessive bail. Irma did not always go on the line but to-day, with the new deputies, she felt it better. She stepped out, her head up with its little arrogant tilt, a little excited with the danger—thinking to herself she must expect to get arrested.

4

Daisy West called to Mamie Lewes.

"You acumin', Mamie Lewes?"

"Shore I'm cumin'."

"You reckon them deputies goin' ter be rough?"

"They're thet onery I shouldn't be s'prised."

The line crept along serpent-like—a wavering caterpillar of a procession. The picket captains ran along the sides closing up the gaps stringing out the people. Dewey Bryson had taken the head of the procession.

"You little girls git back," he said to the two young ones leading. "This is a man's job. Miss Irma, wisht you'd git back too. You'd be more useful seein' the lines kept in order."

Irma humored him a while but was soon back at the front. Every one was nervous. They'd know what to expect from the troops but this was something new.

The long picket line wound down the street and turned a corner which led to the mill. This wasn't the direct approach but a side street which led past houses sliding down hill on a red earth bluff. Women, children and spectators lined the bluff as the procession went along. Some one started singing—

> "Come all ye scabs
> Ef you want to hear
> The story of a cruel millionaire.
> Basil Schenk was the millionaire's name,
> He bought the law with his money and his frame."

The singing which had begun a shrill piping of half a dozen little girls now swelled in volume and came out with a gay taunt—

"He bought the law with his money and his frame,"—and then in a shout,—"*But they cain't buy the Union with their money and their frame!*"

They were at the end of the street now. A whistle blew and a police car with deputies clinging to it drove up, and another, then another. There was a sharp order. Suddenly, without warning, the deputies and police charged the picket line. The picketers were taken by surprise. Always before this they had been dispersed with clubs or blackjacks. More deputies had come up. The strikers broke and ran.

Roger was sitting in a car with some of the other reporters.

"Gosh, this is a riot," said Dick Durgan. "Look at 'em. They're chasing 'em like rats."

Della King, one of the young girls, fell. She was arrested and taken away in the police wagon. Many of the others were being arrested.

The strikers ran back and forth in confusion, screaming. They were beating Dewey terribly. Hitting him on the stomach with a blackjack. There was an element of unreason, of madness, in these police.

The reporters' car drove along slowly. Roger wanted to get out.

"Don't be a fool," said Hoskins. "They'll get you next. Don't lose your head like that. Use some sense."

"Look at that woman," said Dick. "She's bleeding." A woman with a long neck, her head held high up in the air was screaming.

"He jabbed me! He jabbed me!"

"They're hunting them along the street."

A group of strikers, followed by deputies, ran for the relief store and pushed into it, the deputies after them.

A panic seized Mamie Lewes. She tried to think,—"There's nothing to be afraid of. They cain't do nuthin' to me." Daisy West's phrase, "They kin kill me, but they cain't eat me," kept coming to her mind. She heard herself laughing. Her own laughter terrified her.

5

Women and men were struggling with deputies and policemen. A deputy was twisting a boy's arm. The boy screamed. Anger filled Mamie Lewes. She wanted to go up to the deputy and snatch the boy from him,—but she couldn't. She was being hunted. Running. She saw Daisy West, a deputy on each side. They were taking her away now. They had arrested her. Mamie Lewes thought,—when they catch me, they'll arrest me, too.

She ran toward the relief store. There was a crowd waiting in the relief store for the evening distribution of food. People who hadn't been on the picket line at all. The hunted people, Mamie Lewes with them, ran into the relief store. The policemen, Murck and Zober after them. With them were six deputies with bayonets. They hunted the strikers. They charged and drove all the people out with their bayonets.

Two of the boys working on the Relief Committee were behind the counter,—Dan Marks and Wes Elliott. Wes was sitting reading, waiting for the supplies to come in when the distribution would be made. Murck ran towards him and lunged at him over the counter with a bayonet. Wes Elliott was taken by surprise. He had been expecting nothing. He had been told to keep off the picket line for a few days, for he had already been arrested twice and was marked by the police.

As Murck lunged at him with the bayonet, he dodged. The bayonet stuck in the wall. Murck pulled out the bayonet and chased Wes. The bayonet stuck in his hip but as he saw it coming, he turned his leg. The wound was slight, but as he afterwards said, "It ruined a good pair of pants."

Outside Dan was asking Murck to let him go back to get his books.

"I got t' git my books," he said. "I got t' git 'em." They let him go back in.

As in some absurd moving picture scene, the people who had been chased out and who had gone in back yards and up alleys, were coming back again into the store. Again the deputies chased them out. Mamie Lewes leaned against a wall. They hadn't arrested her. They hadn't caught her, but several of the women in the crowd had been scratched with bayonets.

She found herself crying with rage.

"We didn't do a thing," she sobbed. "We didn't do a thing."

6

No striker had lifted a hand; no striker had thrown a stone; no one had been armed with even so much as a stick.

"I wisht they'd hed their guns," she thought. "I wisht Irma and Fer hed let 'em hev they guns." Her legs were trembling under her. The street cleared a little,—the deputies were still herding people further down the street. Mamie Lewes saw old Mrs. Holly walking down street.

"Awful, ain't it!" she cried to Mamie Lewes. "I wus jest acomin' to get my supper an' they chased me. Look yere." Her dress flapped on one side. Bloodstained.

"They chased me and baynited me, en I wusn't on no picket line. I never did go on no picket line," she chattered along in a high frightened voice.

"Look out!" screamed Mamie Lewes. Murck was chasing people down the street. He was beside himself in a frenzy of punishment. He stopped old Mrs. Holly and struck her. Mamie Lewes screamed. Mrs. Holly was mute.

Mamie Lewes saw him striking the old woman again and again.

Her face was purple, her eyes were closed. Mamie Lewes screamed again. She could hear the sound of Murck's fists battering the old woman's face. It seemed like something in a bad dream,—something that couldn't happen on the streets of an American town. Finally Murck let Mrs. Holly go. He shoved her aside and rushed off down the street after some more of the fleeing strikers.

Suddenly the street was cleared of people. Police wagons with arrested strikers had clattered off. Every body was off the street,--only Mamie Lewes stood there, holding up Mrs. Holly, from whose face the blood streamed. The old woman was moaning but she made no outcry. Down the street came a tall man,—Holly. He had been at home. Mrs. Holly's son had come out to look for his mother.

Doris and Irma were in jail. Most of the picket captains had been arrested. Ten people had slight bayonet wounds; many more had black eyes — they had been chased, kicked, beaten with blackjacks.

"And the queer thing is," said Roger, "there didn't seem to be any resistance."

"I told you," said Hoskins, "the workers are unbelievably patient."

The streets had been cleared of people except for small groups outside the stores, who stood chattering together in their anger. The people who lived in East Stonerton were small shopkeepers and the few people who owned their own homes, beyond the track, were with the strikers.

"They ought to do something to them laws."

"It's a disgrace and shame, — what these pore people hev got to stan'. Workin' twelve hours a day fer nuthin' en then get beat up an arrested when they strike."

"En when they jabbed at that woman, — like she's a pig, — just lunged right at her with a long vicious baynit."

"I never thought I'd live to see the day when I'd see white women abein' chased along the streets."

"Yes, en I'm an ex-service man and he's an ol' slacker en he chased me with his baynit. I wisht I'd hed my gun."

"They'd ought to be shot — them laws ought."

9

1

THE CHAMBER OF COMMERCE was giving a luncheon to the newspaper men to meet the prominent business men and to familiarize them with the problems which confronted them.

Long tables were spread in the Chamber of Commerce hall. All the newspaper men had been requested to rise to their feet and make known their papers or magazines. There were sixteen of them. They came from big New York dailies, from news services, from small local papers, from liberal weeklies, and even from some monthly magazines. They had been drawn here, first by the chopping down of the headquarters by the mob and were kept here by the spectacular arrests and bayonet jabbing on what one of the tabloid men called "Bloody Monday."

The way the Northern press had handled the situation had not pleased the South. It was felt that an education was needed. Daniel Jameson, well known in the textile industry, was to be the principal speaker. The various business men introduced themselves to the reporters. Every one was there, even some of the big mill men from Lafayette.

2

After the luncheon, a cold and friendless one, the professional booster of the city arose to his feet.

"This is no time, folks," he told them, "no time to be thinking about the small disturbances occurring in this community which is no more than a pebble would be on the great wide sunny ocean.

"Our little town which at the time of the World War only numbered eleven thousand inhabitants has passed in ten years' time the twenty thousand mark. If you go up and down the streets of our county you will find we have got one hundred and twelve mills. Over forty per cent of these have been built in the last ten years. Around the cities of Lafayette and Stonerton are more than fifty mills. There are new buildings everywhere, showing that millions are being made and spent.

"The war gave an impetus to our industries, and in spite of bad conditions the last two or three years, we have never let it die. And are we now going to let it die? Not while this spot remains the garden spot of the world. The natural advantages are unparalleled in any part or territory of the great United States.

"Now, folks, what we've got to do is to make such an attractive offer to the Mendleburg Rayon Co. that's looking for a place to locate that we will get it—as we ought to have got the Bendberg, Glensdorf Co. Tennessee beat us to that. A little town in Tennessee beat Piedmont, the heart and center of this splendid country. Tennessee got Bendberg and Asheville got Enka. Now we've got to get Mendleburg Rayon.

"I want to say to you gentlemen of the press right here and now that this city is going to be the choicest center of the textile industry. We have made a start with our rayon mills. We've got the city, we've got the water, we have transportation, and we've got the labor and plenty of it. Don't let's be misled by these small happenings, nor don't overestimate them. Keep your mind on prosperity." And with that he deluged his hearers with facts and figures of Piedmont and North Carolina, and especially of the unparalleled prosperity of Stonerton which in a brief time would push the other textile towns off the map.

The Quartette now arose and sang old favorites in close harmony. "Little Gray Home in the West," "Sweet Adeline," and to show they were modern, "Old Man River."

3

It was Mr. Jameson's turn. He was a stout and genial man, a man built on an ample pattern. He spoke with the carrying conviction of a man sure that he is right. He had had a good time going through life. He was kind, considerate, generous, and he had the engaging quality of a man who looks upon the world as a good place. He told all the people there the things they wanted to hear and gave good reasons for them. After his little preamble he plunged into the subject closest to his listeners' hearts.

"I don't believe that the unionization of the cotton mill employees is among the steps necessary to bring about better social and industrial relationships between employers and employees.

"Society is filled with reformers who, without making a diagnosis of our industry's ills, are offering their cures. The unionization of textile workers is one of the panaceas suggested. I am very clear in my own mind that under the present depressed and complicated conditions nothing could happen that would result more disastrously to employer and employee alike than an attempt by foreign influence and outside unsympathetic organizations to unionize our cotton mill operatives. No fair-minded man will deny the right of any citizen to join a union.

"The right of a man to join a union is not only in keeping with the constitutional guarantees but it is one of those sacred and inherent rights based on justice and individual freedom to which all men are entitled where not in conflict with the best interests of society. The question, however, of the extent to which the rights of organized labor may be allowed to proceed in our social and industrial structure is an issue of grim content, and around this question much of our recent conflict of opinion and turmoil centered."

The speaker presented statistics showing that during the last decade, while many major industries were making large profits, cotton textiles the world over had been in the grip of a depression.

"As to the cause of the general unprofitableness of the industry," he said, "it was due largely to the policy of many mills which failed to realize the importance of adjusting their operations to demand. Mills of this type lose sight of the fact that, while in former years production problems arose from a need of increased and more economical productions, at this time the production problem is one of accommodating itself to consumer demand. It is regrettable that so many manufacturers persist in a policy of flagrant disregard of the law of supply and demand.

"The wage scale may be low but the ease with which workers can be trained must be taken into account, so must the agricultural wage scale in the South. Inasmuch as textile labor largely originates from the farms we must essentially take into account the low income from which these tenant classes are fleeing. They are overrunning the mills out of an impulse of economic self-interest. Wages are higher, hours are shorter, houses are better, comforts and conveniences of living more abundant, and general conditions vastly better than prevail on the farms."

He quoted United States Department of Agriculture reports as showing that there are in the Piedmont section one hundred thousand white farm families with an average cash income of three hundred and thirty-six dollars a year.

"These same families," he said, "conceding two workers to the family, can earn one thousand dollars a year in cash at the start of employment, with the prospect of an increase to two thousand or more, according to skill and efficiency. In States from Maine through Pennsylvania farm wages average three seventy-five a day, and in North and South Carolina, Georgia, Tennessee and Alabama one forty-five a day.

"The labor problem in the South is principally agricultural," he went on. "The phase of it which exists in the mills can never be fully handled until a solution is found for our farm population. Let us not fall into the mistake of giving attention to the superstructure when the foundation is crumbling.

"A majority of mill owners favor abolishing night work. This, however, brings up a tremendous social and industrial problem. Thousands would be thrown out of work if it stopped.

"Increasing wages with decreasing profits is as economically out of the question as it is physically impossible to bring two poles together. On the basis of present earnings the mills are paying the highest possible wages consistent with sound business principles, and the only way to raise the general wage level is to develop the industry so it will earn larger profits."

A feeling of contentment and comfort went through the audience at these familiar words. Mr. Jameson was reassuring. He had told every one the things they wanted to hear — the stretchout — it was a good thing only it had been introduced tactlessly. The day was over when the employers could impose their will on the employees — that wasn't the way to make cooperation between workers and management. This was the kind of a talk for those Northern newspaper men. This was the kind of a man to have — genial and temperate in their utterances.

"Well," said Hoskins as they walked away, "I hope this has enlightened you, Hewlett. You can understand now that because the farmers do not make enough that is the reason why the mill workers shouldn't Q.E.D."

4

As a result of the Chamber of Commerce meeting Roger with some of the other reporters was invited to visit Hastings. Hastings was one of the model mill villages. Whenever Roger met Mrs. Parker on the street she always said:

"And have you visited Hastings yet?"

Whenever any of the comfortable people talked about conditions in the mill towns they always ended up with saying:

"But you should see Hastings."

It was a vindication of the system. It showed what a mill village could be.

The Hastings family had built up the industry. The older Hastings had begun with a small mill. Now they had a town of eight hundred families. The little town as they drove into it was cheerful and neat. Rows of pretty cottages, each with shrubbery and lawn, faced the front street. There was a church and a school and a store. In the distance lay a charming lake. The town itself sloped down a side hill toward the water. Mountains ringed it around.

They stopped before the office and presently the younger Hastings greeted them. He was a man in his late thirties, agreeable, intelligent. He had none of the quality one may frequently find in old-fashioned employers—in Basil Schenk, for instance. That:

"This is my mill and I'm going to do what I want."

"Of course it's far from an ideal system," Mr. Hastings said. "There are plenty of imperfections about it. But I don't know in what other way the industry could have come about in the beginning. When we built the mill the workers came to work. They had to be housed. It was inevitable for the mill owners to build houses for them and to provide a store, help with the church, even with the schools. So much power will naturally be abused in certain cases. It doesn't conform with the democratic ideal. But can you suggest in what other way the industry would have grown, granted the circumstances?"

"What's your feeling on unionism?" some one asked.

"It's not a question that's come up as yet. We shouldn't be opposed to it if the textile industry were organized by a conservative union. We shouldn't want the Textile Union here, naturally."

Roger reflected that he happened to know that there was quite a bit of organization even in this best of mills.

"We should be glad to see the hours shortened. We can't shorten them beyond a certain point ourselves any more than we can raise wages beyond a certain point without going out of business. Union or no union we could give the workers very little more than we are now. The Hastings Co. has never paid a dividend. We practically own the stock ourselves and we put back into the town all we make. We have spent thousands of dollars on roads. We maintain a model farm. We don't try to make the farm pay for itself. We sell milk, vegetables, everything to the workers at cost. Sometimes we run at a loss."

"Your people don't have pellagra, I take it."

"No, I think it's practically unknown in the town. If any one has pellagra they would have had it before coming here." He went on to tell that the industry paid for the maintenance of all the lawns and shrubs on the main street, that it furnished trees and shrubs to the workers. "They have a golf course over by the lake."

"Do many of the workers play?"

"About thirty. We maintain the golf course and keep it in order for them."

"Could a worker own his own home here?"

"That has been one of the constant criticisms of the industry that workers can't own their homes."

"We wouldn't have any objection to a worker owning his home if we could be sure it would remain a home. We tried the experiment of selling pieces of land outside the village to workers but they immediately sold at a profit to people who wanted to put up things like hotdog stands with gambling games on the side. Our village is comparatively prosperous and there would be a quantity of these pests preying off the workers if we would allow it. We haven't even wanted the Gastonia bus to come through the town, disturbing the quiet of the village and putting it in the heads of the young people to ride into the city for no reason. Now if they really have a reason they have a little trouble. The bus comes near enough."

They went through the farm and the mill and drove around the beautiful township. Roger could easily imagine the pride of these two men who had actually created a town where there had been nothing. What fury they would feel if they knew the Union was there among their "happy and contented" workers.

10

1

MAMIE LEWES got up at five in the morning. She put on her petticoat, a dress and stockings—all cotton. There was some gravy to be warmed, and some bread and grits. There was no coffee or milk. She prepared beans with a piece of fatback and put them on to cook for the children's dinner. She hummed as she stirred around in the kitchen. The baby, who was two and a half, sat up in bed rubbing her eyes. It slept with Mamie Lewes and the three other children slept in another bed. The two beds took up almost all the room. Rosie, the oldest girl, slid out of bed and began to dress.

"Rosie," Mamie Lewes said, "you keer fo' the chillen an' watch these yere beans. Keep on addin' water so they don't git sco'ched none. Ef youall want enny more braid, you'll hev to bake hit; they's flour and they's lard."

"Ain't you comin' home, Ma?"

"I ain't comin' home till nightfall. I'm on the strike committee now, honey."

"Oh, Ma, is you?" Rosie didn't know what the strike committee was, but it sounded grand to her.

"Yes, and I'm on the relief committee," Mamie Lewes bragged.

"You is?"

The two little boys waked up and tumbled out of bed, scrambling into pants and shirts. Mamie Lewes dressed the baby, straightened the beds, washed up the dishes and swept out the room.

The strike committee meeting was at nine o'clock, though generally it didn't get started until about halfpast nine or even ten; but it was five miles away. Maybe she would get a ride, maybe not. She couldn't count on a ride.

She started out towards the highway which wound smooth and gray towards Stonerton. Puffs of red dust rose up from the road at each step. Mamie Lewes' cabin was on a side road. Bare fields stretched on either side, blazing blood red. One field was green with wheat— screaming green and blood red. A mountain reared itself straight up before Mamie Lewes, deep green-blue against a pale morning sky. The sun streamed down. The world smelled of dust and things growing.

A sense of expectancy filled her. Something exciting was going to happen. It was like going to a party to go to a strike meeting. Each different room in the mill chose one worker to represent them on the committee. The strike committee met every day and discussed all the questions of the strike and voted on them. Number Two mill in Tesner had struck. There were five people from the Tesner mills that were sent to Stonerton. It was a little mill with only 300 people. Two hundred of these had struck, and now the mill had closed down; so there wasn't much to be done about it except to keep up the morale of the strikers. Irma went over to Tesner almost every day. They held meetings in an empty field.

2

There were about forty members on the strike committee. For the most part they were young; there were a few older women and a few older men. Ma Gilfillin was on the strike committee, so was Kate Trent and Victor Jolas.

Mamie Lewes looked around. There were quite a number of the people she knew on the committee, even though they were Stonerton folks. There was Dewey Bryson, who long ago had worked in the same mill with her but who was a weaver. She never had time to learn to be a weaver or any of the things that paid more. You had to be a learner too long and "what with the chillen comin' on all the time, didn't seem lak she ever did have time to larn nothin'."

There was Wes Elliott and Dan Marks, standing strong and able looking, at the back of the room.

Fer didn't come. Irma Rankin rapped for order.

"Brother Deane has been detained, so we will have to have the meeting without him this morning. We will take the things up in the order of their importance. We are going to take up scabs, house-to-house visiting, relief picket captain's report, local speakers"—she went on through the list of strike activities.

"We will hear from Sister Gilfillin on scabs."

Ma Gilfillin rose to her feet, her thin straight nose quivered, her dark brown face with its wrinkles seemed a hundred years old but she sparkled with life.

"Sisters and brothers," she began with the ease of one who had led in prayer numberless times. "They's folks aslinkin' into the mill that no one suspicyons of. I seen lights in Mary Ann's windows this very mornin' and I slunk out and I kep' awatchin', and didn't I see Mary Ann's daughter Nancy, to say nuthin' o' young Joe, atippin' quiet outen the house and goin' of the back way around down to the mill. An' won't Mary Ann be to the union meetin' to-night, en' acheerin' en' ahollerin' fer to bust her in'ards, en acomin' around to the relief store and agittin' her vittles!"

"What do you think should be done about it?"

"Thair ain't but one thing to be done about it," cried Ma Gilfillin, "git some boys and girls and whup 'em and whup 'em so they won't want to go to no mill!"

"I want the report how many people are working at the mill."

Dan Marks said, "I gotta fellow workin' in the mill and he counted wern't more'n about a little over a hundred, wern't enough in spinnin' room to keep work agoin'." He gave his report, leaning against the wall, his head thrown back, his arms crossed. His head with its curly light brown hair was poised on his strong neck,—a proud and quiet man. "Trouble is, Sist' Irma, we ain't got no real figgers about how many *is* in th' mill aworkin'. We ain't got men nor wimmen in every room. Now, my fella' was in the spinnin' room but they don't let 'em git out to get in other rooms,—the boss-man, he sees to that. I think we oughter get up a committee for sendin' folks we can trust back into the mill."

"Will some one make a motion to that effect," said Irma.

Some one made a motion and it was voted on. The strikers had a delight in the formal procedure,—it gave a weight and a dignity to their meeting. It was like a legislature,—they were making rules and laws just how their strike should be run.

Irma called for the report of the picket committee.

"Seems lak as folks, it's hard fer to git men out on thet picket line sence them deputies cum in with ther bay'nits. Seems lak it goes gin their manhood to stand up on thet picket line and be run through and not be 'lowed to defend therselves 'tall. Ef they wus to git their guns an' hev gun fer gun, they'd make it all right." There was a murmur of assent through the room.

"Yeah, les bring our guns."

"Even if our guns wusn't loaded." A light breeze of excitement had blown through the room.

Irma stood planted firmly on her two feet, her chin was lifted obstinately and her hands were clasped behind her.

"Brothers," she said, "you can't take your guns on the picket line. How many times do we have to tell you that there's no use exchanging a rifle bullet for machine gun bullets? It's as silly as exchanging a brickbat for a bullet."

A hum of talk interrupted her.

"Ef they got guns, why cain't we? Hev we got to see our wimmen chased by drunken dep'ties with bay'nits and not lift a han'?"

"Ef we hep oursel'es onct, they'd lay offen us. You don't know what a low lot them dep'ties is. Ef they was to see us strikers totin' a gun onct—"

Irma rapped vigorously for order.

"There is no use discussing it. It would just be committing suicide to take guns on the picket line. You can't do it. There has not been a time in all the history of strikes when any one is shot, that it hasn't been laid to the strikers."

"Well, Miss Irma," a voice called from the end of the hall, "it's jest goin' to clean-cut the ambition offen we'uns to see all them thar skunks and pole-cats out with guns and bay'nits on 'em, and us'ens awalkin' along prayin' fer them to run them long mean lookin' bay'nits into our backsides. This standin' up agin' bay'nits shore is fierce—sense they'se stopped bringin' the scabs in by road and is bringin' 'em in by train picketing is shore fierce."

Irma rapped smartly.

"The next order of business is the report from Tesner," she said, "Will Sister Mamie Lewes please make that report?"

3

When Roger got down to strike headquarters, there was the usual crowd loafing around. Men, women and children were chewing industriously and spitting long jets of tobacco juice. Everybody chewed and "dipped."

"The Relief Committee's meetin' now,—they'll be out soon, I reckun."

A big-shouldered boy named Bunny Wright, who limped a little as a result of an accident in the mill, came pegging up breathless.

"Wheh Mis' Doris? Hev youall seen Mis' Doris? They'se 'victin' a woman ovah to the ravine."

"Who is it?"

"Hit's Mis' Winstead. She's got foaw li'l chillen. You seen Mis' Doris?"

"She's in the relief meeting," said Roger.

"Well, they'se evictin' Mis' Winstead."

"Say, ain't thet a shame with all her little chillen," the men growled as they spat tobacco juice. Bunny, full of his importance, crowded close to the door,—the women clustered around him.

"Yeah, they'se evictin' Mis' Winstead."

It was the first evictic.. in the strike,—an event. The individual landlords, not on the mill hill, had been threatening eviction. The Basil Schenk Company had also gotten out eviction papers but nothing had been done as yet.

Roger noticed a pleasant looking man getting out of a car. With him was a young girl. He went up to the man politely.

"Were you looking for some one," he asked. He had a feeling as though he had some responsibility in the strike and had to do something about the strike visitors.

The man was a minister from a neighboring town. He and his wife, who remained in the car, and the young girl, a student of economics in the University of North Carolina, had driven down to investigate the strike at first hand. He introduced himself as Reverend Howard Kingsley and the young girl, Miss Thurston.

Fer came shouldering through the crowd,—late again, Roger noticed, to a strike or relief meeting, which would make Irma angry. Roger introduced him to the clergyman, who began asking the usual questions.

"What was the cause of the strike?"

"Too low wages and too long hours. They worked eleven hours. The immediate cause was the stretchout."

4

The door of the building opened now and the Relief Committee filed out, while the waiting crowd surged into the dingy room. After all it was a place to stay,—a place where they might meet one another. For them, it was an excitement after all. People met one another and learned to know one another. Here they discussed all the details of the strike; they discussed their rations; the latest atrocities, and in the back of the hall, they sat together singing spirituals and some of the new song "ballits" about the strike.

History was making here and they were proud of it. The long monotony of the mill work was interrupted. Lately there had been rumors that a lot of people had been scabbing in. It had come out in

Relief Committee meeting to-day, and strike meeting, too, that people were applying for relief who had members working in the mill.

Irma interrupted Fer's conversation with Dr. Kingsley to tell him.

"We've got to put a stop to this. They say scabs are coming to get relief. We have got to have a closer check. When do you want to have a meeting, Fer, so we can discuss it?"

Bunny had attained his object. He was telling Doris in an excited tone.

"They'se evictin' Mis' Winstead and her chillen!"

Doris pushed back her hair from her face in a distracted gesture.

"I'll go right over."

"She wan's to know what she's goin' ter do with her furn'tur."

Another striker rushed in.

"Mis' Doris, thet sick woman, Mitty Jones, the doctor's ben there and he says she's gotta go right off and be op'rated on."

"I thought you were sitting with Mitty Jones."

"I wus, Mam, but the doctor, he sint me to tell you he couldn't do nuthin' fer her,—she's got appendicitis en' she's gotta git op'rated on right off."

Doris turned to the telephone and called the infirmary of Stonerton, the closest hospital. They refused to take the patient,—a striker,—without pay. In Stonerton were three other hospitals, all supported by different churches. Not one of them would take in the sick woman.

"There's nothing for it," Doris told Fer. "I'll have to get an ambulance and take her over to Lafayette. Some one else will have to see about the eviction. I'll have to see to Mitty Jones. Some one else will have to stack for me to-day and get the food." She ran around distractedly. Different strikers came up to her.

"Mis' Doris, kin I git the med'cine fer my ole man?"

"Mis' Doris, did them ole clothes that anuther union was a sendin' up to us come? My boy shore needs some shoes, enny kind."

They were gentle but relentless. This, Roger knew, went on all day. The stream of sick people coming and begging for medicine. Doris plowed through the waiting people with their incessant requests.

Bunny Wright kept reiterating,—

"They'se evictin' Mis' Winstead ovah to the ravine, Mis' Doris. She says what's she goin' ter do with her furn'tur."

"Oh! We'll find a place for it. Do be quiet," replied Doris. "Roger, you go over and see about Mrs. Winstead. Fer's got to meet the picket captain."

There was an air of unrest about the crowd. No one seemed to know exactly what to do. People crowded in—to hear and talk about the eviction, about the sick woman, about the men who had gone back to work, about the picket line and the deputies with their bayonets. There was a feeling of disintegration and a slumping of morale. Every one looked toward Fer. Every one expected him to bring with him encouragement, to inform them with their first fine excitement.

As Roger got into the car with the Kingsleys, he heard a woman's voice, — "My sister thinks I'm plumb crazy to be in the Union."

These two people, Eleanor Thurston and Dr. Kingsley, were the first outsiders who had come into the strike area to see the conditions of the workers at first-hand. Dr. Kingsley himself was a Northerner but Eleanor's family were North Carolinians and lived in Charlotte.

5

They drove over to the ravine. In front of the house were piled pell-mell, what had been the furnishings of a home. Dressers, mattresses, beds, chairs, were piled on top of each other; clothing spilled out of bureau drawers; other clothing was heaped on kitchenware and dishes on top.

Two children with yellow hair and blue eyes sat like solemn robins on a pile of bedding. A woman guarded the whole. She was a wide-shouldered, fresh-faced person, her blue eyes set far apart like her children's. Roger remembered having seen her wait in the relief head-quarters. He had not recognized her as Mrs. Winstead.

"Did you come from the Union," she greeted them, and without waiting for an answer, "how'm I goin' ter store my things? I gotta store my things. They'se all I got. I jest cain't lost my things."

"They'll be stored somewhere," said Roger. "Certainly they will be stored."

"I cain't lose my things," she cried. "I los' my cook stove. I paid nineteen dollars on my cook stove and then I couldn't meet my payments and they cum and took it away. Now, I cain't lose my things whut I paid for. How'll I ever get my things again?"

"They'll store them," said Roger as he decided that he would see to it himself, that Mrs. Winstead's furniture should be taken care of. An older child with the same flaxen hair and blue eyes came lugging a baby, who had been asleep over at a neighbor's.

"Was it sickness, that you couldn't make the payments on your stove," asked Dr. Kingsley.

"Yes, sir, my husband he was sick en' hed to get him medicine, course, so's how I couldn't meet my payments. It's awful hard to make payments on anything when you are makin' only $12.50 and you gotta feed six people and pay the rent outen it. My husband, he ain't worked hardly enny fer two yeahs now."

"What's the matter with him," asked the minister.

"Pellegry. There he sets now and he sets lak thet most of the time. Jest sets and his han's ahangin'. Sometimes he won't answer en I think maybe he's a goin' outen his min'—en his mouth—it bleeds awful."

They followed her gesture to where a man sat listlessly, his two pale hands hanging over his knees; his eyes staring vacantly before him; his face was ashen yellow. He was a big rangy man and must have been strong and good-looking before he had pellagra.

"They cum in this mawnin' and they jes' didn't say nuthin' to me but fer me to git out. Shurff and his dep'ties cum in, en shurf he bosses the job. They jes' tuk en throwed ever'thin' out; wakin' the baby en' atossin' hit right to me. My husband he wus layin' in baid and they med him git up and dress. He's ben asittin' there ever sence lak he didn't know whats happened."

"Why didn't you live on the mill hill," Roger asked.

"Hit's cheaper yere. On the mill hill they asks fifty cents a room and ovah yere I pays only $1.50 for foah rooms. Mostly houses offen the hill is higher but they's jes' a few cheaper. Then they won't keep me on the hill. They'se got ter be two han's in the family or the Comp'ny won't rent you no house."

"Two hands?" asked Eleanor.

"Yes, Mam, en they'se only one han' workin' in our fam'ly. That's me an there's gotta be two in the fam'ly workin' or the Comp'ny won't rent you no house. Lots times when a woman's got a baby and cain't cum back to work right off, they jest turn 'em right offen the mill hill."

"They don't always do that," Roger explained, "not all companies but quite a lot of them.

"Cum in the house," Mrs. Winstead invited with bitterness, "cum in and see the kind of place we live in!" Like most cheap Southern houses, it was built without a cellar and stood on the usual brick pillars. The lumber was of the cheapest and there were frequent knot holes in the roof through which the rain poured. It rained in like a sieve.

"When it rains, we had to keep amovin' our baids araound to keep 'em dry." There were electric lights but they had never been turned on.

"Where'd I get my five dollars fer the deposit?" she asked angrily. She was angry,—angry at the house, at the circumstances of her life, at the eviction.

11

1

THEY WALKED along in silence. The women's anger had been contagious. All of them were angry. The indignation which had flamed up in Roger from time to time had become a consuming thing. He could understand Hoskins having "gotten mad" seventeen years ago and not having gotten over it. Roger felt he would never get over this.

Eleanor Thurston burst out, "People don't know about it. People can't know about it. They wouldn't allow it if they did. I'm going to tell people. If it takes the rest of my life I'm going to tell them. And you can, you can better than I," she turned to the clergyman. "You're going to talk to the girls at the University."

"I'll tell," he answered, "how first they overwork them and underpay them. They underpay them so much that mothers of families have to overwork. They abuse them and mistreat them when they try to organize. Finally they evict them. It's the cycle one has to enlarge on."

They had gotten to Mrs. Holly's. A visit to her was part of the strike sightseeing. The minister wanted first-hand accounts of the police assaults of ten days before.

Mrs. Holly's house was much like Mrs. Winstead's but little better built. One of her sons opened the door. She came in heavily, a big, motherly looking woman, meant for pleasant words and pleasant ways. Her eyes were blackened still after all this time and her face still discolored. She told her story.

"I was jest goin' along, aimin' fer to git some supper. I wasn't thinkin' of picket lines or strikes or nothin' when they come achasin' me down with bay'nits."

"Did they wound you?" asked Eleanor.

"Well, I wouldn't say I was hexactly wounded. I was right smart scratched so's my leg bled aplenty. Lawyer Burdette told me how I had oughter keep my dress. But I didn't hev dresses enough so I could lay hit by."

"And thet weren't all," young Holly joined in. "That there law, Murck, come up and hit ma in the face with a blackjack and his fists!"

"If he hit me once, he hit me twenty times," Mrs. Holly stated calmly. "I reckon he was shorely drunk."

"Shore he was drunk! The laws was all drunk that day! Chasin' the poor folks up and down with bay'nits, cutting their clothes and skins!"

There was a silence as Holly finished. No one said anything because there didn't seem to be anything to say. What can one say when an old woman had been beaten on the streets, until, as she described it, her face was the "size of a punkin."

2

Tears of anger were in Eleanor's eyes. She felt that all she had to do was to go out in the land to stop this iniquity. Roger glanced at her with compassion. He saw all three of them as they were, tiny, powerless people, confronting a highly organized machine, part of whose business was to crush workers' organization, committed to the policy of anti-unionism. Back of them, the body of the indifferent people, who when they were moved out of their indifference, only became angry at the workers or the workers' leaders. Comfortable, indifferent people, who, when they were stirred out of their indifference, were soil to grow a mob.

The others had to go. Roger said good-by to them.

"It's going to be almost impossible to make other people believe what we have seen this morning. You can't credit that such things can happen in America," said Mr. Kingsley.

"I'm going to make them believe!" said Eleanor Thurston.

3

Roger went over to the speaking ground. Fer was talking. He was earnest as usual but Roger felt something lacking in his talk to-day. He waited for the appeal to come for the pickets to come out. It didn't come. Fer talked on about the function of unions, of solidarity, a morale talk without the spark in it. He got down from the speaking stand, mopping his face with his handkerchief.

"Gosh!" he said to Roger, "One is put to it some days to know what to say to them."

"Aren't you going to send out the picket line today?" Roger asked.

"Say, Roger, I didn't have the nerve to ask 'em to go out. You just can't get the men out against those bayonets."

"But you can't let your picket line lapse, Fer. You just can't do it."

"I just didn't have the nerve to do it," he repeated doggedly. He stood with his feet far apart, his shoulders bent over with his air of being about to charge through a crowd. "They keep talking about their guns when I talk to them alone about going out. You know how these fellows feel without their guns, Roger? They feel denatured. Do you know what one fellow said to me? 'I feel I ain't got my manhood without my gun.' "

Wes Elliott was speaking. Roger had a feeling of nightmare. He had come upon Fer at his lowest ebb. Fer at this moment didn't believe in his workers.

"Fer, don't you make your captains each responsible for ten men?"

Fer turned away a little petulantly. "You can make them responsible all you want, but you can't get them out now. No use talking, Roger, you can't get the workers out like you can up North. They'll go out when they know they'll be beat up by police. But when these fellows are beaten up, they want to hit back."

"I tell you, you ought to have a picket line," said Roger.

It seemed absurd for an outsider to be arguing with the strike leader. But Roger had grasped from the temper of the people that they needed the visible symbol of their own strength. He had seen the crowd as a mirror reflecting Fer's disbelief. What he sensed was invisible and intangible, yet it was as vividly present to him as though he could see a broken bridge.

"Don't you think they ought to go out on the picket line?" he asked Dewey Bryson. He had a feeling of despair as though he was trying to convince people of a flood which he knew was coming and in which they didn't believe.

Or maybe Fer did believe in it. Maybe Fer had felt the falling away of the strike. Maybe he felt the strike was lost, and wanted to see an end of it.

But there shouldn't be an end of it now. It was like giving up without a struggle. Roger heard himself arguing with Dewey and Fer while Wes spoke, arguing picket lines, fighting for the strike. In that moment he felt as though Fer had actually given it up.

"Look at the crowd you've got this afternoon. Gosh, it's a fine big crowd. You could get a grand picket line out of this crowd."

"You going to speak next, Dewey?" Fer asked. "You be the last. You call out the picket line."

Dewey flushed under his tan. He was just beginning to speak and was very proud of himself. A number of these Southern workers had become quite good extemporaneous speakers. They took naturally to oratory. Roger, still feeling that the whole scene was unreal, talked excitedly with Dewey about picket lines and their function in the strike, — all the accumulated anger of the day of sightseeing streamed out of him.

4

The picket line marched out. Old Mrs. Whenck and Ma Gilfillin, the inseparable companions, brown as leather, thin as witches, spitting brown streams of tobacco juice, ran around among the men and urged them on.

"You all heard what Dewey Bryson said."

"Brother Gil, ain't you agoin' out on the picket line?"

"Come on, Robert McDonald. You cain't but get arrested. They cain't eat you."

"Mrs. Block, whar's yore three boys? I saw 'em loafin' up the railroad track."

It was under way now, more girls and women than men, but a good, stout scattering of men nevertheless. Dewey Bryson and Ma Gilfillin's boy leading, the two old women clacking in their trail, their limp calico skirts flying at their heels, Binney Jolas and May McDonald bringing up in the rear, Mamie Lewes and Daisy West walking together again.

Roger saw them go out with an almost unbearable feeling of excitement. It was his picket line. Some compulsion which he could not account for had made him take this active part, had made him convince Fer, had made him put the words in Dewey Bryson's mouth.

There had not been a picket line for two days. There had been no "laws" present at the afternoon meeting. The picket line walked down the back way toward the factory, very orderly, full of repressed excitement, the two old ladies calling out greetings and sarcasms to the spectators. Roger followed from the sidewalk.

Presently came the police whistles and the sound of the police car. The line turned down a side street. Three carloads of policemen jumped out. Roger, from an embankment, could see them starting to turn the picketers, hitting with their bayonets. The picket line held. It had been turned out and around so that Binney Jolas and May McDonald led the line. Roger was in a group of townspeople of West Stonerton. There was a commotion now, an agitation among the picketers.

"Look what they're doing!"

"Look how they're chasing them with baynits!"

"Oh, it is a shame the way they beat the poor folks!"

"Them laws ought to be rid out of town."

"Them laws are the sorriest folks in town."

"See, they're arresting them!"

"Look what they're doing to her!"

A police auto had stopped in the road almost below Roger. They were dragging a nice-looking woman toward it.

"Look! That's Mary Graham," said the woman next to him.

"I seen her atakin' her little boy out of the picket line."

"Mrs. Graham wasn't picketin'."

"No, she never pickets. She cain't. She's got a li'l nursin' baby."

"Look! Look! Look what they're doing to her!" The women's voices rose in a scream.

The woman was struggling with the police. They wrenched her arms, two men holding her and two of them trying to bend her head, forcing her into the car. The little knot of people swayed to and fro as the woman struggled. Not a sound came from her as she fought with the four policemen.

The woman next to Roger, who had screamed, clutched his arm trembling. The woman on the other side of him was crying. Murmurs ran from up and down among the spectators.

"They'd ought to be shot."

"They's going to be murder if this keeps up."

"Oh, they's atearin' at her hair!"

"Her husband's up in the crowd. See him, see him there! Mr. Graham's up in the crowd. How can he hold his head up ag'in if he don't go to her now?"

"They ain't no sense in his going. They'd only shut him up too."

"There is too use! There is too use! He had oughta!"

And Roger felt that she was right. He felt he ought to go personally. It seemed as if this swaying, fighting mass of people stayed there for a long time, while the spectators watched with horror.

At last they had vanquished the woman. At last they had thrown her bodily into the police car and had driven away with her. Roger walked along with his neighbor on the bank. She was still trembling. They came on to the main street where a knot of people gathered who were told what had happened. Other people brought in details.

"Mrs. Graham, she wasn't on the picket line. She was fighting like that because she was afraid to leave her little baby."

"Now they've took her off to jail, her with a little nursin' baby to home."

They were overcome with the injustice of it. The woman who had caught hold of Roger's arm, took hold of him and said with earnestness:

"I don't know what's going to happen in Stonerton. What's going to happen to folks? I cain't put my mind to anything. I can only go to the meetings."

"Are you a striker?" Roger asked.

"No, sir, I ain't. I keep boarders. Most on 'em mill hands. I ain't got courage to work these days. Not with things happening like we jest seen." And she stopped to tell the story of Mary Graham's arrest to a newcomer.

"Are you with the Union?" she asked Roger.

"No, I'm just a newspaper man."

"But you're fer the Union. You're writin' to the folks in other places what these poor folks is going through." She put her hand on his sleeve impulsively. "I wish youall would come and board to my house. You'd be lots more comfortable than in a hotel. I sure would be pleased to have youall."

5

Before Roger could answer Victor Jolas charged through the crowd. "Hev you seen Fer?" he asked. "Have you seen Irma? Binney arrested! Binney's arrested and I can't seem to find anybody!"

"Have you looked for Doris?" Roger asked.

"Yes, I looked fer her. I think she's gone to see about Mrs. Graham. I think they've gone to take her baby down to jail."

"How did they happen to get Binney? She's such a little thing."

"Well, you see when they turned the picket line 'round, Binney was aleadin' with Mary McDonald so they jes' took her in. I know it ain't right. I know there's plenty jes' as young and tender as my Binney's that's been arrested. Yes, and stayed in jail all night. I know ef I let my Binney go out on the picket line I ought to be hardened to hev her in jail. But I jes' cain't bear it. I jes' cain't stan' to hev my Binney in jail. I feel something crazy rise up inside of me at the thought of them thar laws atouchin' her. They's girls been in jail like Della Barstow and Eva King. The laws has come up and said vile and insulting language before 'em. Ef enny one was to do it to my Binney I think I'd tear 'em apart with my own hands."

"Come on down to the jail," Roger advised, "and we'll see what we can do. We'll try to get Binney out before night. There's some bail money around and I know Lawyer Burdette can use it at his discretion."

They found Burdette at the hotel. He had already come over from Lafayette. Together they went to the jail. Jolas was an ashen gray. He showed his age. The skin over his thin, humorous nose was stretched tight. He was very quiet in his manner as he told his story to Lawyer Burdette. But none the less he seemed to Roger like a high explosive.

They had no difficulty getting into the jail. It was a modern jail and fairly clean. The two little girls were sitting on the bed behind the bars. In the cell next to them was the Tetherow boy and his buddy, Bob Postwait.

"Binney," said Jolas quietly, "you all right? You ain't skeered?"

"Sure I'm all right, paw." Her eyes were bright. Her tiny elflike face was gay. It was a great adventure.

"There weren't no one speak rough to you, Binney?"

"No, paw, there weren't nobudy spoke rough to me. They all been right kind yere to the jail. Weall 'av' been asinging, the boys and us."

From another cell came the mutterings of a drunken man. The boys giggled. "You ought to have heard him a while ago," said the little Tetherow boy. "He was aravin' fierce."

The children were glittering with excitement.

"Well, I sure am going to bail out that there desperate character if they won't fix the bail too high. But the boys, I'm goin' to let them stay in all night," said Burdette.

"What's happened to Mrs. Graham?" said Roger, who had forgotten her in the presence of Jolas' distress.

"The Union got me on the phone and I advised them to march right down to the jail with the baby and for them to take the baby right in. Well, suh, when they seen that there small howling baby coming they hastened to let that woman out."

"How long before you kin get Binney out?" asked Jolas.

"Oh, I'll be right back. It won't be but a little while, Mr. Jolas."

"I'll wait yere in the jail for her," Jolas said glumly. He couldn't stand the sight of Binney behind bars. He couldn't stand the thought of her in that jail. As he went away Roger felt again the bond that was between the two of them. He could not imagine what would happen to Jolas if anything should happen to Binney.

12

1

AT THIS TIME the strike was being played against a background of the social life of the comfortable people of the community. In prosperous schools all over the State young girls were being graduated— pictures of them in the papers, pictures of fine college buildings, stories about graduation ceremonies.

A little while ago in Virginia there had been an apple-blossom festival; the Sunday papers had told charming stories of the peach orchards of Georgia. The flowering fruit orchards and the young girls flowering out of schools and colleges were all part of the social order which had its dignities and charm.

All around the Piedmont mill towns these graduations and festivals were going on. All around Piedmont, the mill hill people went on in their own way, partaking not at all of this other life, though they helped to support it. Where would the prosperity have been without them? Where would the celebrations have been without the mill people and the other people working for small wages throughout the State?

Roger would have enjoyed the spectacle of these celebrations. He wished impatiently that that were what he was South for. If he could only have that kind of vacation. If you could only turn your memory off and forget about strikes. If you could forget about Mamie Lewes and Ma Gilfillin; forget about the men with bayonets and the straggling picket line—of the kids they put in jail and the men they beat up. Just get it out of your mind for a little while, and go to a party where there were young faces and girls in pretty clothes against a background of flowers—some writer has said that the peach blossoms of Georgia were as beautiful as the cherry blossoms of Japan.

2

Roger was strolling down the main street near the relief store thinking these things. Mamie Lewes and a group of the strikers were coming toward him from the opposite way. Then there came the noise of a truck and shrill screams of delight. Little girls in white dresses and boys in Sunday suits, all waving flags and shouting.

"Where are they going?" Roger asked Mamie Lewes.

"That's the school pageant. All the chillen around Stonerton are goin' to the school pageant. Here comes the Basil Schenk trucks."

Children from the schools near the Basil Schenk Mills, all loaded into trucks and singing, going to the pageant. Everybody going to march in the pageant or to watch the pageant.

"Your children going, Mamie Lewes?"

"They never hev been to school. I never did hev shoes for them and we live too far out."

"I thought they made you send them to school."

"They do, ef you live on the mill hill. They never did say nuthin' to me. I wouldn't be able to go to work ef I couldn't leave my little girl to take keer of the little 'uns."

Roger heard them talking behind him.

Another truck had taken its excited, shouting children to the pageant—blond heads and blue eyes predominating over the darker heads. The "country's wealth," as the commencement speakers called them, going to the pageant. A delightful time of seeing beautiful things and singing beautiful songs. All the children of all the schools would see each other to-day—comfortable people's children and the mill hill children met only at such times, otherwise they never saw each other.

"How many of the mill children belong to the high school?" Roger asked Dewey Bryson.

"Not scarcely any gits to go to high school of the mill han's. The mill han's children they jes' hev to go to work. A few gits to go but jes' a very, very few."

These gay shouting children that had just gone down the street singing songs would presently be in the mill. Roger had seen children who were already working in the mill who did not look more than ten or twelve years old, although they all claimed to be fourteen as the law provides.

3

Roger stood looking at the last of the trucks which took the children to the pageant,—then a woman touched his arm. It was one of the women who had stood beside him on the picket line the day before.

"You never did come to see my sister," she said. "My sister's real disappointed. Why don't you come with me now? She on'y lives across the railway tracks."

"All right," said Roger. "I'll go."

"You'd be lots more comfortable livin' to my sister's then to Bisphams. She's only but one boarder now. She's been so upset sence the strike, she jes' didn't hev the heart to keep boarders. Two or three boys she had, wuz strikin' and then they went off to git work somewheres else."

At the other side of the railway tracks lived people who owned their own houses. The people here were small trades people, or workers in other trades than that of the mill. Over by the ravine were a few houses which were even more flimsy than the houses around the mill hill. A handful of families also lived here who worked in the mills,—the infrequent people in a community of drifters who bought their own homes and stayed in them. The houses along the track were as bleak and bare as the houses in the mill village. They, too, stood upon their brick posts.

There were two houses which stood out from all the others, as they were surrounded by trees and roses.

"That's my sister's house," Mrs. Soams told Roger. "She jest sets a store by her flowers. An' you'd ought to see how that woman works around her roses. Seems lak she makes her life outen her flowers and garden. An' where she gits the time—don't seem like I can make no time aplantin' enny garden. I got nuthin' but a few flags. Don' know how she'd make out ef weren't fer ole Mr. Cuthbert next door didn't give her a han'."

Mrs. Thorn met them at the door.

"I certainly am pleased to see you yere. I wuz beginnin' to be skeered you wuzn't acomin'."

"I found him up awatchin' the children's parade and brought him down."

The house was cool. It had a hall through the middle, like most of the houses, and an "L" gallery off the kitchen. As he stood there a neighbor came up on the veranda. There was the sense of a community life going on. Suddenly Roger was tired of the bareness of his room at Bispham's. The room that Mrs. Thorn had shown him was comfortable and homelike. The linen was cared for and there were hand-some quilts on the bed. The walls of the room were decorated with water colors. It looked like the colored pictures of children in a modern school. It turned out that Mrs. Thorn had suddenly taken to painting watercolors last year and she had framed them. Under a sudden im-pulse, Roger said:

"I'll go and get my things right away." The price he was to pay was six dollars a week for board and room.

"Cain't ask more'n that—mill workers won't pay."

He sat down to a supper of fried ham, cold beef, beans, hot bread, coffee, preserves and strawberry cobbler. At the table were Mrs. Thorn and her daughter, Lissa, Harry, who was a scab in the mills, and one older man who worked as a carpenter and was a permanent boarder.

4

Lissa stared at Roger all through the supper. A curious, scrutinizing look as though she could not get enough of him. She had eyes that looked dark but were gray; her eyebrows were too heavy and her hair grew low on her forehead, and unlike most of the women in the mill towns, she wore it short. Her neck was slender and her wrists and ankles delicate, but in spite of that, she had a look of power unusual among the women of the mill hills. And in spite of this quality of latent strength, her color, the way she moved and all made one realize that she was very young. Young by Northern standards but not by Southern standards. Lissa was eighteen.

"When I wus her age, I hed worked in the mill five years and hed been married five years." This from Mrs. Thorn. "Those days we went to work in the mills early,—about as soon as we could stand up,—went in as cleaners-up, doin' little jobs. We hed to, what with Paw and Maw amakin' what they used to, we hed to. You git my sister, Mis' Soams, to tell you about workin' in the mills. She worked twenty-eight years before she was married,—didn't git married till after she wus thirty-five. She can tell you somethin' about the work in the old days; twelve hours a day year in and year out, astandin' on your feet, twelve hours all night long. It's a wunder, it's a clear wunder these folks ain't struck before. Would hev struck if they ever been able to stick together. That's what ails 'em now,—they won't keep together. Look at him!" She nodded her head at the retreating figure of Harry, the scab, who had bolted his food hurriedly and gone his way.

"He was astrikin' at first and he wus in debt to me for fifteen dollars. He makes sixteen dollars a week en he gits in debt to me jes' the same. I'd hev kept him on if he was a good striker, but I knowed all the time, he wusn't a good striker, runnin' aroun' with women and girls en adrinkin' en stayin' out nights. His bureau's all covered with hair tonic en cold cream en tolcum, so he ken keep himself beautiful. I wouldn't give dish-rinsin' fer him."

"Did you ever work in the mill?" Roger asked Lissa.

"No, I never did." Her eyes smiled when she spoke and her voice came deep and resonant, unexpected, — a lovely mature voice.

"Lissa went to High School a year. I wanted her to go longer but she wouldn't, — claimed I wus workin' too hard for her. An' 'tis hard work, takin bo'ders en ef the house ain't full, it don't pay me none. I got to hev eight bo'ders fer me to clear fifteen dollars a week." But in spite of her deprecating tone, Roger felt that she thought this was a fine sum of money and that she was proud of her house and her garden with its fruit trees and roses; and she was very proud of Lissa, who had been to High School. Mrs. Thorn was married at thirteen to a man fifteen years older than herself. Later, Roger gathered, he had left her this house, all paid for, and other real estate.

In East Stonerton, she was rich and fortunate, though she got up to work every morning at half-past four and her work wasn't through until evening, though she did a huge washing each week out-of-doors, boiling the clothes in a huge iron pot, as was the custom in this part of the country. Her house had been built a matter of eight years, a new fine house of seven rooms with front and back galleries. There was no water in the house. Every one washed in the back yard under the spigot, and even the dishwater had to be brought in.

She had dishes and linens in unusual quantities, nice furniture and ornaments for her walls, yet no one had given any thought to saving the woman of the house. Roger sat down on the front gallery with them. Neighbors came in. There was no talk of anything but the Union and the strike. All the people who lived in the neighborhood had been mill workers at some time or other. There were several mill boarding houses of the better kind up and down the street, mostly boarding houses for single men and women and for couples without children. Mrs. Thorn was a second generation mill worker. The passion of her interest was a gauge of how the community surrounding a mill village felt about mill conditions.

5

"I belong to the Union," Lissa told Roger.

"But you never worked in the mill."

"Lots of folks belong to the Union who never worked in the mill nowadays. They's carpenters, tailors and all kinds of folks has joined the Union."

"But they don't stick together," said Mrs. Thorn. "Thet's the trouble with these folks, they won't stick. They's fer the Union en' strikin' one minute and you ken skeer 'em out the next minute. I've kept telling 'em that right along. They'd before now, if they'd stuck together."

"You see some of the girls I know," said Lissa, "they'll go in a couple of weeks to make a little money and then they'll come out again."

"Yes, and their Ma's agoin' to the relief store all the time to git supplies. Thet ain't being a good Union. You go talk with thet Harry. He'll tell you about what's happenin' to the mill. He says they's a lot of em gittin' sore and ready to walk out."

"How many are working in the mill?"

"He says they ain't producin',—jest amakin' a show to git 'em to go back. I ain't agoin' to keep him after he's paid me his fifteen dollars. I don't trust him none."

They were sitting on the piazza now after supper. Lissa said in a voice which made Roger think of little Tetherow's voice the first day he had come, "There comes Fer."

"Yes," said Roger. "I told him to come around here to see me after supper. And I want him to meet that scab, too."

Lissa sat absolutely still as though she could not realize that this had happened, that Fer was actually coming to her house, to sit upon her porch. When he said to her genially, "Oh, I know you. I've seen you at meetings lots of times," it was almost more than she could bear.

"Say, Roger," Fer said, after they had talked a while, "I've got to get over to Brookington somehow. We've sent one of our organizers over there and they report that they want me to come over and speak. I ought to get around the country more, anyhow."

"You mean the Union's gone clear to Brookington?" said Mrs. Thomas, bending forward.

"It's got to more places than Brookington," said Fer.

"You mean we're really going to get a Union right over the South? You think you're going to get them?"

"That's what we're going to try to do."

"Ma," said Lissa, "why couldn't he drive over with uncle and me to-morrow?"

"Why shore nuff! Lissa's goin' to visit kin over to Brookington for over Sunday! She'd take you along and welcome and Mr. Hewlett, too, if he should want to go. It's a right pretty drive and it's a good chance for you to see the country."

6

They started early the next morning in Mr. Horner's old Ford. Roger sat in front with the old man and Fer and Lissa sat behind. Brookington was up beyond Asheville, up toward Tennessee. The plant was a new plant and manufactured automobile fabrics. They had drawn their labor supply from the nearby mountain families and like Elizabethton, the workers were independent. They had not yet been broken by the mill.

Roger could hear Fer talking eagerly to Lissa. He was telling her about his plans for the Union. He was letting his tired mind play with things as they ought to be, making his dreams come true.

Lissa was a perfect audience. She had faith, she believed. No doubt clouded her mind. What Fer was saying was the flowering and the establishment of Mamie Lewes' simple couplet:

> "We're going to have a union,
> All over the south,
> So's we kin hev good clothen
> And live in a better house."

The road unfolded between red fields. A side hill with the sun shining on it was a blare of color like music. Here and there young fields of wheat made a clear, translucent green spot among the dark red of the fields. The hills were clothed with trees. Everywhere the pink and white of laurel decorated the woods. Everywhere there was a spurt of orange azalea growing wild. There are no such woods anywhere as those of the Carolinas, Virginia and Tennessee.

"I sure love to drive up through these woods. They's flowers all the time from early April," said Lissa. "First it's boxwood and Judas trees. Now it's laurel and azalea, and in June there'll be the rhododendrons. You oughta drive up here, Fer, when the rhododendrons is in bloom. It sure is pretty here."

"I certainly'd like to, Lissa. Say, Roger, wouldn't it be great to come up through the country like this just to see the rhododendrons? Not to have to think? Not to have anything on your mind except how fine the woods looked? Wouldn't it be great to go fishing?"

"Yes, it would," said Roger flatly. Fer had spoken in the voice of the homesick. In a voice which said, "Wouldn't it be nice to be like other fellows my age? With a nice girl by my side. Not to have to think of strikes or how the other fellow is going to be fed. Not to have to worry about organizing. Not to have to worry about people in jail. Not to have to worry about mobs or men toting guns."

Well, he had his little moment of freedom now and he enjoyed it. He sat back and for the first time he noticed Lissa. She was young and strong and yet delicate, something like the laurel. She knew that he had noticed her. It was almost like an explosion within her. An indescribable thing had happened, that Fer was sitting beside her, noticing that she was a pretty girl, glad to be with her.

He said, "I'm sure glad your mother asked us to come along. It makes it so much nicer to have you here." He had a sincere, honest way of saying a thing like this which put it beyond flattery. "You know, I'd forgotten what it was to feel this way. You get so wrapped up in anything like a strike you forget you're living in the world. My, it's beautiful!" He reached out for Lissa's hand. It lay in his palm, slender and firm. Tears came to Lissa's eyes.

A swift knowledge had come to her that this was her only moment. Soon the drive would be over. Soon Fer would be swept back into the strike. He wouldn't have any time for her and when he saw her he would see her through the veil of the strike. He had principles, too, she had heard. Dewey Bryson had said, "Fer don't believe in messing up with girls in a strike." Some of the boys and girls had taken advantage of the opportunity the strike had given them to have love affairs. Fer was one-pointed. There would be his one moment of emotion, the promise of something that might have been, there could be nothing else.

13

1

THE STRIKE was entering on its sixth week. The management of the mills had declared the strike was over and that they had as many workers now as they needed. The newspapers had printed this repeatedly. They had been printing something like this from the very beginning. The strike was passing into a quiet phase. Every afternoon a little picket line wavered out. Every afternoon the little picket line was broken up but now with less brutality, with fewer arrests.

Roger and Hoskins stood at the outskirts of the crowd. The lot sloped slightly down hill towards the speaking stand. Beyond the speaking stand was a flat space and beyond that a high railway embankment. Back yards of shabby stores bordered it.

The crowd to-day was definitely smaller. It was less compact. Down towards the railroad track families sat on the ground, their men standing. Children played around on the outskirts. There was a little milling around among the people, a slight restlessness even though Fer was speaking.

"When I came a month ago," Roger said, "nobody stirred or moved while Fer was speaking. What do you think, Hoskins, do you think the strike's lost?"

"I've always thought this strike was lost technically. At least in the sense that you're going to get the management to talk with the Union."

"What does Fer think about it? Does he know it? What's he going to do?"

"I don't think he knows it. The leader of the strike doesn't meet the faint-hearted ones. He is always surrounded by the ones who won't believe the strike is over. Just at this point too, unless there's been an actual break—"

"There's been no break here."

"No, there's just been a seep, seep, seeping away. People leaving for the mountains. People going back to work. Some of the best people are going back up to the hills and some of the worst ones are going back to work. There's another thing, the folks here are fond of Fer. They hate to tell him anything disagreeable. They hate to know about people going back and they don't repeat it. That's another thing. These folks don't want to quarrel with a person they respect. You put anything up to them and they say, 'Maybe you're right.' That doesn't mean they agree with you. It means they respect you."

2

Roger wandered on through the crowd. He got the sense of something shaky underfoot, hard for him to express but definitely there and more menacing than the bayonets of the deputies. The picket line, weaker than it had been, started out. Roger ran into Irma.

"You look tired," he said.

"I haven't had time to ñave any lunch to-day. I was up early. I had to go over to Tesner. Mamie Lewes was at the meeting. My, that woman's wonderful. She sang."

"Come on and get some coffee and a sandwich," Roger suggested.

They went down the street and went into a small and dirty restaurant. It was an odd hour and empty but for themselves.

"What's the matter?" he asked.

"Oh, it's the awful state of things," she said. "It's Fer. It's that we need more people. It's that we need to broaden out. It's that we get calls and calls from other towns and we haven't anybody to send."

"What do you think about the people here?"

"I don't think, I know. It's that they're going back to work. If we just had a few more people down here to talk to them! Northern people don't know what it means to these people to go out on strike. Northern people when they strike usually have a little money in the bank, or credit. These people come out without twenty-five cents in their pockets. They trade at the company store and they haven't any credit. Northern workers generally have some one in the family working in some other industry. Here the whole family works in the mill. They haven't anything. I've got to go see Ma Gilfillin. She wants to talk to me about Mrs. Whenck."

3

Roger went with Irma to Ma Gilfillin's. The house was full of the strike. The women, both Daisy West and Ma Gilfillin, had been too excited to clean up much. On account of the boys who lived there, there were always strikers traipsing through the house, as Ma Gilfillin said. There was a sense of people coming and going perpetually. Life was disorganized, restless and disorderly.

Ma Gilfillin, her eyes sharp as gimlets, chewing solemnly on her cud of tobacco, beckoned them into the kitchen with a finger which was as meager as a bird's claw. She shut the door.

"Miss Irma," she said, "you know my buddy, Mis' Whenck, her and me that was always running around together?"

"I haven't seen her for a long time," Irma said.

"No, you even't seen her for a long time. And why? Because she's got the pelagry. She's aspittin' blood. Then soon's she got a little better, her daughter got a baby."

"We ought to do something about the baby," Roger said. "I thought there was going to be a fund for strike babies. There always is. It makes good copy."

"That baby ain't a strike baby," said Ma Gilfillin.

Irma asked, "Why not?"

"Because the boys is gone back to work! Yes, ma'am, they's gone back to work and that's what I wanted to talk to you about. You know they's ascabbin' but they ain't scabbin' in their hearts. There's two or three grandchildren ennyway under ten years old, and now they's this new one. An' God only knows where *he* is. I mean the paw of this baby. He ain't ben yeard of fer six months. Stepped out from yere as so many men did befoh the strike. An' now Mis' Whenck down with the pellegry, the boys just naturally went back to the mill. My boy Will, he sez, 'I'm goin' to git a bunch and whup them Whenck boys,' and I sez," she darted her head forward like a serpent and stamped her foot, " 'You ain't agoin' to do no sech thing, Will Gilfillin!' He sez, 'I ain't, ma? Who's goin' to stop me?' And I sez," she shot her head out at them and stamped her foot, " 'I'll stop you, and I'll see to it that none of your whuppin' crews molests them Whenck boys. I'll talk to the Union about it.' And that's what I'm doing this minute, Miss Irma. An' I want fer you to tell Fer. A new baby, and its paw gone and the pellegry, and all them little chillen. One of 'em never has ben nothin' but a cripple."

"You tell Fer 'bout it," Irma told Roger. "I've got to go down and see about the distribution of food."

4

Roger found Fer in the back office of the relief store which served as strike headquarters now. The evening crowd was waiting for the distribution of the food. As Roger slowly made his way through the crowd, he again got the sense of something of their quality, something pungently different from any group of people anywhere.

Part of the difference is the extreme meagerness and poverty of their outward lives which have driven them inward, into affection one for another, and into religion. They were living all of them in the eighteenth century. Their conception of the world was an eighteenth century conception. The place of man in the universe had been untroubled by the age of reason. For them Darwin had not written his disruptive philosophy.

Williams, the old preacher, and some of the boys were sitting together on a counter of the store, their shoulders relaxed, their heads bent together, singing a spiritual.

> "My Lord, what a mornin',
> My Lord, what a mornin',
> My Lord, what a mornin',
> When the sky come tumblin' down."

People from the crowd were perpetually coming up to Fer who was sitting on a high stool in front of the desk. They were bringing him requests which properly belonged to Doris. Could they have medicine? There had been threats of eviction. The boss man had been around to threaten the women folks. The people coming with their complaints, information and requests really wanted to warm themselves in the presence of their leader. They loved him.

Burdette had said to Roger, "Make no mistake, they'll follow him anywhere. They'll do anything he says."

They were a great clan and he was their chief. They gave him the single-minded, undivided emotion of simple people. He was their David defying the Goliath of the mills. And this devotion of theirs was comforting to him at times and at times the weight of so much affection and trust almost crushed him. There were times when he could hardly bear the affection of their eyes. He knew how powerless he was. He knew how mighty were the forces arrayed against them.

He knew, too, that if the strike was lost they would blame him. He knew it, knew what things would be said against him by the boss man and by the papers. To-night was one of those times when the people's closeness was intolerable. He greeted Roger with relief, and gently, very kindly, got rid of the importunate men and women around him.

5

Roger told him about the Whenck boys and Ma Gilfillin's request.

"I'm going to have a meeting with some scabs tonight," Fer said. "Right away I'm going to have a meeting. They think that the mills are getting ready to come out again."

"Do you think they'll come out?"

"I don't know," said Fer in a matter-of-fact tone. "It's the only thing that's going to save the strike if they do."

Roger felt his heart give a jump.

Fer, then, had faced defeat.

Fer was conscious as was Roger, of the slow, imperceptible disintegration of the strike. The Whenck boys going back to work was just one symptom, just one more family starved back into the mills.

The Union was doing all it could, all any union could be expected to do. It had kept the agreement as to the food it would furnish. This wasn't enough if almost any disaster happened in a family. Fer said with quiet matter-of-fact emphasis:

"They've got to come out again. You know the strikers here aren't like those in any other strike I ever saw. You know I always told you this strike wasn't like any other. It's a hell of a queer strike: when you get one old woman like Ma Gilfillin calling off the strong arm boys from the Whencks. Most strikes, that old woman would be rushing at the other old woman and sicking her boys on. There's quite a lot of strikers to go back to work for a week or two and get a little money to go on with, and then come out again."

"If you could only organize them," said Roger, "you could make a regular strike of it. Let the mills support the strike in a way."

"It'd take more organizing than what we've got. You know, Roger, these folks don't know yet what a union is. They don't *feel* unionism. They think a Union is like a church. It's kinda like salvation. You belong to the Union, and somehow or other, you're saved. They have a mystical feeling about the Union. But that feeling of solidarity, that real heart of it, that 'all for one and one for all,' and the kind of feeling that the scab is the lowest thing on earth,—these folks here haven't got it yet."

"Some of them have got it," said Roger. "Wes Elliott, Max Harris, Dan Marks, the Tetherows and Dewey. And some of the women are good unionists like Mamie Lewes. She's certainly got it."

"But what gets me is that at night when we have the night meetings, some of the scabs will come up to me. One last night said, 'Fer, I'm terrible sorry I had to go back to my work but there just doesn't seem to be any way out of it.' And he went on and told me the usual story of sickness in the family and a new baby. You know the usual pressure. But then they come up to me and say, 'Fer, we're coming out again as soon as we can.' "

They walked out of the ill-lighted room together. People were receiving their bundles of food. The relief workers were sweating behind the counter. Roger parted with Fer at the door. He went away for the good supper up at Mrs. Thomas's flower-covered house, Fer's words, "If they only come out," echoing like faint hope in his heart. His feeling of apprehension deepened. In a thousand inappreciable ways he could feel the strike weakening. Its fabric of compact human beings being dragged apart. The strike spirit bleeding to death, starving to death. And yet there was always the hope that they might come out.

14

1

FOR A MONTH past people had been receiving eviction notices from the Basil Schenk Manufacturing Company. These notices told them to vacate their houses. A worker in North Carolina cannot be evicted between night and morning. An eviction notice must be given a certain number of days before it becomes legal to remove his things. Eviction notices had been served upon more than sixty families.

In the relief store Henry Tetherow said to Doris:

"I got my eviction notice, Miss Doris."

She looked at the paper in his hand.

"Why, it's made out to you!" Henry was seventeen, but looked fourteen.

"Yes'm. I'm the head of the house. My paw he ain't aworkin'. He's ben sick a long time, so I'm the head."

"How many of you are there working?"

"Me an' m' sisters. They's older'n me. We rent half our house to Truemans. When we're evicted they'll be 'victed, too. They say we'll be about the fust to go, caze at the beginnin' of the strike the Union meetin's used to be held to our house."

"The date on this notice is old," said Doris.

"Yes'm. They was holdin' off the 'victions I guess caze they thought the strike would be over. Now I guess they's agoin' on with 'em sho' nuff."

It seemed definite that they were going on with them. Sixty families evicted would mean three hundred people homeless, if one counted only five in a family. Very often there were more than two families in a house. Unless it was a big family people did like Tetherows or Ma Gilfillin and rented rooms. There would be more than three hundred people if they were all thrown out.

Three hundred people homeless in a town as small as Stonerton would be classed as a major disaster if it had been caused by flood or fire. The Red Cross would come in. Food and shelter and clothes would pour upon the homeless people.

These evicted people would be looked after only by the Union. None of the charitable agencies would help them.

2

The evictions were scheduled for Tuesday. Roger came down to strike headquarters. A car with Otis Bingham and two camera men was standing in front of the relief store. A big crowd of people choked the store and filled the street.

"They say they's 'victin' over to Truemans!"

"They say Marks is goin' to get 'victed right off!"

"They's agoin' to put out thirty families on the mill hill!"

"Where all they goin' to go?"

"Where all they goin' to store the things?"

"I got my 'viction papers. You got your 'viction papers, Ma Gilfillin?"

"Lawdy yes, I had my 'viction papers long time ago. 'Spect we'll be out in a day or two if we don't get put out to-day."

"Whar all we agoin' to stay?"

"Fer says they's goin' to have a tent colony. They sent for the tents."

Roger pushed his way through the crowd and found Mamie Lewes inside and some of the other workers on the Relief Committee.

"Do you know where they're evicting?" he asked.

"To Bellows, I reckon, and Tetherows."

Roger got in with Bingham and the other reporters from Lafayette. The news service man driving turned up the road leading toward the mill. Mill guards came out and held a hand up. It was a public highway.

"Where youall agoin'? What youall want?"

"We're newspaper reporters. We're going over to the mill hill."

One guard went back within the mill gates, and the other one remained beside them. In a moment he came out and made a signal and blew a whistle.

"All right," said the mill guard.

"Can they do that? Can they hold up a car moving on a public highway?" asked the picture man.

"Sure they can," said Bingham, who was the reporter who had been knocked down by the policemen. "They can keep you off the mill hill if they want to. It isn't legal but they do it. If we had come from the Union we wouldn't have been allowed through."

3

Bellows first. Here piled out upon the ground was all the material of a gutted household. A dresser was balanced drunkenly on one side. Men were still bringing things out of the house. Bellows wasn't there. He was a serious man, middle aged, who had always taken an active part in the Union and who was a member of the strike committee. Roger didn't know him well. He had only spoken to him once in taking an affidavit for Burdette of how he had been beaten up in the jail after he had been arrested.

Three children stood to one side gazing with surprise upon the things all put out upon the grass. A man came out with a big doll stuck into an empty pitcher, his arms choked with household effects.

The company doctor, a big man with pendulous jowls the color of raw beefsteak, stood puffing among the furnishings now strewn all over the yard. He was a paunchy man and short of breath.

Mrs. Bellows sat upon the porch holding a child wrapped up in a blanket on her lap. There were spots on its face.

"What's the matter with the child?" some one asked the doctor, who was there to see no people who were really sick were evicted. This was against the law. Moreover, the judge in declaring these evictions legal which Burdette had protested had recommended a special mercy in case of sickness.

"Smallpox," said the fat doctor.

"Why isn't she quarantined?" asked Bingham.

"Ain't no quarantine for smallpox in this state. Compuls'ry vaccination and compuls'ry schools is 'nough without quarantine."

"Aren't you afraid she'll give it to some one?"

"Naw, she ain't contagious no more! She's past that stage!" The child's eyes were vague with fever. Her head drooped limply on her mother's shoulder.

"Ef I waited for her to git all well they couldn't 'a' evicted 'em for a couple weeks."

Photographers were taking pictures. The reporters said among themselves that the child looked pretty sick. Mrs. Bellows and the evicted children said nothing.

"The mill's been mighty kind to these yere folks. It's been mighty patient. It's been awaitin' and awaitin' for them to come back to their senses before evictin' 'em. It's sent foahmen to their houses to reason with them. They put off evictin' them for ovah a month. Everything

Basil Schenk can do for his hands he does. But there's a end to every-thing."

"How many you goin' to evict to-day?"

"Well, maybe 'bout eight or ten families, I reckon. Goin' to take the Union leaders firs'. Goin' to spot 'em all over the mill hill so the rest can see what's acomin' to 'em. Ought to be a lesson to 'em. Yes, sir, there's a end to patience."

4

Truemans and Tetherows next. An old piano organ, a motto, "God Bless Our Home" done in crewel work, piled against chairs and bed-ding, all the miscellany of life jumbled together. Men walking in and out bringing out beds, kitchen things, clothing, trunks. Trueman stand-ing there watching the men. Henry wandering around among the things in a vague, uncertain sort of way. Mrs. Tetherow with a child wrapped up in her arm.

"This one's got sore throat. She hed it in bed. Likely there will be a sick person in bed in every house we go to. Fresh air won't hurt 'em. The mill's been mighty patient. This place has been a hotbed of unionism right from the first. They'd oughta been cleaned out long ago."

The Union should have done something about all this, Roger thought. There should have been a demonstration ready. Perhaps it was part of the moral degeneration of the last days. If they had had a picket line of strikers singing Union songs following the police around.

It was a miserable business watching the houses gutted one by one, seeing people turned out among their poor little belongings, how they lived and how they didn't live, all spread out for everybody to look at. It was indecent to expose them so. It was a lonely business too, no friends around, just the police and an isolated family, police who had the power to turn a home into a rubbish heap. Neighbors peeking through windows, neighbors standing on the front porches, some scabs and some Union people, watching Basil Schenk's lesson on what price unionism.

Mrs. Parker would like this. She would be glad that Basil Schenk had gotten over being soft-hearted and patient. "Throw them out, drive them out! That'll teach them something."

5

The mill hill of the Basil Schenk Manufacturing Co. looked like a gypsy camp by the end of the week. The streets of the mill village ran crazily up and down hill. Red roads, steep and rutted, formed its streets.

Thirty families had been evicted. They reckoned at Union headquarters that nearly two hundred people were homeless.

The eviction officers went around accompanied by the paunchy company doctors systematically evicting ten families a day. They had paused a day after the first evictions. Apparently they expected there would be a rushing back of people to the mills.

It didn't happen. The workers were angry. The evictions stiffened the morale of the Union leaders and the morale of the workers. The strike which had begun to disintegrate knotted itself up into a hard fist.

"It's a shame what they're adoin' to the pore people," Mrs. Thorn said to Roger. "Everybody in all Old Stonerton's mad at the Basil Schenk Co."

"Yeah, folks who ain't unions is mad at 'em."

"Folks that ain't unions has pity on these poor folks throwed out like they is."

Harry, the scab, was still staying at Mrs. Thorn's.

"Harry he says that they's buzzin' in the mill. They ain't nowise contented at the mill." Lissa said:

"Harry thinks they's goin' to come out. But I don't put no confidence in him. He ain't got no honor."

Roger knew that Fer and Wes Elliott, Dan Marks and Jolas were holding meetings with scabs from the mill. Suddenly, sharply, the strike had taken another turn since the evictions. It was like a living thing which had a life of its own. It was strong and lusty, it almost bled to death, it grew feeble, and again it became stronger.

6

Roger went out with Lissa and Doris Pond visiting on the mill hill, seeing how the people were, seeing what could be done to help them. The families with young children were to be given shelter first. The work was colossal. Every one on the Relief Committee was strained to capacity finding even the most necessary rooms. Where the strike had hung a little slack after the excitement of the first days now it was again filled with excitement. There was again a rush of events carrying with them a flood of detail which overwhelmed every responsible striker with immediate practical problems to be solved.

Mamie Lewes voiced it as she walked along.

"You certainly got enough to do, Miss Doris," she said. "Have you been up to the Robertsons yit?"

Doris stubbed along, her head bent down, her shoulders humped a little as if she were carrying a sack of flour on them. Her dress was longer on one side than the other.

"No, I sent up one of the boys."

"Did you yere about Robertson's?" Mamie Lewes asked Roger.

"No, I didn't."

"Robertsons when the laws come naturally barricaded they do's, and Robertson he got his gun and he 'lowed how he blow any depity or law to blazes if they bust the do' of his house. Well, then they got shurf and he come up and Robertson he held off the whul of 'em for mose twenty-four hours."

"Then what happened?"

"Then the kids got cryin' and old Mis' Robertson she lives with 'em, she begged and she implored him to give in. They shoved everything in front of they do's and they put the mattresses on 'em. An' Mary Robertson she jest ahollered and ayelled. She sung and she sung and they didn't give in until the old lady made 'em on accounta there bein' nothin' lef' to eat. She says, 'You gotta give in some time. Ain't a might a sense in makin' the chillen suffer. Ye jest cain't see 'em starve to death.' Shurf he says, 'ef you don't open soon I's goin' to git tear gas bombs.' "

Up on the mill hill everywhere the household goods were spread out. Now throughout the place there was a sense of lively movement. The whole population was walking up and down the mill hill to see who had been evicted. From the distance came the sound of singing. Groups of strikers now followed the evictions and sang hymns and Union songs. Irma had organized this. She didn't approve of them singing hymns but she had to put up with it.

They went first to the Wrights. Here in the general sense of the excitement and confusion there was a pool of quiet. Mrs. Wright, a pretty woman, sat calmly writing a letter to her husband. Her baby slept in a clothes basket. Of all the furniture that Roger saw this was the only furniture that looked new. He thought that some time they must have had a little money, not much, but the furniture looked painted and cared for. The dishes that were carefully piled were a set with flowers on them. There was a neatly folded pile of fresh curtains on one of the dismantled beds.

7

Across the field and down the hill Mrs. McClure was being evicted.

"Look, Miss Doris," said Mamie Lewes. "They's puttin' out Mis' McClure. Didn't they promise youall they wouldn't put her out?"

"We thought they'd have to let her stay. She's going to have a baby so soon."

"Any minute, I's told."

In the midst of the turmoil of eviction sat Mrs. McClure. Her eyes were closed and tears ran down her face. She cried on silently without end. Her children, five of them and all small, were gathered about her. The baby was only a little over a year old and now a new one might come any time.

"When do you expect your baby, Mrs. McClure?" Doris asked.

"Any time now. I jes cain't think what I'm agoin' to do."

"Don't think," Mamie Lewes cried, patting her. "Don't think. The Union's goin' to find you a room right off. We'll jist come and get you all." Doris said:

"We've got a place for your furniture, too, Mrs. McClure, so you won't have to be worrying about that all the time you're sick."

"Seems like I cain't think what to do. I jist didn't think they'd come after me right off when they'd see how I was. I say, 'Doctor, I cain't go and leave my house with all my children and another one acomin' enny minute.' He says, 'You got plenty of time to be in the Union and you got plenty of time to find you a room before you need it.' And since then I been all dizzy and confused like."

"You see her husband's off collecting Union money in the mills down toward Asheville, and he's jist been arrested. And that's got her upset, too. Now this come."

"We'll see about you right off, Mrs. McClure," Doris said.

"I'm jist agoin' right off, honey, and agoin down to the Union and find you a room, and I'll come for you and the children and send the movin' truck for your things." Mamie Lewes hurried off.

Doris and Roger continued visits through the mill village seeing about the old people and sick people who would be evicted. Many of them had rheumatism, many had gotten up from their beds. There were sick children. But no one grumbled. The Union had been knitted firmly together by the evictions. It was getting dusk when they went back to headquarters. Stoves had been lighted out of doors. People were getting supper. The kids were having a pretty swell time of it. Down by Truemans when they passed some one was playing "Home Sweet Home" on the cabinet organ.

8

That night it rained. When Roger went into breakfast early:

"Ain't this terrible," Mrs. Thorn said. "Jest kept me awake this rain apoundin' on the roof. All them poor people aliein' outside and it arainin' like this. Did you find Mis' McClure a room?" she asked Lissa.

"Yes, maw. We got 'em all to bed and fixed last night."

"Did you git her furniture in?"

"Yes, we got that in, too."

Binney Jolas appeared in the door. "Mis' Mamie Lewes wants to know kin you go down and hep about breakfast and the folks? Miss Doris she's been up most the night on account of the rain."

"Mamie Lewes stays down to Landers and her sister takes kere of her children sence the evictions and she's ahepin' out so much," said Lissa.

They went over to the relief store.

"How are they standing out under the rain?"

"They're doing fine," said Doris. "They didn't get as wet as I was afraid. They pulled the beds under the houses. A few of them broke in. I've got almost all the younger children under cover."

Every one on the mill hill and many people not on the mill hill who had an extra bed had offered it to the evicted people. They filled the Ford full of packages, coffee, sugar, milk, beans, flour, fat back, supplies for the day. They stopped first at the house of some strikers Roger had never seen. The children looked Irish, they had red hair. Now the sun was out again they had pulled the beds out of doors. The children looked up from out-of-door beds, bright-eyed. The woman was starting breakfast on the range that stood in the middle of the yard. Everybody seemed to be having a good time.

"My boy John when the laws come he went for 'em. He tried to hide out ag'in' 'em. He chased up off and was agoin' to whup 'em, and he set his hound dog on 'em. It's a lucky thing his daddy's away. He wouldn't 'a' let 'em come nohow."

Down the street Mrs. Robertson was making an oration. She was standing on an embankment near her house for the hillside was steep at this point. Down the street the laws were already at work evicting. She threw back her head and talked as though from a speaking stand about the nature of the Basil Schenk Manufacturing Co.

"Wasn't it Robertson who barricaded himself?" Roger asked.

Doris nodded. They could hear Mrs. Robertson's voice, deep and defiant. People were beginning to gather around. The laws tried to look ostentatiously indifferent.

Everywhere it was the same. The rain seemed to have affected the spirit of the people as if they had been plants and had enjoyed it.

In the picket line and parade, wherever workers meet together and have one another's support, it is easy enough to be militant, but when you are alone in the dark and your things all out on the ground being rained on you'd expect people's spirits to be dampened. But these people's were not. All of them had courage. It was as if they said, "Nothing you can do to us is going to shake us."

Doris, as if she read Roger's thoughts, turned to him and snapped at him in a voice that was rendered hoarse with fatigue.

"These women are militant workers."

PART

III

15

1

Even BEFORE the eviction occurred, the Basil Schenk Manufacturing Company had evicted the strike headquarters. After the wrecking of the headquarters, the relief store had served for office also. The little old man who owned the store seemed friendly enough. Almost every one in the village of Old Stonerton sympathized with the strikers.

"Shore is turrible how the laws treat these yere folks."

"Don't know huccum they'se so patient."

"Hit's a wonder to me they ain't shot up none of them police yit."

"They shore should be give high pay. The hours is turrible long."

People on the street corners were always saying things like this. Mr. Duncan, the owner of the store, talked about the "pore down-trodden people," too—but he went to Doris and told her the Union must move after the end of the month. He seemed ashamed when he told her and looked away muttering to her in a low voice.

"I'm feered the mob'll wreck this yere store, too."

"Have you heard anything?" asked Doris.

"No, ma'am. I ain't yeered nuthin' yit but I'm 'feered. They do say the Committee of a Hundred is gittin' stronger en they do say the Basil Schenk's gittin' tired the way the Union hangs on, an' they'se boun' to be agittin' up some ruction. I don't dast let you hev it." And although Fer went to see him, and though Roger went together with Mrs. Thorn and Lissa, who were great friends of his, he remained firm. Mrs. Thorn told Roger:

"Reckun he's had his orders from Basil Schenk all right. Reckun he must hev been tol' he'd git his ef he didn't move out the Union."

They moved next to a tiny shack a few doors down the street. The place had a corrugated iron roof. It was only half the size of the former place and the windows were nailed up. It was sweltering, but even this poor shelter was soon taken away from them. And though there were plenty of down-at-the-heel buildings with signs "to let," they were not to let to the Union.

The harried owners made shifty excuses. They told the Union committees that were sent out to try to hire something, any kind of a place, that "their place wasn't to let," "It had just been let," "They were about to make repairs" or baldly—"That they warn't agoin' to let to the Union." Word of some kind had gone out from the mill owners. Threat or warning,—that was enough to make the Union taboo to any one who had an empty loft or store.

"They're skeered they're agoin' to be burned out," Mrs. Thorn pronounced.

There were some days when Doris had to make the food distribution in the open, backing a truck up in an open space in an empty lot where the people got their supplies.

2

They were struggling with this problem when the evictions came. Fer, from the beginning, had promised a tent colony if there should be evictions.

"We don't care for eviction, we'll just go and live in tents and have a nice vacation."

"Summer's cumin' and we'll just live in our own tents." People repeated it,—"We'll just live in our own tents"—and the tents had been sent for.

But the housing of the people was after all a matter for the relief committee, while the housing of the Union, that was Fer's business. In a union meeting, they decided to hire a lot and build their own union headquarters. An electric shock went through the workers, especially the men and boys.

"We're goin' to build our own union hall."

"Yeah, we're goin' to hev a place of our own whar they cain't throw us out."

Special funds were raised for lumber from the carpenters' locals, sympathetic with the strike, but still they hadn't found an available field to rent.

It was Lissa Thorn who finally found it. The field belonged to friends of her mother. It was off Main Street on Braddock and on the other side of the railroad track, a wide field, stretching between two new houses. Belonging to the same people was a woodland glen surrounded by high trees, at the other side of a ravine. A little stream flowed here, where people could get water, and the open spaces in among the trees would be a perfect place for the tents,—when they came. Facing the highway was the meeting ground, on which was to be built union headquarters.

Lissa led Fer around. She had done something for the Union. Fer's face had the clear look which it had when he was happy. He saw it all as it would be,—here they would build a union hall; here the people would come to the speaking. Here would be the tent colony.

"Our own ground and we can keep the laws off it, if we want to." Here the children could play games and here would be the tents.

"Lissa, this is a peace of a place. How did you get him to let us have it?" They were standing in the glen among the trees,—he took both her hands and swung them.

"Ma talked to him," she said shyly.

"We're walkin' on our own ground. It's the first time we've had a place. It's a peace and you're a peach, Lissa." And at that, from sheer liking of her, he kissed her lightly.

Lissa's face flushed—the incredible had happened. Fer Deane, the great leader, had kissed her. Her heart beat so she could hardly breathe. Her good sense told her he had kissed her but lightly in a moment of gayety and that there had been more gratitude in the kiss than affection. But he had kissed her. He never sweethearted with the girls. He was interested only in the strike and the strikers. She had been singled out above everybody. The kiss was something no one could take away from her, nor the moment of companionship when he had taken her arm in his, and they, all by themselves, walked alone through the sunlit woods.

3

Violet Black had gone back to work. It was a great shock to everybody. Violet Black had gone North with a group of strikers, collecting strike funds from the Unions. Her husband, who was a scab, had tried to sue the Union for "alienation of affection." It had been a phony suit, intended only to embarrass the Union and to prove to the community that the Union Reds who believed in and practiced "free love" and went about breaking up families. The case had been thrown out of court, and Violet Black had proclaimed that she had gone North at her own suggestion and of her own free will.

Now she had gone back to work,—bribed or bullied, no one knew. Just how many people had gone back to work, no one knew. There was no break in the union ranks at any time, nor any spectacular number of people going back all at once.

Old man Mason had gotten up in the strike meeting one day saying that the strike was lost and he thought they should call it off.

He had been woofed out of the meeting.

They were not trying to bring truck loads of scabs from other counties now, as they had at first. On the day of the largest eviction when there were about sixty homeless families, the management had said that the strike was over—that it had been over for a long time and that they had all the workers they needed.

At the same time there was a concerted drive on the part of the foreman to see all the principal union families. Especially the women. Formal calls were made upon them. They were begged to come back to work. Letters, too, were sent around, saying that no notice would be taken of union activities. Although the word "union" was not mentioned, the idea had to be conveyed in a roundabout way, because the employers and the Manufacturers' Association did not recognize that the Union existed at all.

The local paper commented upon the magnanimity of the Basil Schenk Company which had also stated in a page of advertising that it would at any time take back its individual employees and listen to their grievance.

Everybody knew about Violet Black going back in. Other people had sneaked back quietly. They stopped coming to the union meetings like old Mis' Whenck. The papers took up Violet Black's case. They had statements from her, injurious to the Union. She had found the Union wasn't going to help the people any and that the management was the people's best friend.

Strikes are strange that way. Some one person going back, being bought off, will make more effect than a dozen others. Violet Black had seemed sincere. She had been active on the Relief Committee. And there she was, back at work. There was a movement of unrest among the strikers, crowded in narrow quarters, watching their few belongings anxiously.

4

Wes Elliott felt a quiver go through the people. Fer was absorbed in the routine of the strike, in the details of the leasing of the land and the getting of the materials, in perpetual problems concerning the evicted strikers.

Wes, however, sensed a moment of danger. The strike could not end like this. The seeping away of people had to stop. He threw himself into the task of keeping up the morals. He and Cuthbert, young Trent and a committee of others made personal visits on every one. They singled out a half dozen of the most staunch of the evicted women to visit. They put arm-bands on the arms of all the evicted children and sent them up and down the streets conspicuously. The reporters took it up and pictures of the children went through the press. They had them go in a parade, in bands of two and three, finally forming into line as they neared the hired field.

A core of people was being formed who would not yield to terror, police brutality, eviction or mob. A small group bound irrevocably to unionism. Men and women who would remain unshaken—a nucleus to work from.

Around them frightened people. People who could be bribed. People who could be gotten at by the ministers. People who thought one way one day and one way another. People who were of the mind of the last orator they had heard. For the Union if they had heard a Union argument, and against it, if they had heard an argument against it.

5

Then just at the right moment, the lumber arrived for the head-quarters. Fer, himself, was a good workman. The field now was full of activity. A framework was going up of a fair sized building with windows and a door, all of which belonged to the Union. A promise to the people that the Union had come to stay. A threat to the employers that the Union was here for good. Their own place, the outward sign of the solidarity of the Union. Given by other Unions to the Union of the Textile Workers.

There was always a crowd of people around the little building. The sound of hammers was music to them. The hammering went on from morning till night. While the food was being distributed the hammering still went on.

Every one in the Union watched every nail being driven.

The feeling of insecurity was gone. The local papers were made ridiculous with their editorials.

"Remember how they sed in the beginnin' they wusn't goin' to be no relief?"

"Yeah, they sed they wusn't goin' to be no relief."

"Remember how they said Fer wusn't goin' to be back, the time he went ovah to the meetin' in Johnson City?"

"Yeah, sed he'd done run off."

"Now they sez they ain't goin' to be no tent colony."

"Shore! Thet old Stonerton *Times* oughta be called Stonerton *Hard Times*."

Fer went around grinning, the actual making of their own head-quarters gave him a sense of permanency and security he had not had before. His own doubts now had vanished. He had new plans and further schemes. And he also had the sense of security in Wes Elliott and his boys and the women around these boys—the people he could absolutely rely upon and who would not slip away.

He had gotten to know his people—he no longer felt afraid. The little building was symbolical to all of them. They were building not only a roof and a wall but they were building a building. For the Union it took on a significance far above its cost and above its size.

The first union hall belonging to the Union in the South, given by union labor and built by union labor. Floods of oratory were poured over it by Fer, the organizers and the strikers who could speak.

6

It was Doris who was having a bad time of it. Already all the spirit of rebellion and resistance which had been the first result of evictions, had worn thin. The high courage of evictions had disappeared. Mrs. Robertson, who had stood trumpeting a challenge at the officers, now whined perpetually. Mrs. Wright, who had set so fine an example, writing a letter to her husband while the baby slept in the clothes basket, a fact which Ed Hoskins and Roger had made much of in their articles, had quietly disappeared and gone back with her nice furniture to the mill hill.

Her husband had gone back to work and repudiated the Union. Now, everybody thought he was a stool pigeon. Mrs. Winstead com-plained night and day and talked about nothing but the mountains. Doris doggedly made a round of all the places which the Union had hired to house the evicted workers and the other places where they had been given shelter by friends. Her temper was getting as thin as the people's who talked with her.

"When's the tents comin', Mis' Doris?"

"For heaven's sake! You know as much as I do about it."

"What all do you thinks become of the tents? Some one sez how Basil Schenk hes had 'em all sidetracked sumwheres. Reckon thet's true, Mis' Doris?"

"For heaven's sake! You know as much about it as I do. The tents will be here when they get here."

"The paper sez tents never goin' to git yere, Mis' Doris."

"The papers always tell you the truth, don't they? The papers told you there wasn't going to be any union headquarters. Now look at it—most done."

"What am I agoin' to do 'bout storin' my furniture, Mis' Doris?"

"Well, I can't see about everybody's furniture. You all got to do something for yourselves."

The long years in the mill village, the paternalism under which they had lived, had taken initiative from many. They did not seem to be able to cope with their difficulties alone. Some of the strikers distributed their furniture among their friends or found places to shelter them. In many places the pathetic pile of furniture and household goods had remained in the open for days. The mattresses were moved under the houses, so they would not be soaked but they were getting damp. The furniture was becoming warped. But there were always people who depended upon Doris to do their thinking for them. When she was at her wit's end, they would say:

"She's mighty short and sharp."

"Yeah, she's mighty uppity."

"Hit's all right for her. 'Tain't her furniture that's out in the open."

"No, 'tain't her things that's gotta suffer." The women as they sat in their crowded quarters and talked of the eviction had already begun to magnify their losses and to pretend that they had had things which had been theirs only in imagination.

7

The tents came at last, and there was a great spurt of activity. Thirty tents were put up in two rows along the ravine. Every one in the Union was drafted into service. Floors had to be built for all. Sanitary arrangements had to be made. Fer had been too occupied with the building of the headquarters to pay attention to the grumbling of the women and refused to listen to Irma.

At last the families had been moved into the tent colony. The congestion in town was relieved. The weather was fine. The people took the tent colony as a great lark in those early days. There was always singing in the little tent village.

During the daytime, the "laws" came in to the strike meetings but as the morale of the Union grew stronger the rumors of the activities of the Committee of a Hundred also became stronger.

Roger Hewlett had been off on a trip to South Carolina and Tennessee. When he went everything was at loose ends. The strike was sagging. It had stiffened after the eviction. The eviction made resistance. The people informed by Wes Elliott's courage were fighting mad.

Fer had let himself go with Roger as he had with no one else. In one discouraged moment he had seen himself and his little handful of workers in relation to the vast Cotton Manufacturers' Association. He saw the puny people, their heart-breaking courage, and himself equally puny, leading them nowhere.

He was sure through a hundred small events that the strike was bleeding to death.

The people who went to work in other mills, while not technically scabbing, were leaving the Union. The people going back to the hills were leaving the Union.

"They're only leavin' the cripples, the old people and the weakest people behind. Pretty soon this won't be a strike no more. It will be a charitable institution," he said.

And the tents hadn't come and the tents hadn't come. After the big eviction, the newspaper men left one by one, saying:

"Well, the strike's about over."

"I guess there won't be much more here."

"S'pose they're going to get the tent colony?"

"Don't make much difference—it's over, anyway."

Roger left, feeling that courage had seeped out of the strike. It was strange, too, how swiftly this feeling of depression came after that early morning of unbelievable heroism of the evicted women.

8

Roger came back with the memory of this ebb tide of emotion clear in his mind. He found his way down to the new strike headquarters. It was Decoration Day. He met a procession of children led by Irma and Lissa. They had American flags in their hands. A small children's parade going down as near the mills as they dared. Two newspaper photographers drove beside them. Around the new strike headquarters, placed in the middle of its field, was a crowd of people which had a holiday air about it.

Fer hurried forward to meet Roger. He seemed like a different person. When he was discouraged, he seemed fatter, and slumped into himself but his moods expressed themselves in every muscle—in the folds of his clothes, in the very color of his hair and eyes. He was eloquent in the variations of his moods. Now hope streamed out of him. Wes Elliott, his eyes glowing, dark, thin face more ascetic than ever, followed him like a shadow.

"Isn't it great?" he said. "You haven't seen half of it. Come on and see the tent colony."

"You look quite different," Roger said. Fer nodded, with a quick, emphatic gesture.

"I got my second wind! We're just beginning to fight. So have the strikers."

Binney Jolas came past with her father. She had hold of his hands in the way she had, as though she were still a little girl, and looked up at him adoringly. There was something about the affection of these two that always stirred Roger.

"Binney," Fer called out. "Oh, Mr. Jolas, Roger's back. Come and show him the tent colony. The Jolases have got a swell tent, haven't you?"

"Yes, we have," Binney chirped. Mr. Jolas smiled and nodded his head. He carried with him a benign contentment that nothing had been able to shake. He leaned a little on his cane, for his leg had never gotten over an accident he received in the mill.

They walked across the ravine. The tents were dappled in sunlight. Children were playing in the open spaces before the tents. Ma Gilfillin was stirring something in a pot. The numerous McLaughlins were clustered around another tent. Mr. McLaughlin's peg-leg stuck out straight on a stool. Mrs. McLaughlin's dark eyes glowed. She looked younger and more at ease. Even Mrs. Winstead had forgotten to whine for once. Fer smiled benignly upon these scenes, as though he were the author of it.

The incredible labor of getting the discouraged, dissatisfied people moved in had not been his. The responsibility of it had fallen on Doris and Irma and their little committee. Now Fer showed it off to Roger as though he had said, "let there be tent colonies and there were tent colonies." It was an attitude of his of which he was not conscious, but which infuriated the girls. They, and not Fer, had been responsible for the welfare of each baby and the safe transportation of each piece of furniture. They and not Fer had listened for days to questions like—

"Wheah's my dresser gone?"

"They's a slew of my dishes I cain't fin', Miss Doris."

"If I don't git a payment on my furniture, they'se acomin' fer hit."

"I'm goin' to need that mattress I loaned you fo' Mis' Wheelock."

9

The existence of the colony, the actual presence of the new hall had given the Union a new standing. A new feeling about the organization had swept through the whole mill hill. People in the village of Old Stonerton were saying:

"Well, the Union's come to stay."

"Yes, they're going to fight with Basil Schenk to a finish."

"They say they'se a lot of them workers in the mill's awful dissat-isfied."

"Yeah, I wouldn't be s'prised if they'se agoin' to come out again."

Mrs. Thorn preached union in Mrs. Soams' boarding place.

"If youall had stayed out like I tol' you, you'd had 'em licked by now."

The people of the mill village saw themselves as opposed only to Basil Schenk. It was a simple proposition in their minds. They didn't know anything about the market. They didn't know anything about the power of the Cotton Manufacturers' Association. They had only one thing to fight. That was the mill against which they were striking. It was as if this confidence had swept into Fer.

"There's going to be another strike, Roger, as sure as you're living."

"Do you mean they're coming out again?"

Fer stopped. He looked around him. Binney Jolas and her father were at a little distance. Only Wes, his shadow, was close by.

"Cuthbert and young Trent are back in the mill. They're rousin' up the people. I'm having meetings with scabs from different rooms every day. The women are doing house to house visiting. After nightfall, scabs come over visiting in the tent colony. We're sure goin' to get them out."

16

1

THE ANIMOSITY against the Union had flamed up again. The feeling against the Union existing in the hearts of the comfortable people seemed dependent on the vitality of the Union itself. When the strike waned, the feeling against it waned. Now that they knew the Union had come to stay, now that they felt the core of resistance among the workers, their anger spired upward, fanned by the mill people.

There was vitality in the strike. More organizers had arrived from the North. The Textile Workers Union had sent another organizer in Wood's place. He was a mill worker from New Bedford named Charlie Clint, blonde and freckle-faced and young. He got on well with the Southern mill workers from the first. He had been on many strikes and liked to tell stories about what the Northern mill workers had to put up with. It gave them a feeling of solidarity with the Northern workers to listen to him.

Paul Graham and his wife were two young radicals who had hitch-hiked down to help with the strike. They roomed at Thorn's, and Irma had a room there, too. All these new people coming in cheered the strikers and gave the Union a feeling of stability. It infuriated the mill people and their friends.

It was bad for the Basil Schenk Manufacturing Company to have the tent colony with meetings every afternoon, when they had gotten out a statement that the strike was over. The Committee of a Hundred organized by the mill had come back to life. It was composed of people who were mill hangers-on. Young men of the kind who like to hunt niggers; a small group of business men, and their friends.

"Something's got to be done."

"We oughta do our duty and tear up that rat's nest."

"Oughta ride 'em out of town."

"The town authorities oughta take notice of that there tent colony an' disperse 'em."

"Ef the town don't take notice of 'em, the citizens ought to."

"The citizens gotta right to clar out them tramps and hobos."

"Yeah, but they got guards."

They did have guards. Roger asked Fer, "Aren't you afraid that they are going to tear down your new headquarters the way they did the old?"

"The Union decided to guard the grounds. We noticed when we were putting up the tents folks were maraudin' through the bushes at nights. We couldn't afford to have the kids scared."

"No," said Wes, "we couldn't afford to lose our work for nuthin' and hev our headquarters chopped down or maybe burned, so after nightfall, we jes' have a patrol go raound."

"Why didn't you ask police protection?" one of the reporters inquired.

"We'd be liable to have police protection! The only protection we'd ever git from them, wuz to beat us up. Do you recollec' how on the night the headquarters was tore down, it was us boys thet wuz arrested? We gotta right to have a night watchman watch our property like any one else has a right to."

2

All through the factory, foremen were on the alert. Discipline was relaxed. Acts which usually would have called for a sharp reprimand were passed by unnoticed. The factory was running not above two-fifths capacity and the workers were sure that they were getting but a minimum of the production which they should.

There were, of course, spies and they had reported unrest among those who had come back to work. The new workers who had replaced the old were restless also. Within the factory there was a core of resolve. This was represented by the foremen and the so-called "loyal workers." This was the minority of workers, most of them in the higher-priced jobs, who had not struck or who had quit work unwillingly.

These "loyal workers" were irritated at the lack of production, at the disquieting slackness which made them feel that the industry was not a going concern, and that something might happen at any moment. The foremen zigzagged in their conduct from overlooking slackness and minor infractions of the rules, to a blustering severity. These extremes sawed on the nerves of the workers. The long hours sat uneasily upon those who had come back after the vacation of the strike. There was a feeling of discontent throughout the mill.

It was a discontent hard to put your finger on. Where did it come from? The superintendent and foremen — the boss men — tried to find out. Impossible. Its source was nowhere and everywhere. It permeated the whole organization. Something was going to happen, every one felt.

"If we could tear out thet tent colony, things would be better."

It was well known that on Saturday afternoons, the scabs working in the mill went to the meetings. And that after nightfall, they attended the meetings at the union grounds.

"Better not take that up," the management decided. "We can clear out that whole colony. Ef we could start a fight there now, — start some shooten, we could clar out the whole crowd. The police would come in, then we'd mop up the rest."

<h2 style="text-align:center">3</h2>

There was a change in the atmosphere of the tent colony. The first day that Roger had returned, it had been a peaceful place. It had a sense of sunlight, of children, people happy to be living in tents after their eviction, after being crowded into small quarters. Within a few days, there was a feeling of excitement. You could see it even among the children — Binney, going along with her hand in Jolas', her startlingly pale gray eyes staring out of her brown face.

The older men came to see Jolas under cover of night. Jolas and others also made night visits through the mill hill. Jolas was a man much respected in the mill village. He was somewhat of a lay preacher also. He could preach Union as well as any one. He had a compelling gay way in telling his experiences. It was he who started the experience meetings, "How I came to be a Union man," modeled upon the "How I came to be saved" meetings. His own story went:

"Brothers and sisters! I heard a voice asayin' to me, 'jine the Union! jine the Union!' It warn't a still small voice, — it war a loud hoarse voice acroakin' like a crow. It war Brother Wes Elliott's voice. It kep' afta' me night and day asayin' 'Brother Jolas, ain't youall jined yit? Brother Jolas, why ain't you ajined up with us?' an' one day it come to me, I jest couldn't beah to yere that voice acroakin' to me no longer, an' I started in an' with my lame leg, I run for two miles an' I nevah stopped runnin' til' I got to union headquarters, an' jined up. An' I see Brother Wes Elliott's head with his hair acroppin' up all ovah his haid, acomin' to me an' before he opened his mouth to let out ary croak, I hollo'd right to him. 'I is, Brother Wes! I is jined!' "

4

The meeting was over. It was already dusk. Roger had been trying to put his finger on the reasons which made him feel so keenly the excitement latent in these meetings. It held something different than the rapt attention of the strikers in the first weeks of the strike. The meetings now were very different from those dwindled meetings in the days of Fer's depression. Again they had something different from the indignation of the meetings directly after the eviction. Then people in great numbers had come to hear what the Union had to say about dispossessing sick people and children.

There was now a sense of something taut, people getting ready for something. Yet what they were getting ready for, was hidden in the committees to which only a few belonged. Committees who were in direct touch with the scabs and with Trent and Cuthbert.

Roger was walking along with Fer and Wes. Wes asked:

"Why don't you bring him along?"

Fer said:

"All right."

Roger was conscious now that they were going somewheres of importance and had, perhaps, not known quite how to get rid of him.

"I'd better leave you here." Wes looked at Fer.

"Oh, come on," Fer said. "It's all right, Wes. Roger belongs to the Union, don't you?"

"He'll know all about it soon," said Wes.

They were now walking along a dark road. No one was in sight.

They went on a roundabout road to a house at the extreme confines of the mill village. There was not a sign of a light anywhere; it was silent. In some of the mill hill houses there were still lights. Most of them darkened. The only sound was of a dog yapping. They went to a side door. Wes scratched on the door rather than knocked. It was opened by a woman only a fraction of an inch and almost no light came out of the crack. Wes said:

"I is."

The woman murmured:

"I is," and let them in. Roger had a feeling of discomfort as though he had gotten there by hanging on to Fer and Wes, who hadn't known exactly what to do with him.

Ten men were gathered together in the kitchen by the light of a shaded kerosene lamp, which they had put on the floor, so it would not shine through the green shades. He recognized Jolas, Trent and Cuthbert. The others were key men in various rooms. They were here to report on the committees they had formed.

"They're all fixed to come out," everybody reported. "They'll come out nex' Saturday!"

5

In labor situations everything gets known. There are always leaks, there are always indiscretions. And especially, there are always spies. There are always people who can be bribed—men with faint hearts, weak men at the mercy of the last people they speak to. Of necessity, some of these spies are plausible. Experienced leaders are wary of the too zealous. There is little tradition of the underground work in the labor movement. Such underground work as there is is transparent and amateurish.

Of course the management knew what was on foot. It had penetrated down, seeped through, until every one knew. People know everything anyway. It is doubtful if such things are ever secrets. The newspaper men knew that something was on foot.

"They're coming out again, aren't they?"

"Are they?" asked Roger.

"Well, they're trying to get them out."

"When do you think they are planning to get them out?" Roger asked.

"At the end of this week, they say."

The reporters began sifting back to Stonerton again on the news of disaster. The reporters of the big state dailies had returned and the Washington papers had sent men.

The days of the week dragged along slowly. Roger went up to call on the Trents. The young couple lived with Mrs. Trent's much older sister, Mrs. Wilcox. Mr. Wilcox had been a piano tuner; now he sold radios, victrolas and records. They owned their own house, which was built on the same general scheme as the other houses on the mill hill, with slightly larger rooms and one extra bedroom. They had a sitting room, without a bed in it, and a piano. They were in sympathy with the Union but were quiet about it on account of Luke Wilcox's business, and they were well enough pleased when young Trent returned to work. They were not in on his secret.

The day shift was over when Roger got there. Trent should have returned. Lucy Trent, whose head was heavy with its great mass of long hair, and whose face was pale, greeted him with:

"Dan ain't back yit." There was a silence between them. Roger knew instantly that she knew why he had gone back. He hadn't been able to keep it from her, of course. She leaned against the wall, flattened her hands against it and bent her head forward, listening.

"Every time he's late," she whispered, "I'm skeered. I'm skeered they'll do somethin' to him. I'm skeered." Her eyes were fixed as though she were looking into the future. When Trent came, he folded his arms around her in a protecting gesture. Roger turned away. These two young creatures really loved each other. She lived in a torment for his safety.

"Honey," Dan said, "what's yo' skeered of?"

"Oh, I do' know. I'm jes' skeered. I'm skeered of ever'thin'. I'm skeered o' Saturday."

6

Everything was working up to the climax of Saturday. Every one took the excitement differently. Fer grew more steady. His face was shining and his feet seemed rooted to the ground as though he were a tree, when he stood on the speaking stand.

Irma was skeptical. Hopeful perhaps, but skeptical also as she was in everything that Fer did.

"There hasn't been organization enough inside the mill. They're not sure enough of the scabs. I feel as if something more was needed," she told Roger privately. But she was good to Fer in these days, and besides she was afraid of being considered a "defeatist."

Roger had a feeling of excitement and of dread. He could not tell from where this premonition of disaster came. Maybe from Ma Gilfillin. Maybe from a talk he had with Mrs. Cuthbert. He knew, from the local reporters, that the committee of a hundred had definitely planned a counter demonstration. Just what they were going to do, he couldn't find out exactly. Probably they themselves did not know beyond the general program of "clarin' out that rats' nest." There was what Durgan, the Baltimore *Planet* man, called "a lynchy feeling."

On Saturday afternoon, people came early to the Union grounds. The slack main street of the little village was filled with men drifting up and down and standing in knots. The Committee of a Hundred? Roger asked himself. He couldn't tell.

The speaking began later than usual. The grounds were crowded. Irma spoke first. Suddenly there was the sound of crashing. An egg had broken on the stand—and another egg. Irma, her face flushed, continued to talk. There was a growl in the crowd.

"Throw 'em out."

"Whar are they?"

"Yere they are." But in the crowd, people continued to throw eggs and vegetables.

One of them hit Irma. Her eyes blazed.

"Don't do anything violent," she warned. "Just let's get rid of these trouble makers. If we make trouble, the police will come in and break up our meeting."

"Keep on throwin'," she cried. "Keep on throwin'! You'll soon finish what you've got! You can't terrify me! You can't hurt me! You can't stop our meeting! You can't pick a fight!"

"We got one yere, Mis' Irma! We seen him throw."

"Put him out," said Irma. "Quiet now!"

Fer got up on the stand. There was a report of a pistol. A shout went up.

"They're tryin' to kill Fer!" A roar went through the assembly. Shouts —

"Yere he is."

"He's got a pistol in his han'!" An hysterical woman's voice from the edge of the crowd was heard, shrill and high.

"Oh! Oh! Oh! they're shootin' in the speakin' lot! They're shootin' in the speakin' lot."

Fer stood above the crowd, tranquil and quiet.

"That'll do!" he called. "That'll be about all! I guess they're through with their ruction. Quiet now. You all know what this fuss is about this afternoon. You know why they've come here, bringing eggs and rotten vegetables to throw at us. They have an idea that's how they can scare us. They think by shootin' off a popgun, they can scare this Union. But they came here for more of a reason to-day. They came because they know there's a strike going to come again to this mill! You know and we know that the conditions in this mill are rotten, and we know that the workers inside are discontented. We know there's no production! And what we've got to do this afternoon on the picket line is to go down to the mill and get them out. When they see our picket line, a strong picket line of their fellow-workers marchin' by the mill, the people inside are agoin' to come out and show them."

There was a breathless silence in the audience. It had calmed down from the confusion to this moment of menacing quiet.

"I want everybody to go out on the picket line," Fer called. "Every one on the picket line! *Every one!*"

"Every one on the picket line!" they echoed.

7

The picket line evolved itself from the crowd. Irma was at the head of it. Wes Elliott disputed the place with her.

The picket captains, boys and girls, young men and older ones, ran up and down the line, arranging the sequence of the marchers.

"Back yere, you little girls. You cain't lead the picket line to-day."

"Oh, sho', let us lead 'em, Wes."

"We ain't been 'rested for a long time, Wes."

"Git back! Git back, you little girls! Yere, Ma Gilfillin, you be captain of these little girls and herd 'em backwards."

The picket line had a blunt, hard nose. Nearly twenty men marched first.

"Are those the guards?" Roger asked Fer.

"Some of them. Almost all the men take turn and turn about guarding the place."

There were a few women interspersed among the men, women not too young, not too old, the steadiest and most hard-working. Roger saw Mamie Lewes and another woman walking behind Dewey Bryson, and one of the Tetherows walked behind her as though to protect her. Mamie Lewes' eyes shone with excitement; inside of her she had a feeling of quiet. Without putting it into words, there was something in her that was like Fer's unshakable qualities—only Fer wasn't unshakable, as Roger knew. All of a sudden, it would seem as though the earth opened and swallowed all of Fer's confidence.

The line wound slowly along. The people of the village, the onhangers of the meeting, crowded around the line and banked themselves high in the fields above the road, as they started down toward the factory. It wound out long like a ribbon. Roger's heart beat painfully. This picket line meant more than any other he had seen.

If only they would come out!

8

Fer had expected them to come out before and they hadn't come, only a score of people at one time had joined them. Yet all of them brought reports that people inside the factory were waiting for some one compelling moment. It was late afternoon. This was the afternoon when they paid off the hands and they would be late coming out of the factory. It was for this moment they had waited.

Some of the newspaper men in a car called to Roger and he got in with them. They drove down to the factory. Halfway down the public road, the guard stopped them and the man went back to consult some one within the factory, then signaled to them to come on. They swept around the factory and back up toward the picket line. The picket line had crossed the railroad track and was coming on quietly in an orderly fashion, two by two. In one place, crossing the street, they had become bunched up into a crowd, the others at the opposite side of the street were strung out.

There were shrill police whistles. A police car came charging up, filled with officers. Another one with officers and deputies and another one with more officers and deputies.

"Hey!" said Dick Durgan. "Look at 'em. It's goin' to be a massacre!"

"They break up the picket line every day, don't they?" some one asked.

"They haven't been having much of a picket line lately. Just a small demonstration."

"I don't believe the officers were looking for many to-day. They didn't have the roads patrolled."

There was a sudden charge of the police and deputies.

Some one cried: "Rush 'em, boys!"

Murck grabbed Irma and choked her. Roger could see her being shaken back and forth like a rag. Then Murck threw her to the ground. Ma Gilfillin, a tiny brown wisp of fury, was coming to Irma's aid.

"Leave her be! Leave her be!" Murck put out a huge arm and Ma Gilfillin was rolling on the ground.

Another deputy was chasing some of the little girls. The assault seemed to have been made chiefly on the women but there were a few of the men also who suffered. From nowheres, policemen sprang out, banged with blackjacks and chased the screaming women again.

The picket line had kept a brave semblance of order but now it melted under the combined attack of police and deputies. The crowd was forming rapidly. A cry went through the fleeting strikers:

"Look out! Look out! The Committee of a Hundred!"

17

1

AFTER THE picket line left, the tent colony had been almost deserted—only a few people getting supper and putting the small children to bed had been left behind.

Old Peg-leg McLaughlin watched for news on the strikers' lot. He felt too tired to go out. Outside the headquarters door, on an overturned box, sat Mis' Winstead's husband. His face made a yellow spot against the field; his big earth-colored hands hung down slackly and he looked at nothing. The pellagra was bad.

A little boy came running. From where he was, Peg-leg could see the people milling down the street. He craned his neck. Beyond the railway track he could hear noises: a shouting, a roar; police whistles; a dark, menacing knot of people.

"What's happened, son?" he cried to the boy.

"They're chokin' 'em!" Bunny cried. "They're chokin' 'em!" he cried again. "They're chokin' Granny! She wus alyin' on the groun' cursin' awful! Those laws are chokin' ever'body! They choked Miss Irma!" He fled, as if followed by panic, across the meadow toward the tents.

Peg-leg stumped down to the entrance of the lot. The stragglers from the picket line had turned and were coming across the railroad track in knots of twos and threes. Far down he could see Irma striding along.

"What happened?" Peg-leg called. "Did they come out?"

"No, no one come out!"

"We never got near the mill."

"If we hed and they'd seen what we wuz agittin', they'd stayed where they wuz!"

"Is any one 'rested?" shouted Peg-leg. Voices answered from the crowd.

"Yeah, youah wife's arrested."

"No, she ain't."

"No, Mis' McLaughlin was jes' choked!"

"Yeah, they wuz chokin' us to-day."

"They choked Mis' Doris!"

"They pounded the women with their fists!"

"Yeah and blackjacks."

"They cracked men on the haid with blackjacks."

Fer, with two or three of the responsible strikers who had been detailed to stay off the picket line, came out of the headquarters. He stood waiting. Young Tetherow came panting up to him. There was a moment's silence between the waiting group and the boy. He was the first one of the trickle of returning pickets. In the evening light, they looked black as ants as they came down the road. From where Fer stood, he could see Irma, her head back, her hand at her throat.

"Well," he said in a muted voice. "Well, they didn't come out." Tetherow shook his head.

"We couldn't git near the mill!"

Wes Elliott spoke: "We'll see Trent and Cuthbert to-night."

"Yes," said Fer. "Jolas said he was sure they'd come out when they saw the picket line. That was to be the signal. But you never can tell. You never can tell about things. As far as we could get it, they was all set to come out." They spoke rapidly and in a low tone.

"Dewey Bryson was meetin' with a set of scabs?"

"Yeah," Fer nodded. He went down the walk slowly to meet Irma. Young Trent contributed:

"They choked Mis' Irma. They choked a heap of women. They threw Ma Gilfillin on the graound and choked her!"

2

Irma said to Fer dryly: "No, they didn't come out."

"I know," Fer nodded.

"The next time we try, we'll have to have more organization."

Fer hated her for this. Triumphing over him was like triumphing over the strikers. At this moment, he felt himself indivisible from the strikers. He felt all the disillusion that the men felt who had worked so hard and who had had such high hopes.

He knew how the strikers inside the mill felt. He knew what it was to almost come out and not quite dare. To be on the tremulous verge of flowing out to something you wanted and to something you desired, and then have the frustration of not daring. Some small thing lacking. Some enthusiasm failing to flame quite high enough. Some mechanical bit of organization gone wrong. A traitor in the wrong place. The key man not there. Straws, matches, an adverse wind, enough to halt the tremulous waters quivering on the edge of overflow.

If one could have started only a trickle, it would have been a cataract and a roar, — the factory would have emptied itself. In that bleak moment of insight, Fer could feel within himself each individual fear, each individual hesitation and uncertainty which in their sum had frustrated the workers within and the workers outside the factory. Fatigue swept over him. The thoughts he had came irrelevant and purposeless, jamming one another. Only the feeling of the defeated workers remained with him.

He stood quietly, standing with that steady pose of a man who speaks a great deal in public, and therefore knows how to stand quietly on both feet. The light was out of his face, but here with the sun going down, it wouldn't show. It wouldn't show that he was the empty shell which, for the moment, he felt himself to be. He would have to stand there and wait until the strikers came up with their reports; until the picket captains had come back. He would have to wait afterwards and have a meeting inside the shack and listen to Irma and listen to Doris and their thinly veiled sarcasm. He stood alone, while the people crowded around.

3

Lissa came up to him. It was comfortable to feel that in her eyes at all times, he was good and that he made no mistakes. Her faith was like a pillar and he leaned against it. She smiled at him, a look of triumph in her eyes. It was as though she said — "It's all right. It doesn't matter whether they come out to-day or to-morrow. You know they're going to come out!"

He didn't want to feel himself soften. Better stay as he was. Better stay in this neutral zone where he wasn't himself but where he was part of the strikers and their indecision — the strikers inside the factory who didn't dare to strike, as well as the strikers outside the factory. He didn't want to feel. And he felt the strength of her feeling and her own faith in himself. He put the safety of speech between them:

"You were on the picket line?" he asked.

"Yes," said Lissa.

"Tell me what happened."

"The police clubbed them and they ran."

"That's what always happens on the picket line here."

"Did they arrest anybody?" Wes asked. "They say Mis' McLaughlin was arrested."

"No, I don't think they got her."

The people from the picket line crowded around the door of the office, each with his own clamoring, with his own story. Each with a different rumor as to who had been arrested.

<h2 style="text-align:center">4</h2>

Wes, with his hands deep in his pockets and his shoulders hunched, slipped up to the side of Fer.

"Come on in the office," he said. "Le's git out of this." Jolas and Binney came, and Dewey Bryson. They went inside the office and put one of the boys at the door to prevent the strikers from swarming in. The room with its bare walls had a corner in it which was used for an office. There the leadership could get a semblance of privacy. Unless the door was closed, the headquarters was full from morning till night,— the people that were loafing around, people who came with their complaints or with their wants.

They sat down in their chairs, Fer tipped his back against the wall. Binney stood beside Jolas, her arm around him. Doris plunged into the room, slammed the door after her and said: "Well!" She threw back her hair, grabbed a chair and sat down with her legs wide apart.

They all looked at Fer. Two of the other boys came shouldering in,—Fer's bodyguard. Jolas spoke:

"We'll git 'em out yit." It was a quiet statement as though the old man had voiced a decision, as though he had spoken for every one here. He was the core of the strike. In these dozen men and women here was the strike's center of obstinate resistance.

This time they hadn't succeeded. Never mind, they would next time. These people and a few more like them were the directed portion of the strike. People who would go on unafraid, undisturbed. The people who were dedicated to Unionism. For them it was a religion for which any sacrifice was to be made.

The mass of the workers, uncertain, fearful, easily turned aside would have to be leavened and led by these few. They opposed the mighty forces of the Cotton Manufacturers' Association, and through them, all of the vested interests in the South which by mobs, by police and by the Courts, resisted the Union. They hadn't measured the strength of the enemy. They could never know it. But what they did see with a passionate clarity, was the immediate job. They sat together and planned their work, not admitting defeat. It was getting dusk.

5

The boys who were going to go on guard came into the office. Wes was to go on guard that night.

"Are you going to git out to-night?" he asked Dewey Bryson.

"No, I was guard las' night. I gotta sleep some tonight."

"Well, come on fellahs," Wes said. There was a noise outside and two of the girls came running up to the headquarters. One could hear them outside—

"Let me in! Let me in! I want to speak to Fer!"

"What's the trouble?" asked Wes.

"The Committee of a Hundred's formin' down near the mill."

"How'd you know?"

"We wuz down there an' we yered 'em."

"They sed, 'Cum on, let's go clean 'em out.' "

"Who said thet?"

"Out in the crowd they said hit!"

"But they're jus' atalkin'. We cain't go down on the street any night without yereing folks say, 'le's clean 'em out.' "

"Well, they said, 'Le's git Fer an' hang him up on a tree, an' le's git Wes too, and hang him up!' " The girls shouted at Wes.

"Who said that?"

"I don't know who said hit. I yered it."

"Hit's the same folks thet was tryin' to shoot Fer on the speakin' stan'."

The light was fading but the grounds were full of people. Some of the young fellows now came up.

"Fer, we wuz down on the street and hit seems they're formin' up a mob to tear down our headquarters, shore 'nuff."

"Yeah, they ses as how like they'se agoin' to come an' tear down our headquarters."

"An' they're goin' to try to git you, Fer!" Fer had been standing in the doorway, one hand against the jamb, standing with his usual quiet and without speaking. His face was blank and vacant and he looked almost stupid. He saw Roger and Hoskins coming and he shouted:

"What's all this talk about a mob on the street? Have you been down, Roger? Do you think they're goin' to try anything?"

"You can't tell," Roger answered. "They just seem to be fussing around down there. It isn't much more than there's been other nights.

They might, and they might not! I just thought I'd come out and get you. Come on down to Lissa's with me."

"No," said Fer. He wanted to go. He wanted the quiet of Lissa and the flowers and the lack of responsibility. "No, I can't go to-night. I got a lot of writin' and a lot of work to do." His voice was flat and he sounded tired.

"It's gettin' dark," said Wes. "Let's clear out the folks that don't belong yere."

"The folks that ain't colony folks gotta git out now. Youall gotta go. We gotta guard the graounds now." There was a trickle of people going out.

"You don't need to go," said Fer to Roger.

"I think I'll go along," Roger replied. "I've got work to do, too. I've got to write a piece about this afternoon."

There was a general feeling of flatness mingled with a sense of apprehension. More of the colony began ebbing back. Everybody brought with them the account of a mob forming.

The guards began patrolling over by the tent colony.

Fer made the rounds. Then, over at the end tent he heard a woman's voice screaming:

"Who's thet out thar?" Again the woman's voice called.

"Thet you, Wes? I yered some one amaraudin' 'raound in the bushes. They'se some one skulkin' 'raound down'n out thar,—I yered 'em."

The events of the day,—the egg throwing, the mob, the pistol shot, the brutality of the police, the rumors that the mob was coming to clear out the colony, had put everybody on edge. Fer, Doris and some others were sitting in the headquarters. Fer was finishing some work. The younger boys, Charlie, Clint and Frank Gilfillin were guarding the front entrance which led to the strike grounds.

6

An automobile with five policemen drove up. In it were Humphries, Murck, Zober, Philip Hunt and Grosman. Had the neighbors phoned for the police? That's what they claimed later. Humphries got out and said:

"What seems to be the matter here?" He was followed by Murck, Zober and John Grosman. They had been drinking. Philip Hunt stayed behind in the car. He had a sawed-off shotgun in his hand.

"Thar ain't any trouble," the guard, Clint, said. "You can't come in now. No one can come in after hours."

"To hell I can't," said Humphries.

"You can't come in after hours without a warrant."

"To hell I can't," said Humphries again. "Put down thet gun. Take thet gun from him," he said to Murck.

A shot came from the direction of the police car. It passed over one of the guard's heads.

He fired.

There were more shots. Now from the darkness on both sides, there came a fusillade.

Terror seized the colony up in the tents. Women moaned and cried. "They're shootin'! They're shootin'! They've come after us."

The boys—the guards themselves, didn't know what had happened. They only saw the dark figures below.

They only heard the shots. Men came out and fired shots into the darkness. The policemen answered. There was a sense of nightmare through the whole colony.

Up in the headquarters there was silence. Fer said:

"God! They've come for us!" Irma said:

"Put out the lights." Then they waited. Irma went to the door and looked out. The shooting that seemed to have lasted for hours, lasted only a few moments. Down by the rear door entrance, Humphries had fallen face downward. They lifted him up and he said:

"Boys, I'm done for!" The other officers were wounded. So was Clinton but he managed to get away and came up to the headquarters panting—

"Fer! Fer! Humphries is dead an' so is Murck an' Zober! Come on, Fer, they're goin' to try and git you." Wes came running up.

"Gosh! This is a terrible business!" he said. "The Committee's comin'!"

Already there was panic through the place. A ghastly silence for a few moments—then panic!

7

Fer stood with his accustomed quiet, standing firmly as if he were on the speaking stand; his head lunged forward. He hardly heard Irma, who pulled at his sleeve.

"You've got to get away, Fer," she said. "They've killed three police. The mob's coming. They'll lynch you."

He didn't answer. It's come, he thought, it's come at last. He felt as if he had been expecting this moment from the beginning of the strike. He had known always that a gun would go off. Some one would be hurt. Then he would be blamed. Irma was at his side, saying in a low, excited tone:

"Fer, Fer, you've got to go! You've got to! They'll lynch you!"

He answered quietly, as though from sleep: "There's no use in my running away." It was though he had said, what's the use in trying to get away from something that's all decided?

"Hurry, Fer."

"Any of our boys shot?"

"Only Clint. Clint's shot in the arm. He isn't hurt bad."

"They'll be here any minute now. The police and the mob."

He stood there not moving, absorbed in his thoughts. It was all over now. Now they wouldn't come out. All the effort, all the suffering wasted. Put an end to by a shot. It was what the enemy had been waiting for. Yet he couldn't leave the tent colony unguarded. They had a right to defend themselves.

8

Madness had broken loose in the tent colony. Women were screaming. Children crying. A sudden silence. Then screams again.

"They shot the boys."

"The boys is lyin' daid on the ground."

"What happened?"

"They've shot Humphries."

"Humphries is daid."

"Murck and Zober's daid."

"Our boys is lyin' daid on the ground."

"The committee's comin'."

"It's comin' to git us."

"Lawdy! lawdy! lawdy! what'll we do?"

"They'll lynch Fer."

"They'll git us all."

"Le's hide in the woods."

Women screamed and wept. Mrs. Winstead had hysterics, her cries came through the dark unsettling, horrible.

Mrs. McLaughlin kept saying to her, "Shet up, honey, shet up!"

Jolas said, " 'Tain't safe yere. You Binney, come with me."

She put her hand in his. They walked through the frightened, crying women, tranquilly, out to the wood and away, before the police arrived. Before the mob came.

"We'll go to Thorn's and git Roger," Jolas said softly. Binney held his hand tight. They walked down the road—a lame old man and a little girl.

"The police'll be here in a minute. They'll telephone headquarters first thing they do. For Chris' sake, Fer, git out!" Wes Elliott said.

"What's the good of my going?" said Fer. "They'll sure get me!"

"Ef they'd only arrest you! It's the mob—it's the mob, Fer!"

Turmoil and screams from the tent colony. A moment of waiting, of suspense. Suspense that was freighted with knowledge of coming disaster. Lissa came running.

"Fer, my uncle's out yere with a car an' Roger. You go. You go over to Burdette's. He'll tell you what to do."

"Yeah," said Wes. "Go over to Burdette's."

Irma, her hands clenched as if she would shake Fer, said:

"Go on! Go on! Isn't it bad enough without you getting lynched?"

Her fury penetrated through Fer's numbness. He didn't care much, now, what happened to him. They hadn't come out; and the shot had been fired which he had been looking forward to, down the avenue of days, since he had come. The two girls, Lissa and Irma, each took an arm and pulled him along.

Sounds of police whistles. Screams from women. A dark mob of people. Hoskins and Roger, waiting in a car.

"Toss a penny, will you, Roger?" said Hoskins. "Which one of us goes with Fer, and which stays to see what will happen."

Fer said dully, "I don't think I ought to go, somehow."

"Don't be a fool!" Irma cried to him.

Lissa said nothing, as she tugged at him.

Now there was the roar down the road of the approaching mob. As if to himself, Fer said:

"I'd sorta like it to be over with."

18

1

THE MOB CROSSED the railway tracks and surged down toward
the speaking stand. Some of the guards had scattered. People from the
tent colony were running for shelter among their friends. The police
arrived before the mob. More police followed. A large number of people
had been hastily deputized. The man hunt started.

"Here's one! I've got him!"

"Arrest the gang!"

While a few of the people of the tent colony had scattered, most
of them had stayed and were rocking together in a frightened huddle.

"What're we goin' to do?"

"They're acomin' fer us!"

"Humphries is daid —"

"Murck and Zober, too —"

"They're acomin' fer us!"

"Oh, oh, oh! They're goin' to git Fer!" Mrs. Winstead's voice, loud
and screaming.

"Hesh, honey, hesh! Don' be skeered."

"I yere 'em! Come on, le's run!"

Children crying; women screaming.

"They're lynchin' now! They're surely lynchin'."

Sounds of a scream. Blows.

"Somebody's bein' beat!"

"Come on, le's git away!"

The frightened people of the tent colony ran. Large trees and underbrush surrounded the tent colony. Women took their children and hid in the ravine. Women and men ran into the woods.

2

Only Peg-leg sat still in the midst of the almost deserted tent colony. And with him stayed Ma Gilfillin, who said:

"Ma Bill's on guard. Reckon his gun went off."

"You reckon he killed Humphries?"

"I'd rather he'd killed Zober and Murck. If Bill had to go ashootin' up enny one, I hope 'twas them laws."

"Don' know who shot who."

"Don' no one know anythin'."

"They're comin' now. Yere 'em yellin' an roarin'."

"They got any of our boys?"

"I dunno nothin'."

The roar of the mob, led by the deputies, was in the colony. Rough hands. Loud voices.

"Come on, you."

"Whar's the others?"

"The rest is cleared out."

"Come on, git along."

Ma Gilfillin's voice screaming, "He cain't go no faster! Cain't you see he's a peg-leg?"

"Shet yo' haid."

"Whar's the others?"

"Come on!"

The sound of crashing. The sound of rending. Tents were being demolished. They were throwing furniture around, and kitchen utensils, in the destructive manner of mobs. The crashing of the tents delighted them.

"Clar 'em out!"

"Roust 'em out!"

"I found some one!"

Children's screams. A man's loud voice: "Deane!"

"Whar's Deane! We want Deane!"

They dropped Ma Gilfillin's arm as she struggled, and she hid behind some trees. Electric torches flashed like giant fireflies. They were attacking the tents with fury. There was a terrifying savagery about it. The tents symbolized Fer. They were razing the tents as they would kill Fer.

"Lawdy," she thought, "if they ketch pore Fer they'll shore lynch 'im."

White bulk of tents crashing down, billowing and flapping. The clatter of kitchen utensils. Shouting. Men calling to one another. In the distance shrieks as of a frightened animal. Some one of the tent colony caught in the woods. A flashlight on Ma Gilfillin.

"Yere's one! Yere's one!"

"You take 'er in, Joe. You're a depity."

"Arrest 'em!"

Ma Gilfillin said nothing. It was a lynch mob. She shut her mouth firmly and walked along between a deputy and another man. Behind her was disaster and confusion. Crowds of people had come from the town who did not belong to the Committee of One Hundred. A cordon of police had been strung around the headquarters.

Rumors had floated through the city. Fer had lured the policemen to the place. He had sent a telephone call asking for the police. Then the strikers had lain in ambush and shot them down. It was a conspiracy, a plot of the anarchists and bolshevists, and Fer the arch-conspirator.

Exaggerated reports had flown in. Three or four policemen had died. Humphries was dead. The excitement through the town was like a conflagration. The news spread from one comfortable house to the other in advance of the newspapers. No one in New or Old Stonerton, in East or West Stonerton, who was ignorant that Humphries had been shot.

Humphries not only shot but lured to the tent colony and murdered in cold blood.

That was what comfortable people in Stonerton believed.

The disorder of the strike had spired upward to its culminating act of murder. It had begun in disorder and ended with slaughter.

Slaughter was what the strikers merited. Blood was what the people of Stonerton demanded in exchange for the life of their policemen.

3

Up in the tent colony nothing remained but heaps of canvas and piles of household belongings. It was no orderly eviction. It looked as though a whirlwind had come through, as though the elements themselves had destroyed the strikers' shelter. With dozens of the men deputized, part of the mob had stopped to destroy the tents. The strikers had fled and hid in the ravine. Some who had friends in town scattered to their friends' houses. Many hid in the woods.

The man hunt was in full cry.

It was fun to hunt the people through the woods.

"Yere's one!"

"Yere's one hidin'!"

"Bring 'im in!"

The tent colony was completely demoralized. They were a fleeing, hunted pack.

It was fun to find a woman lying flat on the ground. The women with small children fought back. They left such people alone, for the most part.

Mrs. Winstead was arrested, screaming for her baby, screaming for her children. Winstead raised his vacant face to say dully:

"I'll keer for 'em."

It made no difference to him whether he was hunted through the woods, whether he lived in a house or a tent, whether his wife was arrested or not. He always cared for the children, more or less, while his wife was at work. He sat in the midst of the rioters with children about him, the baby in his arms, indifferent to the excitement of crashing underbrush, the flash of torches, the screams of women, the vast unquiet of the night.

A small child, separated from his family, ran crying through the woods, sobbing loudly. Henry Tetherow came out of his hiding place in the ravine. He caught the child.

"Whar's yore maw?" The child screamed. "What's yore name?" More sobs. Loud, high wailing.

"Yere's one! Yere's one!" A man grabbed Henry.

"You leave me be!"

"Yah, I seen him with the strikers."

"I gotta find this kid's mother!" Henry protested.

The child broke into panicky weeping. They were dragging a man who had been knocked senseless, through the underbrush. Figures of nightmare. Sounds of nightmare. Nothing seemed real in this fantastic world.

The mob had abandoned itself to the man hunt.

Each moment more people arrived at the jail. They were arresting the entire tent colony. The hunting went on through the night.

The monstrous rumors grew.

Among the tent colony no one knew what had happened to any one else.

Women saw their young sons arrested and beaten. The mob itched for more than arrests. People were beaten and their arms twisted. The mob howled for Fer.

4

The jail was filled to overflowing. As many people as could stand were crowded into cells. Six or eight people in one cell. In all, when morning came, there were seventy-two people arrested. Young girls and boys, grandmothers and infirm old men. Every one who could be found, who was remembered to have belonged to the tent colony, was arrested.

Fer had not been arrested. No one knew where he was. No one had seen him. The strikers talked about him among themselves.

"Whar's Fer at?"

" 'Spect they got 'im."

"Ef he ain't been seen I 'spect they lynched him."

"Bet they got Fer."

"He's daid."

"They shore was lookin' for him."

"They was out to lynch 'im, awright."

They hunted Dewey Bryson out of his lodgings. They grabbed Del Evans. The boys were savagely questioned. They knew nothing about Fer. The certainty that Fer had been lynched grew among the strikers.

Irma, Doris and Ruth Graham were all arrested. The Grahams had been rooming at the Thorn's. When Jolas brought the news of the shooting she had gone up to the tent colony. They had arrested her. Irma and Doris had stayed with the strike headquarters, awaiting the oncoming mob. They had kept the boys together, with the help of Wes Elliott.

"They cain't do no more than arrest us. Better stay right yere."

Some younger boys had fled. Two of them had gone in an old Ford which the Union had been using. One of the boys was the Union's chauffeur. They were caught in Carabbas County and put in jail there.

The three girls, Doris, Irma and Ruth, were in a cell together. They talked in low tones about Fer. There was no doubt in their minds that if the mob could catch him they would lynch him.

No one was allowed to visit them in jail. Hoskins tried to get to them; he was refused admittance. They were held incommunicado.

The police seemed to have gone insane. They threatened and cursed the prisoners. The death of the police chief, which they all believed to have been a planned murder, gave them all a feeling of insecurity. The people whom they had baited, choked and arrested had turned upon them. People whom they had prodded with bayonets had retaliated. They had never thought that the meek, docile strikers would defend themselves. The order of the universe had been upset. The harmless rabbit had proved to be a man-eater.

Terror reigned in the jail. There wasn't food enough for the prisoners. They suffered from discomforts of every kind; from hunger, from thirst. Those inside feared for those outside. It had seemed during the night of terror that the desire to lynch could no longer be kept in check. That from one moment to another the mob would begin to kill.

Finally a tear gas bomb exploded in the jail. The strikers screamed. Panic followed. Their eyes streaming, women howled in fear. Irma called out trying to quiet them, telling them it was only tear gas, hands before her streaming eyes.

Later the authorities said that the gas bomb had exploded by mistake.

Hoskins managed to get in touch with Burdette by telephone. He told Hoskins to come at once to Lafayette.

"I wouldn't let Roger go back," he said. "You come over, too. Feeling's running too high. You're identified with the Union. Just cain't have you boys makin' any trouble. Trouble enough a'ready."

In a roundabout way he managed to convey to Hoskins that Fer was safe. He had refused to allow Fer to go back to Stonerton and had sent him on to another county where, if he were arrested, there would be no lynching. What he hoped was that Fer would be taken into custody in a jail outside of Stonerton County. When Hoskins appeared at Burdette's office Roger was sitting there.

"Nothing more's going to happen now," the old man said. "Youall are known to be favorable to the Union. It jest isn't safe fer you to go back. My friends have told me to keep you out of town for a day or two till things simmer down."

"Are you going to keep out of town?"

"I ain't goin' to be able to. I got to bail out some of those folks. Tear gas bombs are goin' off. I got to git 'em out. But youall keep away. They's nothin' more you can do. You got yore stories. You stay in Lafayette. No use goin' back, you'd be railroaded out ag'in. It ain't a question of bein' brave, it's a question of not giving any more trouble."

During the day anxiety for Fer grew inside the jail and out. Word had streamed through the country that Fer was missing. Every one was sure he had been lynched.

5

Fer was arrested in Carabbas County, together with Clint. He hadn't tried to hide. He had taken a room and waited while the police scoured the Carolinas for him. Two days had gone past.

The feeling in Stonerton was still in spate, but the mob had disintegrated. Every one was in jail, and the mob that had razed the tent colony and taken part in the man hunt had been dissolved into individual human beings. People who were fathers, brothers, went to church on Sundays and to business the rest of the time.

The orgy of the mob seemed already remote. It was, to many of the people, as though they had moved in a dream; but it had been a satisfying dream, and the isolated drops of the current were ready in a moment to flow together again.

Fer was taken from Carabbas to Stonerton county without mishap. Clint and he sat stolid and without speaking. He was still stunned. The catastrophe which had happened so unexpectedly and swiftly left him dazed with disaster. They had been so close to victory. Now it seemed to him that everything had been done in vain. As on the first night, he wished that the mob would put an end to him. And yet as they drove Fer's body was afraid. The world to him had suddenly become a gray and hopeless place. All the efforts of these people, all their sacrifices, seemed to him to have been for nothing. Step by step they had gone steadily forward toward this fatal shooting.

He knew, too, that the people of the community thought that this was a premeditated plan, that he himself and the guards and the local union leaders had planned the murder.

This, he thought, is an awful thing to accuse me of—murder. It doesn't seem possible that any one could think that I planned to murder a man. Yet it was so. He had not known at the time of the shooting whose guns were fired. He had been sure that it was the guns of the Committee of One Hundred yet he knew that no one could believe in his innocence. The strike leader under such circumstances is always arrested.

Every fiber of his body longed for rest. He wanted to be out of it. He wanted to be out of it so much that death seemed to him a welcome release; and yet his body was afraid. Something within him turned sick. He had a sensation of being empty as a gutted fish, as they drove through the quiet Piedmont highways. At the sight of two or three men at the roadside he felt physically sick, and his heart pounded painfully. A cold feeling came about his mouth. Dispassionately he noticed this. He looked on his shrinking flesh as if it belonged to another person, with a mild and astonished disgust.

6

Stonerton continued to rave.

"Oughta hang up every one o' them seventy-two."

"All of 'em oughta be strung on lampposts."

"They oughta be burned like a ho'nets' nest."

"Killin's too good fer 'em."

"The chair's too kind for 'em."

"They says it was knotholes they was firin' through."

"Yah, they bo'ed holes they could stick gun ba'els through."

"They been plannin' murder sence they come."

"Oughta ridden them No'thern agitators out on a rail."

"Oughta tah 'n' feather 'em."

"Wish we could ride 'em out now, 'n' tah 'n' feather 'em."

When after two days Humphries died their fury flamed out afresh. Humphries had been liked in the town. People called him a good sheriff. Humphries personally had kept his head. He himself had not been brutal to the strikers. The dirty work had been done by deputies and by sadistic policemen such as Murck and Zober.

Men in cars drove about the town, looking suspiciously at any stranger. Rumor had gone forth that the Textile Union was going to send down more organizers. Locals of the union existed in many other towns. The stoning and razing of the tent colony had not destroyed the fruits of unionism.

Stonerton City, a reporter said, had ceased to be a place—it had become a state of mind. It was a state of mind since the hatred of the Union leaders had become a mania.

"Comfortable people in Stonerton believed," said Hoskins, "that agitators and Reds were hiding behind every burdock ready to bounce a bright red bomb off their beans." In the minds of the comfortable people, Communists, bolshevists, anarchists and socialists were all the same thing. In their minds, a colossal plot was existing whose very essence was assassination. That is all bolshevists, anarchists and so-cialists wanted to do—they wanted to kill people and incidentally destroy the State and industry. All Union people were low, skulking, murderous radicals who wormed their way into simple-minded work-ers' confidence, with a view to using them as tools in their dastardly works of destruction. So went the editorials in the papers; so went the thoughts of the comfortable people. It was born, as such fury always is, of fear and nourished by fear. They imagined plots spread like a network throughout the country.

Strangers were requested by posses of men to leave town, in no uncertain fashion. A sociological investigator from a young women's college was thrown in jail, and asked to leave town.

"We ain't gonna hev no mo' strangers."

"We ain't gonna hev no mo' trouble yere."

"Any one wants to make trouble can git outa town."

"They ain't nobody gonna make no mo' trouble fer us yere."

"We don't want no mo' agitaters in this yere town."

"We got 'em all in jail now, and whut's outa jail kin keep outa Stonerton."

Self-appointed posses as well as deputies watched the Union grounds.

A reporter arriving was all but mobbed. They bore down upon him, yapping:

"Git 'im! Git 'im!"

"Ride 'im out!"

"Ef he's a new organizer, tie him to a tree!"

"He oughta be croaked!"

"He oughta be shot!"

It was a ticklish moment. The leader of the mob looked with suspicion on the credentials which the reporter handed out, and he was roughly told to leave town.

7

With the release of most of the seventy-two arrested people, the hysteria in the town rose instead of declined. It manifested itself in no overt way. A stranger driving through would have found it a quiet place. Groups of men talking on street corners; no disturbance. But the people were caught at the breaking point waiting for something new to happen, for the reds, the agitators, to appear. Hysteria.

The three girls were held longer than most of the others. Finally through Burdette's efforts they were released. Most of the girls of the tent colony were out of jail, but nine boys were accused of murder.

Ferdinand Deane was accused of murder.

Conspiracy with intent to kill was the charge against him. This was the charge against Wes Elliott, Ma Gilfillin's son Bill, Dan Marks, Will Tetherow, cousin of Henry Tetherow, Lynn Cathcart and Sam Truitt. Accused, too, was Paul Graham, who had come down of his own initiative to help out the strikers, and Charlie Clint, who was sent down from the North by the Textile Union as organizer.

8

The weeks dragged along. The hysteria became dormant, it did not die completely. The boys in jail were now being well treated, the phase of brutality had passed by. Burdette had fought the holding of them incommunicado, he had fought the tormenting of the prisoners. He had fought everything. Finally a more or less peaceable state of things had resulted.

Lissa went to the jail regularly on visiting days. She and Fer would have talks.

Fer said: "I can't get used to the idea of thinking I tried to shoot anybody."

"It don't seem lak any one could do that," Lissa said.

The feeling in the town against the strikers ended down in the part of the village where Lissa lived. The working people in that part of the town said:

"Sho', they shot in self-defense." She told that now to Fer.

"Folks all know you jes' shot in self-defense, Ma Gilfillin sez. Her an' ma wuz talkin'."

"It won't be possible to get a fair trial in this town. I thought they was gonna git you."

"Ma Gilfillin comes over quite often. She's kinda proud o' her Bill bein' in jail. She's shore they warn't no jury ever gonna convict a young boy lak Bill that never did no harm to no one."

"There isn't any jury in Stonerton County that wouldn't convict us. It's going to be bad unless they manage to change us over to another county."

9

The time for the trial approached. It was July. With the approach of the trial fury against the Union flamed up again. The Union had gone on quietly organizing. There were locals both in Tesner and in Stonerton. There were locals in Lafayette and High Hill, and in many other towns.

Now when Burdette appeared on the street he was threatened. Anonymous letters were sent him. Men came up to him as he sat in the restaurant and told him if he defended them murderers and bastards he'd better look out for himself. Witnesses were being intimidated. The day of the trial arrived. The boys filed into the dock.

Burdette applied all his fine Southern eloquence to tell the young and fine looking judge that a lawyer in pursuit of his calling has been, suh, intimidated and threatened on the streets of this yere town. Witnesses had been intimidated.

The place of the trial was removed from Stonerton to Lafayette. The boys went back for another dreary wait in jail.

19

1

AFTER SOME WEEKS the tent colony had finally been built up again. With the aid of the newspapers and publicity, they had succeeded in getting the Stonerton authorities to give up the tents which they had confiscated after the raids.

The Union was giving a barbecue to raise money for the defense of the men in jail. The row of tents as a background to the barbecue looked gay and gypsyish. All slicked up as they were to-day they seemed more like the decoration for a fair ground than placed there by the reality of eviction. No outsider would have thought of them as the only homes of the former workers in the Basil Schenk Manufacturing Company. To the mill workers the tents meant evictions, they meant the mob and the night of the shooting.

Indeed this barbecue might have been like any other barbecue except for the tents and what they meant. The tents meant that there had been a strike. The tents meant that the workers had been evicted from their homes. It was in guarding these very tents that the tragic battle with the police had occurred.

No one at the barbecue could forget the shooting or the night of terror that followed. They could still see the mob which had hunted the strikers through the woods.

In the eyes of the workers who attended it, this barbecue, which was to raise money for lawyers for the jailed men, was different from all other barbecues.

This barbecue was important.

All the people who had been connected with and sympathetic with the strikers were brought together in this one crowd. Their emotions were focused on the boys in jail, as though under an incredibly brilliant lens. The boys who were in jail were more here than the actual people. The thought of them was everywhere. There wasn't any one who wasn't thinking of them all the time.

Children ran around. Over in one corner they were playing a game with Miss Emma, who had come down from the North to take charge of relief work after Doris had been arrested. She was a dark girl with heavy brows and a heavy, dark face. The games they played were all new games. Games like "Picket Lines and Cops." The children made that up themselves. Under some trees men were pitching horseshoes. There was a crowd around the barbecue stand and people went about with pop bottles at their mouths.

Then there was the speaking stand.

Dewey Bryson had a sudden feeling in his solar plexus as though a star had exploded in it, when he looked at the speaking stand. He was going to speak. That was one of the things that made this barbecue different from other barbecues. It was as though its outward manifestations were the same as other picnics of its kind except for the speaking stand and the tents. But its inner meaning, what it stood for, was extraordinarily different.

The barbecue stood for the boys in jail. There went two of the boys' mothers, Ma Gilfillin, with her sharp face, the color of old leather, and Dan Marks' mother. No, at this barbecue no one could for a second forget the boys in jail. If they were convicted, they would burn in the electric chair. The thought of that shadowed everything else. The trouble had happened two months ago. Now the trial was already going on. They were picking the jury.

2

Scraps of talk about the night of terror filtered around through the crowd as one will find fragments of wreckage long after a storm.

"The Committee o' One Hundred come and chased us through the woods. . . ."

"When the shots come I lay down on the floor. . . ."

"They wrecked the tents. . . ."

"Was you near the shootin'?"

"I was a eye witness. I seen shots come from the police wagon. I'm agoin' to be a defense witness."

"Ole Mis' Holbrook tuk a kettle o' water. You git outa yere. . . ."

"I wish to Gawd I hadn't never jined no union. . . ."

The talk drifted slack through Dewey Bryson's mind as he thought about the Union. He hadn't thought about anything else for weeks. It was something he had "slept and et with." Since the arrests, they had made him an organizer. A feeling of pride would choke him up and make him swallow.

The feeling would come sweeping over him before he would know what it meant, then he would remember, I'm an organizer. He knew it was hard and dangerous work. He didn't care. He had soft brown eyes and a wing of soft lanky hair over his forehead. He was barely literate. He didn't know where places were. All he knew was north and south. N'Yawk was north and N'Awleens was south. His mind didn't move east and west. He had been in school until he was twelve when he had gone to work in the cotton mills. He was twenty-four now. He used this in his speeches.

"I'm twenty-four and I ben to work half my life so when I say that the boys are in jail fo' us I shore know what I'm atalkin' about."

That was the core of what he was going to say. "The boys are in jail fo' us and we go to build the union fo' them." These thoughts seemed to him new and valuable. They gave him all the shock of delight that the discovery of a tremendous idea gives to a thinker. The words he would say from the "speakin' stand" strung themselves into glittering sentences against the dark woof of the chatter around him.

3

Then suddenly some sentences of talk pierced him as with a knife.

"Say, does they really burn in the chair—"

"Sho' they burn, an' befo' they goes to the chair they turns on the current. They tries out the current an' the lights they all go dim in the death house because it's all turned onto the chair."

"Does the fellahs in the death house know it's being turned on the chair?"

"Sho' they know it's being turned on the chair! Cain't they hear the dynamo when the lights grow dim?"

It was to Dewey as if suddenly he himself had been in the death house with his friends, and by what narrow margin of sheer chance had he not been in jail with them! As though he heard the high whine of the dynamo and saw the lights grow dim.

It was as though behind the field with its border of tents, its playing children and shifting crowds was the shadow of the death house, with it a huge whining dynamo which meant death by burning. It was like a bad dream. He had to wake himself up.

Standing nearby was Mamie Lewes, her hands on her hips and her head thrown back laughing. He had often seen her but he had never talked to her. Usually he was shy with women, but the shadow of the death house had killed his self-consciousness. He walked up to her as for release.

"Ain't you Mamie Lewes?" he asked in his soft voice, "that I yeard sing so of'en?"

"You shore hev," she answered. "An' I yeard you speak. Yo're Dewey Bryson, the organizer!" No one had called him that before. It gave his position substance and filled him with pride. "I hope yo're agoin' to speak to-day," she went on. "I shore want to hear you speak some mo'."

"That's mighty sweet o' you. I'm just new aspeakin'. I never did speak befo' the Union came yere. They tell me you make up yo're own song ballits."

She nodded her head two or three times in bright assent. A pretty gesture.

He thought, "Why, she ain't old,—Mamie Lewes ain't old." Some way he'd always thought about her as old before. She had lots of children. Her husband "walked out on her," folks said. Folks said that he liked another woman.

She stood before him rather short, eyes wide apart, curling hair, and something free and released about her. Something young and happy and playful. She looked as if the band were just going to begin to play.

"Yes," she said. "I make up my own song ballits. The songs they just seem to come to me now since the Union come."

"Jus' lak I tuk to speakin'."

"Seems everythin' different since we got a union yere. I just went on workin' and workin' year in an' year out like a dumb beast. There wasn't no time for nothin' 'cept to feel tired, was they?"

"No, they wasn't." They had made a contact. He sensed that she had the same passion for the Union that he had. The time before there was a union to fight for seemed far off and shadowy and uneventful. Since then new thoughts had come to him, a new loyalty. It was like being awakened from sleep. She felt this way, too.

4

The people had been drifting toward the speaking stand. A band of children, their hands on each other's shoulders, marched past shouting at the top of their lungs:

"Zober, Zober, never's sober!"

"I hope them laws years that," said Mamie Lewes. "Listen to this one." The children were singing:

> "Old man Zober sitting on the fence,
>
> Tries to make a dollar out of ninety-nine cents!"

"Some of them children is going to get themselves choked and blackjacked," Mr. Jolas prophesied to Binney.

"They sure hate that dep'ty Zober," said Dewey.

"Mamie Lewes!" some one called. "They want fer you to sing!"

"I 'spect I gotta go an' sing now." She nodded at Dewey with a bright friendliness, and went over to the speaking stand. She sang from her diaphragm with her deep, sweet, untrained voice.

> "They locked up our leaders, they put them in jail,
>
> They shoved them in prison, refused to give them bail.
>
> The workers joined together and this was their reply:
>
> We'll never, no, we'll never let our leaders die.
>
> We're going to have a union all over the south,
>
> Where we can wear good clothen and live in a better house.
>
> Now we must stand together and to the boss reply,
>
> We'll never, no, we'll never let our leaders die."

She sang with utmost sincerity and conviction. The words sank comfortingly into Dewey's heart. It was as if the long shadow of the death house was dimmer, the whine of the dynamo fainter.

"We'll never, no, never let our leaders die!"

He felt the bulwark that the Union was against the death of their leaders. It appeared to him present and vivid and potent, and he was a part of it, and Mamie Lewes was part of it and so were the children who sang their taunting songs; and all the people who were at the barbecue. It seemed almost as if the boys in jail could hear it.

"Never, no never—"

Now she was singing at him. He joined in the chorus and they sang together their chorus in an assertion of defiance against the mill and the courts. She sang again, her voice came from deep within her, shouting out gayly and defiantly.

> "Listen all you scabs, ef you want to hear
>
> The story of a mean millionaire.
>
> Basil Schenk was that millionaire's name.
>
> He bought the law with his money and frame,"

and here her voice rose loud and exultantly like a banner with trumpets—

> "But he can't buy the Union with his money and frame!"

The people shouted, *"But he can't buy the Union with his money and frame!"*

Now they were all together. Her songs had brought them together. They were no longer separated people. They were a great audience banded together in a great cause.

No longer individuals, mean, frightened, stunted. They had all been released and felt full of one common generous aim. Their hearts beat with the Union. They were part of it. There was loveliness about, and beauty and hope. Hope for a better day, as Mamie Lewes had sung, "When we can have good clothen and live in a better house."

Mamie Lewes was pulling Odell Corbett up on the speaking stand. She was a thin little girl, her hair cut in a Dutch cut and hung almost to her eyes.

"Odell made up a song ballit too," said Mamie Lewes. "You sing it, Odell." The child piped up at once in a voice that was sharp and piercing and tiny as a needle.

> "Will you let us sleep in your tent, Fer Deane,
> For it's cold lying out on the ground.
> They turned us out of our houses,
> And we haven't no place to lie down."

Dewey felt his heart twisted within him. Mamie Lewes jumped down from the speaking stand and was beside him again. He pressed her hand impulsively. She didn't seem surprised, but clasped his warmly in return. They were joined together in loyalty to their people and their hope and their Union.

5

The speaking went on. Dewey spoke. Mamie Lewes sang again. Again people swayed together. Something beautiful had come among them. They were full of hope and comradeship. Happiness streamed from them, for a moment they were powerful for good. A miracle had occurred. The aspirations of the human spirit had become tangible in this assembly of simple people. The Union had done it.

Collectively human beings are at their best or their worst. They climb perilous heights of beauty and sacrifice together. And together they revert to the hunting pack, creatures aslaver for blood. Ordinary man walks between the two extremes.

Dewey felt this. He couldn't have explained it in words. He only knew he was amplified. That he was more alive at this moment than he had ever been, and that everywhere about him were people alive like him. He knew they could have streamed forth at this moment to conquest as with banners and trumpets.

Then came over him a long shadow as though cast from the ramparts of the mill. They were like this here, but outside this field was hate.

Outside was Mob.

Just now Mob was quiet awaiting blood. Licking its chops at the thought of the music of the death house dynamo.

Again he had the feeling as almost of the visible presence of the boys who were in jail, as though the beauty of the afternoon had been caused by them. They were everywhere, in the music, in the speeches.

Their frightful danger and the need of saving them from this danger was everywhere.

But outside was Mob. . . .

Mamie Lewes came up to him. "Mebbe next time we have a barbecue *they'll* be here."

"Mebbe so," he answered. He felt he had some horrible knowledge which she didn't have. He had seen the lights go out in the death house and she hadn't.

He had heard the dynamo.

Suddenly they felt they must soon see each other again. They arranged to meet each other at the courthouse the following Monday.

20

1

THE AFTERNOON at the barbecue signified to Dewey the closing of a life of innocence. He couldn't have put it into words but life before that Saturday and life after he had looked into the face of the mob had split his life in two. An awful knowledge of the evil of mankind had been shown him.

The Union had moved its headquarters to Lafayette after the feeling had run so high against them in Stonerton. But during the two months since the shooting they had kept up agitation in many of the mills in Stonerton and Gaston counties. They were going to hold a meeting Saturday afternoon in front of one of the many mills surrounding the town of Stonerton.

Dewey Bryson and Lee Henderson were the two organizers and they were taking with them old man Quinn who was an old preacher and spoke very well, and two young fellows who had been speaking pretty well for the Union, Robert Duncan and Poddy Smithson, to speak too. Poddy was a tall, stout fellow. All three boys were ready for a scrap if there had to be one.

"You boys know there's liable to be trouble," Duncan had told them. Robert Duncan had come down from the North to take Fer's place more or less. He was a mill worker from the North, a little wiry fellow, unpretentious, totally fearless, without any braggadocio.

They drove along over the lovely road.

"Reckon there's going to be trouble?" Dewey asked.

"Well, they said the mill's got a mob all fixed for us," Duncan said. "If we can't speak here, we'll go right on up to High Hill."

"You got a meeting fixed for High Hill?" Smithson asked.

"Sure," said Dewey. "Weren't you all at the meeting where we fixed it up? We'll speak yere first and then go on to High Hill."

"They have a right smart union nucleus in this yere Heatherston mill we're going to speak before. That's why they're goin' for us. They know it's a right smart union nucleus."

"I'd feel easier if I had my gun," said Poddy.

"Well, none of us ain't got guns and none of us are going to be carrying guns," said Duncan, who had the aversion to gun-toting of the Northerner.

The thought of trouble was far off from Dewey's mind. He had seen the beginning of the wrecking of the tent colony two months before. He hadn't been living there. He had made an early getaway.

He had not been prominent enough for the mob hatred to have been directed against him. He had never felt it as Fer had felt it. He had never been threatened as Wes Elliott had been threatened and some of the more prominent strikers. Up to this time he had been only Fer's bodyguard. Never a union official, and never even a member of the strike committee even in the most intense days of the strike.

They drove along in the car they had hired through the beautiful August country. It was hot but there was a nice breeze. Dewey felt happy. He was thinking of Mamie Lewes' song "ballits" and planning how he would see her at the court room to-morrow. They had planned it. Mamie Lewes was coming from Tesner in a truck to spend a day at the trial.

They came to the Catawba River. "There's the place," Poddy Smithson was pointing out the Greek's gas station, where Zober and Murck had chased the Greek into the river, the day of the shooting at the tent colony.

"They were both tight as drums and they come up to ask the Greek whar they could get some mo' booze. An' he said he didn't have no booze so they goddamned him to hell and they shot at him and he ran away down to the river."

"That's what made 'em in such good humor to come and clean out the tent colony," said old man Quinn.

2

There was a crowd of people assembled in front of the factories which reached down the road. A hundred people in the road, guns in their hands, ripe for mischief, not a crowd but a mob.

A wave of numb surprise shook Dewey. Those men were out to get him. A howl came from their throats.

"There's the organizer!"

"Take 'em out and lynch 'em!"

"Get him, get him! Shut 'em up!"

Isolated cries they could hear amidst the mob roar. A noise unlike any other. An insane noise.

It seemed to Dewey that he looked down a red gullet. These men who were rushing out to them, crying "to take 'em out and lynch 'em, shoot 'em, ride 'em," were all part of a mob. This was the opposite of the barbecue where the individuality of human beings had resolved itself into something which was the sum of all of them and greater than all of them. Now the mob had swallowed up the individuals and swamped them in a common, unreasoning hate.

They swarmed over the cab, screaming their hate. The roar in Dewey's ears was like a sea. A man hit him in the eye with a blackjack.

A man with a pop bottle was pounding Henderson, trying to hit his face. Henderson put his face in his hands. The pop bottle broke and blood streamed down from his hands. Men were reaching over the side of the open car with blackjacks and fists, hitting old man Quinn, hitting Poddy Smithson. The mob pulled the door open and started hauling Dewey out.

"C'mon, let's lynch 'im. Let's take 'em off."

He wasn't frightened. Stupid amazement filled him.

"Take 'em off and whup 'em."

"Larn 'em to be a union."

It seemed incredible it could happen to him. Now his friends were pulling him back. They were dragging him in, slamming the door.

"Step on it!" cried Henderson.

The car bounded forward. The mob clung to it like a cluster of bees, still hitting the men. The car gained impetus. They were strung out after the taxi, a clot of hate. Stones rattled against the body of the taxi. Shots rang out. One by one they dropped off the taxi. Now they were clear. There was just a black spot behind them, a black spot that had a red gullet.

3

Dewey felt dazed. His eyes were both blacked and his skull cut. Blood trickled from it. Every one was bruised around the face. Even old man Quinn had black eyes and his jaw was puffed out.

The taxi driver spoke first.

"That was a close call!" I thought they was agoin' to git us all."

"I thought weall was goin' to git ours."

"I thought so too," said Henderson.

"I sure was skeered when they was atryin' to git Dewey away."

"If they'd got Dewey outa this car, he'd 'a' been a gone gosling by now."

"Do you recken they'd have lynched 'em?"

"Yeah, that mob was a lynchin' mob. They didn't know what they was adoin'."

"Who was they all?" asked Duncan. This was new to him. "What makes them go after us?"

"It's the mill forces and a few of them they call the 'loyal workers,' and a lot of riffraff. They got 'em filled full that the Union talks free love and atheism."

"Where youall want me to take you?" the taxi driver asked.

"Best take us to a doctor when we pass through Gastonia and git our cuts tied up and then we'll go on to High Hill and speak. We're goin' to hol' some kind of a meeting, ain't we, fellas?"

"Sure we are," said Poddy.

"Sure, we're out to have a speakin' and we'll have a speakin'," said Preacher Quinn.

Dewey said nothing. He was glad they were to go, glad to do anything to keep his mind off the mob, screaming with hate, the memory of the clutching hands, from the memory of the mob roar.

21

1

THE COURT ROOM where the trial was held was lofty and imposing. It was wainscoted with dark, polished wood. Huge windows lighted it. It was a dignified and stately room rather than austere.

Roger walked up the marble steps which led into the courthouse. It was a new building, and the pride of Lafayette County. Two wide curving staircases led upstairs from the lobby. Young girls in light dresses were flocking up the stairs. A group of negroes in overalls were laughing together. Some one had just told a funny story. One coal-black negro threw his head back and let out an explosion of "Wah-wah-wah's" which echoed through the wide halls. Country women in calico dresses and little old-fashioned straw hats, perched upon their knots of hair, and wearing button-up boots, were sauntering up the stairs.

People in Lafayette County made use of their courthouse. It had the feeling of a place used by the people as though it were a cross between a theater and a library. It was their theater. Here they came to witness murder trials. Here they came to see their neighbors tried. The sauntering young girls, the women, the negroes, the men in easy working clothes and overalls, the people coming and going, the feeling of leisure, robbed the place of any austerity.

The press had been given seats which ran sideways along the court room, inside the dark, wood railing. Two lines of benches ran along each side of the big room. These were originally intended for the jury. The one opposite, still with empty seats, was awaiting the jurymen. Getting a jury was a tedious business.

2

Roger had plenty of old friends at the trial. Hoskins was here, Dick Durgan, other of the newspaper men who had been down during the early days of the strike.

The court room began to fill. The audience was almost entirely composed of working people, most of them men. Truckloads of strikers had come from Stonerton. There were a few women. Most of them were "kin" of the defendants. Roger recognized old man Tetherow and Mrs. Tetherow and Ma Gilfillin in the audience. Dan Marks' father, Binney and Victor Jolas, Mrs. Cuthbert. The Bisphams were there and the Landors, and Lissa.

The gallery was filled with negroes. Soon the sheriff called them away to make room for whites who wanted to see the show. They shuffled off without thought of protest.

The judge's desk was on an elevation. Behind him the wall had been wainscoted with beautiful polished wood and a handsome bronze clock ornamented it. The dark wood behind the judge, the bronze clock, the high windows gave almost a histrionic dignity to his high position.

The judge was a young man with thin, aristocratic features, a handsome head, almost the head of a fanatic. Deep-set eyes, a man at peace with himself, poised and unified with life. He had faith, with himself, with the justice in his work, and in his God. In front of the high desk were the massive tables of the lawyers for the defense and prosecution. The greatest legal talent of the state of North Carolina had been engaged to burn these boys in the electric chair. The Union and the defense had engaged brilliant legal talent as well.

The young defendants filed in. They all looked very clean and very young. Friends crowded up to greet them. The sheriff was lenient with them. They were allowed to talk to their friends.

Roger went down to speak to Fer. His eyes were clear and he looked rested. They were all glad to have the trial begin after the tedious two months and a half in jail.

There was Wes Elliott with his reddish brown hair, and his deep-set fanatical eyes and his harsh strong features.

Dan Marks, wide-shouldered, his handsome head set firmly on his heavy neck.

Bill Gilfillin, loose-jointed and shambling and only eighteen.

Tetherow, with golden hair and blue eyes and very neatly dressed, for all the Tetherows were neat people, looked like a high school boy, as indeed he should have been if he had not been a mill worker. Tetherow and Gilfillin were both under nineteen.

There was Charlie Clint, the Northern mill worker, who had come down to help with the organizing. Paul Graham, a young intellectual, who had been less than two weeks in the South when the shooting occurred. He had been sent down to take Wood's place. The Union had at last responded to Fer's and Irma's repeated requests.

The boys all sat just within the railing with Irma and Doris and Graham's young wife, a very pretty girl with great blue eyes and dark hair, sat just behind them.

With them too sat Len Cathcart's wife and baby. He was twenty-one and the only married man among the mill workers on trial. There was also Sam Truitt, another mill worker, among the defendants.

3

Two small children had been sitting beside the judge's seat. They were children of three or four years old, the boy dressed in blue and the girl in pink. Their hair was blond with the blond fuzzy aspect of newly hatched chickens. The sheriff and his assistant brought in an enormous iron box. From it the children drew the names of the veniremen.

This was a trial for murder. The ancient usage of North Carolina provided that the names of the jurymen should be drawn by children who could neither read nor write. The sheriff's children drew the names and seemed never to be tired of it. After the veniremen had been then called to the courthouse they then further drew the names of each juror from a hat.

The little girl was self-conscious and pleased with herself. She made eyes at the men of whom there was such a satisfactory number. The little boy was earnest and did not look about him. As often as not he sat upon the judge's knee, a little blue figure with a golden top. The judge held him abstractedly. The little girl wandered among the correspondents who drew pictures for her.

Roger could not forget them. Two bright bits of color and innocence, bobbing familiarly and contentedly about the court room.

The lawyers skirmished in low tones and with great courtesy.

The clerk of the court called out the name of a juror. The juror presented himself; the clerk said:

" 'ss th' book!" and handed the venireman the Bible.

"Do you solemnly swear—"the rest of the oath was lost in a mumble. In low tones and with great courtesy the lawyers skirmished.

It did not seem like a trial where nine lives were at stake. It seemed like a stately ritual, an eighteenth century affair, a minuet with marches and counter marches. A bloodless duel with feints and parries. An elaborate structure built of courtesy and culture, something between a duel and a minuet.

The whole scene, the young impartial judge, the ancient usages, the elaborate formalities, the courtesies of the lawyers, seemed to proclaim to the world:

"This is no Sacco-Vanzetti trial. This is no railroading of young men to the electric chair. This is justice. This is the court of North Carolina. These young miscreants are going to have every chance."

Roger sat watching, but with the knowledge in his heart that this flower of justice grew in mob soil. He could not forget Stonerton as he had seen it two months before.

The process of choosing a jury was endless. Because it was a trial for murder in the first degree each defendant had the right to challenge twelve veniremen. The state had a very small number of challenges compared to the defense.

Roger sat through the long hot afternoons. The prosecution hurled questions at the prospective jurors.

Are you a mill worker? Do you believe or have you expressed the belief that the defendants are innocent? Have you ever read a communist paper? Have you ever read a piece of literature put out by these people? Do you belong to a labor union? Have any of your people worked in the cotton mills? Do you believe in capital punishment?

Curiously, an unexpected prejudice against the death penalty was revealed. It existed among all classes of people. A number of veniremen were dismissed by the judge on that account. When the state finally passed the veniremen the defendants took them over. Often one was dismissed at once. Again he was minutely questioned. Questions were put to him as to his relations with policemen. Did he have any police in the family? There was a check of his entire family history. Finally when every question was satisfactorily answered, the question was finally chanted by the clerk of court:

"JEW-ROR, look upon the PRIZNOR.

"PRIZ-NOR, look upon the JEWROR! Do you like him?"

Then if for some reason, by advice of counsel or by the feeling of the defendants, he did not seem to be a suitable juror, the counsel made answer, "no." Young farmers, unused to court ways, would look surprised and hurt when they were dismissed.

It was a queer cross section of society which filed through the court. A millionaire, anxious to serve on a jury, sure that he could be impartial. Tradespeople. Farmers. Mechanics. Men living within ten miles of Lafayette County courthouse, as dark as moujiks from Russia. Men who had never heard of the famous Humphries shooting, had never heard of the strike, although the entire county had been convulsed with it. The men had tilled their fields and planted their little patches of cotton as though they lived on another planet. Strange!

The long defile continued day after day. More than six hundred were questioned before the jury was finally impaneled. Roger had the feeling he was listening to people of another generation, another century. Yet the distinguished counsel were of these people, they too were of their century. They did not belong to an age of scientific investigation.

4

The long afternoon had netted exactly no jurors. As they went out together, "Why do you think they didn't take that last farmer?" Roger asked Hoskins.

"I don't know. I would have taken him. He looked like a good fellow to me."

"What's the idea of dragging it out so long?" Dick Durgan asked.

"Well, you can see for yourself," said Hoskins. "This county is divided on class lines. There is no more doubt as to how sympathy runs as to which side of a river a given house is on."

"All the comfortable people," Roger explained, "believe that the strikers are guilty. They've always hated the strikers. They think the Union teaches anarchy, free love and negro equality. They are perfectly sure there was a conspiracy to kill the police. There is nothing too fantastic for these comfortable people to believe.

"The working class element, the small farmers and the mill workers believe that the strikers were minding their own business and that the police interfered. They believed that the boys had shot in self-defense. So if these boys are going to have a ghost of a fair chance, they'll have to have a working class jury, and preferably a young jury with an open mind."

Coming toward them was a girl whom Roger thought he recognized. Then it came to him who it was,—Eleanor Thurston. She hurried up to him, pleased to see him.

"Have you been at the trial?" he asked her.

"Yes, and I escaped from my family to get here. I don't have to go back to school for another two weeks."

"How do you mean,—escape?"

"I think they'd die if they knew I came down here," she told him.

"Then you didn't find it so easy to spread the light, did you?" asked Roger sympathetically.

"They don't want to hear it," she told him. "You can't get any one to listen. They don't believe the things you tell them. None of the older people believe the things you tell them.

"You remember who it was—Professor Scudder—during the Lawrence strike, said, 'If the women of Massachusetts knew how the people lived who wove this cloth, they would never buy another yard until conditions were righted.' Well, I used to believe that.

"I thought that all I had to do was to let them know what I'd seen myself, and tell people about it myself as I did, but they didn't. They were furious about the idea of there being a union, especially about there being Northern people down here to organize the South. They think I'm awful and I think they're—awful. It's almost like not having any family any more."

Roger felt that her eyes would have been filled with tears if she hadn't been so angry. "You know," he said, "I've not been able to go to visit friends I have around here. I feel as if I belong to another crowd. I don't know where I belong. I'm not a mill worker. I couldn't be an organizer."

Eleanor Thurston said: "You know when the shooting occurred, I wrote home for papers to find out what really happened. And do you know my family felt that all the seventy-two arrested ought to be hanged to the nearest trees. My father gets purple in the face when he talks about it. My mother's so frightened that she keeps conversation off the subject. I don't think I could live at home if it weren't for that."

"Did you try to argue with them?"

Eleanor gave him a quick look and shook her head. "I'm an awful coward. You know how Southern girls are. You're brought up to be pleasant. You simply haven't the habit of telling older people things they don't want to hear. Anyway it wouldn't do any good at all."

"But there must be a body of opinion among women in the state that wants better conditions among the women and children."

"There is, there is!" said Eleanor. "There was one group of women who tried to make an investigation of the mills last year but the employers and manufacturers wouldn't give them any data and would scarcely let any of them go through the mills."

"Why can't that opinion be organized? Why didn't you do it? Start to, anyway, among the girls in college."

"We started there. There are a lot of girls feeling like I do. And most of their families feel the way mine does."

5

The long days dropped into the horizon, one after another. Slowly, slowly, the jury filled. Long tiresome mornings, long tiresome afternoons. The defendants reading their papers, passing notes to friends in the audience. Morning and afternoon they stopped for a ten-minute recess. When court was adjourned, Fer would stop to talk to his friends, holding a brief reception.

Then the sheriff would say, not ill-naturedly, "Well, we got to get along, boys." To which they paid no attention but continued their talking.

"Well, boys, we got to be stepping," not too insistently.

At last the sheriff was able to jog their attention, and with shouting and laughing:

"Beans! beans! beans—!" they would file out of the court room.

Difficult to believe that it was a courthouse at all what with its groups of lounging negroes and its people wandering familiarly through the high, marble halls. Everything was new and bright and clean, more like a public library than like a building where the life and death of human beings was decided.

6

Roger began to feel he had always been sitting, watching through drowsy, warm days, listening to Lafayette County men being questioned for a jury which never filled.

It finally was filled. A good working class jury, mill workers, farmers, two very small shopkeepers, and all of them young.

There occurred a moment that mounted to high drama. A strange moment, strangely at contrast with the artificial punctilio of the lawyers, even whose mounting acerbity seemed part of ritual. The twelve young working-men, the jurors, were told to arise and look at the prisoners. The nine young prisoners arose also, and they were told in turn to look upon the jury. They stood, the prisoners, the jurors, gazing at one another, profoundly. It was as though silently the accused boys were asking:

"Will you judge us fairly? Will you give us a fair trial? Will you listen without prejudice to the evidence which you will hear? You are our judges. Our lives depend upon you."

Meanwhile the young working-men, the jurors, looked at the prisoners, boys like themselves, younger than they. Very earnestly, very gravely, they gazed back, almost with an air of surprise as though to answer:

"Must we judge you—young working-men like ourselves? Is it possible we must condemn you to death?"

For a minute the court room was in utter silence. No one moved, no one whispered or spoke, while deeply, deeply, the jurors and the accused boys looked at each other.

7

The morning that the testimony finally began, there was an air of expectation in the court room. The local reporters hinted of a surprise in store. It came, unbelievable, grotesque, incredible. Laughter and gruesomeness mixed. The ridiculous and the horrible at one and the same time.

The stage was all set for the drama. After court opened two women entered the court room. They were dressed in deep mourning, Humphries' widow and daughter, faces ravaged with tears, eyes red from unrestrained weeping. Dramatic figures of grief, who had given full rein to their sorrow, after the manner of the community, where no restraint is expected or observed, and where, among the mountain folks, a sort of ritual keening accompanies death.

Exhausted by weeping, haggard and worn, dripping black, the two women advanced funereally. The counsel of the prosecution arose to their feet and helped the sorrowing women to seats. They sat there, figures of grief.

The doctor, who had attended Humphries, now testified as to the number of wounds and their location. In the profound silence of the court room, broken only by sobs of the widow and her daughter, he told the last words of the shot policeman.

"I don't know why they done it. I always tried to keep the law."

The silence continued dramatically. Then there was a rustle in the audience. As usual, the audience was almost completely a working class audience and favorable to Fer and the defendants. Now they swayed like wheat in the wind.

A large mannikin was being pushed into the court. It was covered by a black shroud. The prosecutor, an agile man, darted forward and removed the shroud. The court gasped. The reporters gasped. For there stood a life-size mannikin of the dead police chief. There he stood in full uniform, his waxen face an excellent likeness, the color of death. His clothes spotted with blood, blood on his necktie, a figure of death and horror.

"Not for nothing they saw the 'Trial of Mary Dugan,' " Dick Durgan whispered to Hoskins. . . .

Hoskins stared with the eyes of a man who cannot believe what he has seen. The reporters from New York were all whispering to each other. The *Times,* the *World,* the Baltimore papers were writing furiously.

"Take that away," said the judge firmly.

"But, your honor," said the prosecutor, "we merely wished to—"

"Mr. Sheriff," said the judge, "take that away."

The lawyers for the defense were on their feet aclamor against the manifest injustice of this emotional appeal to the jury. The widow had broken into loud sobs. The daughter looked as though she had been about to faint. Roger wondered whether they had been warned as to what would happen, or whether the prosecutor had reckoned upon the effect that the ghastly effigy would make upon the two women if it came to them with the full shock of surprise.

"Your honor," said the solicitor, "we only want—"

"Your honor!" cried the defense counsel, "we must protest."

"Mr. Sheriff, did you understand what I said? Take that object away!"

The sheriff awaited the solicitor's eye. At last he obeyed the court. Slowly, the ghastly figure waggled on its wheels out of the court. It had been there long enough to accomplish its purpose. The jury, the reporters, the defendants and the audience had all had a good view of the dummy of death.

8

The rest of the day was taken up by the presentation of the blood-stained clothes of the dead man and the examining of the police officers.

The defense brought out the fact that two of the officers had been drunk and disorderly before they went to the tent colony. That the accused boys had been threatened and ill-treated during their first hours in jail.

Mamie Lewes and Dewey Bryson sat near each other. An awful fear had come into Dewey's heart as he looked at the defendants when the Humphries image had waggled in. If Fer and the other boys were loosed, the mob would get after them, as they had gotten after him. He felt glad Mamie Lewes was there.

"What's the matter with your eye," she whispered as he sat down beside her. He didn't like to tell her. It seemed like saying something obscene in the presence of a woman.

"A fella hit me," he said.

"Oh, I know, the mob most got you."

He nodded.

Now they were questioning witnesses. The counsel for the defense made objections, — cross-questioned. The feeling of this being an elaborate ritual still obtained. But with awful clearness, Dewey understood that these polite gentlemen were here to burn his fellow workers. It was as though deep within him he could hear the whine of the dynamo as the lights went out in the death house.

Outside the mob waited. The mob was like an animal sitting on its haunches with its red tongue lolling out. The mob was a crazy man, yelling. This was his own secret hidden knowledge. Mamie Lewes didn't know these things. It was better that way. He felt a quiver of affection and pity at her innocence.

The questioning and cross-questioning went on. The evidence against the defendants was flimsy. One got a picture of the terror of that night, of the bewilderment of the workers in the tent colony. A clear picture of how fortuitous had been the trouble. Terror born in mob fear, had done the shooting.

9

Dewey went back with Mamie Lewes. She lived in a blackened cabin way out of town. She and her children had one room and her cousin and his wife had the other room. The house was empty. The children had been taken to play at the tent colony. She went in and got a kettle of cold grits to warm.

"Set down," she said. "I'll have this fixed for you in a moment. I hope it'll do you, there ain't nothin' but grits and gravy." She sang as she worked.

"That's a new ballit yore makin'? It's awful sad."

"Yes," she said.

"It's awful pretty. You make awful pretty ballits. Sing it out loud, will you?"

His dark knowledge dropped from him. She seemed to him the spirit of everything he was fighting for. She stood before him, her hands clasped.

"Mamie Lewes!" he cried out. "Mamie Lewes!" He went toward her.

"Set down and eat yore grits. Yo're too young a fellow to come around an ole woman like me."

"Sho', Mamie Lewes, you ain't old."

"I don't feel ole this evenin', but some days I feel pow'ful ole."

"You ain't nothing but a girl."

"I sho' feel like one to-day. I don' know what makes me feel so good when I sing that ballit. We'll never let our leaders die! I feel like I'd done somethin' fo' 'em."

"Well, you hev. Songs is better'n speakin'."

"Go on you an' set down." She gave him a shove as he came to put his arm around her.

"Why not, honey?" he begged.

"I don' know," she said uncertainly. "I don' know. We got too much to do to get mixed up this away."

22

1

THE TRIAL dragged on its length. The testimony for the state was vague and inconclusive. There didn't seem an iota of evidence to pin the shooting to any individual among the boys.

"What do you think about it?" Roger asked Hoskins. "Do you think they've any evidence which would convince any jury?"

"Very hard for us to judge," Hoskins said. "How do you feel about it?" he asked Otis Bingham. "Do you think the state has a good case?"

"Well, some one shot Humphries—that's sure, and it's presumably one among the strikers who did it. The question is how did they shoot him? Did the police fire first, and can they prove that the police fired first?"

"I was saying," said Hoskins, "that it's hard for people like Roger and me, who are so close to the Union, to judge about it. We *know*, we don't just guess,—as you know you're standing on the ground,—that Fer, as a good unionist, thought violence the bunk. Whenever there's a shot fired in a strike, the leaders go to jail. Well, the leaders are going to do their best to keep the workers from popping off a gun."

"The first thing I heard Fer preaching when I came down to Stonerton," said Roger, "was that. He told them to keep their hands off their guns when they wanted to tote them on the picket line."

"Why did he let 'em have guards over at the tent colony?" Dick Durgan asked.

"I expect he felt he had to after the headquarters were knocked down by that masked mob. The tent colony was pretty well out of town and the tents near the woods. You wonder what those young jurors make out of it. Here they are, all unused to weighing evidence. I've attended a hundred trials and am used to court procedure and the long listening day after day confuses me," said Hoskins.

"Well, you get a picture, don't you?" said Roger. "You get a picture of terror. Everything leading up to another mob attack. Trouble brewing. The mob the first time at the headquarters, throwing eggs and vegetables at the speakers."

> " 'Don't forget they caught the man with the pistol
>   in his hand,
>   Trying to shoot Deane on the speaking stand,' "

Hoskins added.

"That and choking the women on the picket line. The strikers all believed that the Committee of One Hundred was behind Humphries' car, at the other side of the railway track, and that that long freight from Florida dragged through and separated them. The attack from the mob on the tent colony came mighty soon after the shooting."

"You're mighty sure in your own mind," said Bingham, "that there wasn't any conspiracy?"

"I *know* there wasn't. Fer's as innocent as I. I might as well have been on the ground as not that night, and if I had been, I surely would have been in the strike headquarters from which they claimed the shooting was done. You see it amounts to this—there's no reason in the whole thing. A certain group of workers know there wasn't any murder. A shooting, yes, a regrettable death; and everybody in the community knows with the same violent certainty that there was a conspiracy."

"It seems to me like an elaborate game," said Roger.

"Well," said Durgan, "there's an awful lot more of it before we see the end."

But there wasn't much more.

Suddenly the trial stopped. It was like steaming ahead at full speed and coming into a wall. Something absurd had happened. The grotesque and horrible again. The tapping ghost on wheels had unhinged the mind of a juror. A man who never should have been accepted. He had gone raving insane. Everything was to be done over again. A new jury to be impaneled, testimony to be gone through with again.

The released jurors gave interviews.

Their opinion was that unless the state had something up its sleeve, there was not any evidence before them which would have made them bring in a verdict of guilty.

The jurors went to their homes, the boys went back into jail. The words went over the wires to the whole country that the discharged jury would have acquitted Fer and the other defendants.

2

A feeling of lightness filled Dewey. He hurried home. He lived at the Landors' together with some of the other Union boys. Paul Landor was a carpenter. He and his wife sympathized with the Union. Often they held union meetings in the unpainted big house back of two scraggly spruce trees.

Coming through the town he had an uneasy feeling of something on foot. People were buzzing on the street corners. It was as though that, at news of the jurors' verdict, people had swarmed out like hornets. Dewey had the uncomfortable feeling of lurking danger that had suddenly seized him at the barbecue, as though these crowds of muttering men might suddenly turn on him and open their mouths with the yawp of the mob.

"What's up?" he asked Paul Landor.

"I don't know," Paul answered. "What is up?"

"They's a pow'ful lot of folks out in the street."

"I seen 'em," said Paul, "when I was comin' home from work."

"Kate's atelephonin' about somethin' now. What did you think was up, Dewey?"

"I didn't know," said Dewey. "I just sensed there was somethin'. I 'spect there'll be ructions about what this yere jury said."

"Reckon so," Landor agreed. "Reckon if the boys do git off free, they'll try to git 'em ennyhow." Kate called them to supper. "Who was atelephonin' to you jus' now?" he asked.

"Thet was Jolas. He sa'd they's goin' to be some kind of a parade to-night, —an anti-red parade."

"I guess I'd better go down to Union headquarters an' tell 'em," said Dewey. Paul stirred uneasily and looked at his wife.

"You set yere," she said. "I'll go down. I don't want you men out the house to-night, an' ef any one goes it will be Paul Landor, Dewey."

"I ain't afeared o' 'em," said Dewey.

"You set still like I tell you."

3

Victor Jolas and Binney came in. Rumors were flying around town. Folks had heard the mill people say they were going to get the Union to-night. They all felt the imminence of evil.

Talk died down like a flame when there is no air. Suddenly there was a noise. Every one sat rigid. Cars passed the house hooting and blowing horns.

Jolas said, "That's them."

Paul Landor answered, "Yes, that's them."

The noise of the cars went on and on. Kate tiptoed to the window, flattening herself out against the wall as though she were afraid of a bullet shot. There was no other sound in the room as she crept around the wall. No one stirred or spoke. The house was enchanted in a horrid silence.

"They's an awful lot of them," Kate reported from the window. She scarcely moved her lips, but the words clattered loud into the unnatural quiet. Still the cars passed; a tremendous procession, blowing horns.

"Guess all the mill folks in town is in them cars," said Kate. Then silence again. The noise of the cars, and shouting continued. A long procession of hate. People out to destroy. A mob in cars sweeping through the country. Murder sweeping through the country, open and noisy, searching for its prey. Dewey sat, his hands on each knee, his head sagging forward as if something had hit him. He felt stunned with the surprise of it He had not looked for this river of hate.

Now there was silence. There was a sound toward the back of the house. They looked at one another.

Binney said, "What's that?" in a whisper. They all sat motionless. There was nothing. There was a noise of a car rushing rapidly past the house. Then silence again. They all sat waiting, for what, they didn't know. For the expression in some terms of violence of that river of witless fury which had poured past the door in cars. Silence persisted. Their ears were now attuned to catch the slightest sound.

"What was that?" Paul whispered. "I thought I yeared somethin'. Did you hear footsteps, Binney?"

"I yeared somethin' lak they was some one lookin' in the window."

"Git up and pull the shades down."

"Bes' not move, Kate," Paul cautioned.

"They wouldn't shoot in yere. Not at us."

"They ain't no one there," said Dewey with conviction. "They ain't acomin'. If they was acomin' they'd've come in they cars."

Time passed. They waited.

In their minds, a dark silent mob stole up to the house and surrounded it. Eyes peered in the windows. The tension grew. Kate gripped the edge of her chair. Dewey could see her knuckles shine out white. He felt that at any moment she might scream with sheer terror, scream on scream. He almost wished she would. The infrequent sound of people passing the house, the occasional little noises of the night all meant menace to them. Once they tried to talk.

"They ain't no reason why they should come yere," Kate argued in a reasonable tone.

"No," said Landor, "ain't more'n a coupl'a boys stays yere, — just Syd and Dewey."

Far up the street they heard the sound of running footsteps.

"Listen," said Kate. "Listen! Some one's comin' now, — some one's arunnin'."

4

They all knew, although there was no reason for them to know, that those were hasty panic-stricken footsteps. They were coming toward them. The footsteps turned up the steps. Light footsteps, swift and light.

"Mamie Lewes!" cried Kate. "What's the matter? How'd you git yere?" For Mamie Lewes lived miles away on the outskirts of the next town.

"They're acomin' yere," Mamie Lewes gasped. "The mob's acomin'. They raided the Union to Tesner. I went down to the Union. The mob went in and they pitched the literachoor out. Some one says, 'Let's set it afire.' They all said, 'Let's burn the damn thing up!' and some one else says, 'No, thet's arson, leave it lay. Let's go and clear out the whole goddamn pack.' Some one else says, 'Yes, let's clear out that crowd. Let's start with that crowd to Landor's.' "

"How'd you git yere?" asked Dewey.

"They was a truck coming along and I caught me a ride. They'll be after you, Dewey. You'd best git out of yere. The truck was awful slow. I thought I yeared 'em after us, follering us. You boys git out o' yere."

"Yes," said Kate. "You boys slip over to Lafayette right quick."

Mamie Lewes lay back in her chair, her eyes about closed, her face very pale, spent. "You best git out," she repeated.

"It's too late! Listen! Yere they come."

"You go out the back door, boys. You got time."

"No, you ain't." Mamie Lewes put out her hand. "No, you ain't. No, you ain't! Listen! They're tramping around the house! They're trampin' around the house!"

People hammered on the locked door. The door opened. Men came in. They were solemn and quiet. Their faces were grim and important and there was an air of high excitement about them. They had cleared out the union halls and they were going on with their holy crusade.

The hall and sitting room were filled with tall and silent men. Astoundingly the intruders sang:

"Praise God from whom all blessings flow!
Praise Him ye creatures here below!
Praise Him above ye heavenly hosts!
Praise Father, Son and Holy Ghost!"

"Now, goddam it to hell!" cried the leader, "we'll clean up this pole cat's nest."

"Listen!" said another. "All yo' who wants to come with us, and wants to give up the Union, nothin' is goin' to happen to yo'."

There came a curious noise, tense, sustained and angry, the sound of a killing mob.

"Youall take keer of 'em," said one.

Individual voices snapped out above the hum. Men began rushing around and tearing up union literature. There was a certain frantic fury about it all. A voice snapped out against the general tumult.

"You all take keer o' them, and we'll get Deane outa jail and lynch him."

Kate slid over toward the telephone. A man caught her arm and wrenched it. Kate hit at the man. He struck her with his fist. She slipped and fell. The crowd milled and eddied, aimless and furious. Then a woman's scream and Binney's voice high above the tumult, the constant roar of the mob.

"They're takin' Dewey away!"

"Kate! Kate! Kate! They're takin' Dewey away. They're takin' the boys. They're takin' the boys!"

The man near her shook her violently. She fell against the wall. He bent down and cut the telephone wires. Shouts went up about her.

"Let's clean out Lafayette. Come on to Lafayette and git the lawyer. Clean out headquarters over there!"

5

Mamie Lewes, leaning against the wall, could see a clot of them, dark as a swarm of bees, struggling out on the lawn. The light on the trees made them stand out spectacular like paper trees. The men struggled and swayed. All at once the hall was empty as though they had been sucked out on the tide of their own hate. Mamie Lewes bent down again, stretching the telephone wires which were cut, to join the ends. She had to phone the Lafayette office. She heard Kate's voice calling Paul Landor.

"Paul, whar are you?" And Paul's voice.

"Yere I am, yere I am, honey!"

"Oh, they didn't git you, Paul! Who did they git, Paul?"

Mamie Lewes felt as if her head would split. She put her hand to her eyes. They had taken Dewey. Mamie Lewes bent down again, stretching the telephone wires. "Kate, we gotta get the office in Lafayette before they git thar!"

The mob swept over to Lafayette. A hundred cars, a man hunt now, people out for trouble, people ready for lynching. The sight of a man taken off for punishment whetted their blood. Ridiculous and savage and grotesque and terrible.

They rushed into the hotel where some of the Union people from New York were staying. Henderson stopped there sometimes, and Dillon, charged with defense work.

They demanded to know where Doris and Irma were staying, — and Graham's wife. They broke the electric light fixtures and tore up the hotel registers. They were at once menacing and ridiculous. Now they swept down to strike headquarters which was also defense headquarters. No one was there. The phone call had come through just in time.

Duncan and Henderson, the other Union people, had been in headquarters and had left only ten minutes before. The girls had been warned and had gone to friends.

Raging, but leaderless, the mob swept around the town. They milled in front of the lawyer's house and called him to come out. They wanted to burn and kill.

"Clean out the Union!"

"Break into the jail!"

There was no head to this mass. They wasted their fury in futilities. They had not even wrecked the headquarters as they had in Tesner and Stonerton. They had only broken in and then recoiled back on themselves at finding only emptiness. Gradually futility left them hollow. The mob melted. The righteous mob of comfortable people had made their protest against the boys in jail. They had voiced their intention to lynch them if the state wouldn't burn them.

In all the comfortable houses there was hate. In all the comfortable houses people believed that the boys in jail should burn. The mob was the verdict of the comfortable people. They had streamed forth in fury like angry bees when the hive is attacked. As instinctively as bees and with the same furious ardor. This mob had been no rabble. This had been no undisciplined explosion of emotion. This was something more deadly.

6

All that night Mamie Lewes couldn't sleep. The face of the mob, the furious, cursing men, their mixture of blasphemy and religion obsessed her mind.

A mob is a raving, witless thing, Preacher Quinn said.

She thought of the mill bosses, threatening, frightening, and intimidating. That is how mob came to be.

Hate made mobs, and fear made mobs.

Early in the morning she went out to watch the highway. Why, she didn't know. As though the sight of cars moving on the road and folks going would help the awful anxiety within her. She didn't let herself think of what might have happened to Dewey. She didn't let herself believe that they might have lynched him. She had been standing watching the road since light. It was as though it was a looked for and expected thing when a truck thundering down the road, slowed and drew up. Negroes drove it.

"We got a most lynched man in yere," one of them said. "He sez to stop along by youall. He sez he cain't go much further."

"Dewey!" she cried. "Dewey Bryson!"

"It's me, Mamie Lewes. I'm all right."

They carried him, indescribably battered, inside her cabin and put him on her bed.

"They left me to run naked through the woods. . . . They left—me to run naked—through the woods," he gasped. "There was—a farmer give me—these overalls."

The two negroes stood staring at the wounded man. They helped Mamie Lewes take his things from his bruised and bloody body.

"I ain't hurt so bad," Dewey muttered. "I ain't hurt—like what I thought I would be. I was glad—when they started—only awhuppin' me. When I got—outa the woods—I thought about you, Mamie Lewes. I thought they—wouldn't look for me yere. Till we could—get some one—to come and take me—up to headquarters." The words trickled slowly. He spoke as from some far distant place. He stopped, his eyes closed. Later, he managed to drink the coffee she had made for him. She washed away the blood and dirt.

7

Dewey Bryson lay on his bed in the hotel where they had taken him. The room was always full of people. He liked that. When he was alone and fever made him drowsy, nightmare seized him. He would be back again being whirled through darkness while they threatened him with the torture, the mutilation which they had imagined but hadn't dared.

He could feel like a physical thing, like an emanation, the quality of their hatred. He tried to remember what they looked like. They looked like hate. They looked like murder. Where had the explosion of hate come from, that swirled through these cities?

Dewey lay lacerated and feverish. As he would drowse off at night, what had happened would become all mixed in his mind. Now he was fleeing naked through the woods. Now he was on the seat of the car trying not to seem frightened, mustn't seem scared. Now they were beating him. A curious feeling of relief that they were only "whuppin' " him. They stopped and drove him into the wood. One said:

"This would be a good tree to hang him from—"

One said, "Git a rope. Let's hang him yere."

One went to the car and came back. "There ain't a rope," he said. "Some of the other fellows musta tuk our rope."

One said, "Let's take the tube outa the spare and hang 'im up with that."

They talked about that for quite a while, and then they decided they wouldn't do that. So they "whupped" him some more. They told him to git and he stumbled through the brush. Then they shot at him. He didn't know where he was. He got to a road and found a farmhouse. They wouldn't let him in but they gave him some old overalls. They told him where he was and how to get to the highway. Again he waited by the roadside. The nights passed in such recollections.

Daytimes the story of what else had happened came through the room in eddies of talk.

It was Tuesday after the mob. Nothing was yet clear to Dewey. Nothing but frightful memories of fear and of mob and talk of mob.

Wednesday Dewey woke up feeling empty and weak but clear-headed. Friends began to come in. Two of the Union boys began to argue about the Union meeting which had been scheduled for Saturday.

One said, "We cain't hold it. They'll mob us and shoot us."

The other said, "We gotta hol' the meetin'."

Clear as a pattern of a star a resolution came to Dewey's mind—

"*We gotta hold that meetin'!*" he said out loud. "We gotta have our meetin' Saturday."

Babel broke loose. "We best let it simmer down befo' we have a meetin'."

"We gotta. We gotta keep on ef we are goin' on. Ef we don't have our speakin' they'll say they got us licked."

"They'll shoot you down like dawgs!"

"Lookee yere what it says in the paper. Did ya see this editorial? 'The Union's warned that it will not be safe to hold a Union meetin'.' "

Dewey sat up in bed. He said wearily, "We'll have it all to do over ag'in if they think by whuppin' an' mobbin' us they kin stop us."

23

1

IN LAFAYETTE Hoskins lived in a boarding house nearly opposite the courthouse. Roger lived in the hotel where most of the reporters stayed. The boarding house was a pleasant elm-shaded house; business men, school teachers, salesmen and their wives lived there. It was a small cross section of Lafayette. They were not uninclined to be sympathetic to the boys in jail. Now the wildest rumors flew around among them.

"The Union has brought in machine guns and gangsters. A truck load of arms has been smuggled into the city." There was nothing too extravagant to be believed.

The Union boys were equally full of rumors. A mob army was being recruited and drilled in various mills. The Committee of One Hundred of Stonerton was being duplicated throughout the country. The actual happenings lent a semblance of truth to the Union's alarm. Isolated Union members were threatened at night. A man named Leonard Good was shot at in Hill Town. The Truitts, cousins of the Tetherows in Stonerton, had their windows knocked on three nights running. Little Tetherow, cousin of the boy in jail, was threatened on the street by mill hands. Toughs on some of the street corners had shouted after some of the Union women, "Nigger lovers, nigger lovers!" There was a frightful sense of tension throughout the whole town. No one was free from it. It permeated through all the comfortable people. There was not a mill worker anywhere, whether he was a mill worker or striker, who didn't feel he was in the presence of some imminent catastrophe.

2

Roger and Ed Hoskins went again to see Dewey. They had visited him when he had been brought in almost unconscious, his body black and blue and lacerated. Now he was better, sitting up in bed.

"Are you really going to hold a Union meeting in Stonerton?" Hoskins wanted to know.

"Seems like we gotta. I don't see no way out," he answered somberly, his dark wing of hair falling dankly over his thin face.

"Have you taken it up with the Union yet?" Roger asked Henderson who was staying with some of the other Union boys in the room which was always crowded with people.

"Yeah, we had a Union meetin' last night," said Henderson. "The Union officers had a meeting right next door here."

"Couldn't you put it off a week till the excitement dies down?"

"Of course they ought to put it off a week," cried Doris, who had been returned to Lafayette on relief business. "It's just leading them out to slaughter to have them go on now."

"Shut up and keep out of this! You're not a Union official."

"What does Simonson say?" asked Hoskins. Simonson was a lawyer from the North who represented the Union at the trial.

"Simonson is all against the meeting," cried Doris.

"Shut up, Doris!" said Henderson again.

Clamor arose. People for and against the meeting. It was as though they talked themselves into disaster. They knew they had to hold the meeting.

"What does Fer say, and the other boys in jail? I think they ought to be consulted. Suppose there is another shooting? How is it going to affect them?—that's the question."

"That was decided last night. They're going to take the Union judgment to Fer and see what he decides."

"He has decided already. Didn't he tell Simonson? Didn't he tell Burdette?"

"Yes, but we couldn't see him until to-day. Wednesday is visiting day and they can't make public what he says privately to them."

Some of the other Union boys came in.

"You seen Fer?" Dewey asked.

"Yes, we've jus' come from him. He made a statement to the press."

"Does he want us to hold the meeting?"

"Sure thing, he does."

"You got the statement?"

"Yes, yere it is."

It was a brief statement, smoothly put and definite, almost like a bit of one of Fer's forthright speeches.

3

Roger and Hoskins went down the street together to visit the boys in jail. The jail where they were confined was one floor of the courthouse.

"What do you think about it?" Roger asked. "Do you think they should hold it? Would you hold it?"

"No," Hoskins said. "No, I wouldn't. I'd be too afraid of what would happen to the boys on trial. That's the one thing I think about. If they go on with this, with the feeling what it is, there may be a sort of a massacre. But you can see how the Union boys feel about it. They feel it's putting a premium on flogging and mob action to give up now. As far as I can see, both sides are committed. The Union can't back out, they've got to hold the meeting. The mob can't back out,—they've got to prevent the meeting."

They had gotten to the courthouse and waited for the elevator which took one to the jail. Ma Gilfillin was waiting there and old Mr. and Mrs. Tetherow. There was a group of colored women with baskets bringing things to their men. In this North Carolina jail the prisoners were not allowed to come out to speak to their families. They talked through a grating. As Roger went up to speak to Fer, all the other boys crowded around. Their heads bobbing up and down behind the grating made you feel they were strange fish in an aquarium. There was a glass behind the grating and a hole in the glass. It was necessary to talk right into the hole right into the person's ear. You could not see them as you talked. It was almost like talking into a telephone.

The people crowded all around. There were four different places where shouted conversation went on. The boys had a spiritual look, almost like young members of an order. They were depressed because of trial having to be done over again. It was as though freedom had been within their grasp and a trick of fate had taken it from them.

"I wish you'd put the meeting off, Fer," Roger said.

"Well, the Union's decided that they'd hold it," said Fer.

"It seems terribly dangerous to me. You can't know what the feeling is in the town, shut up in here."

"How is it?"

"You can't describe it. It's not like anything I've ever known. It's waiting. Waiting for something awful to happen."

"Well, we can't stop all Union activities. What's the use of the trial, what's the use of anything, if the Union doesn't go on?" Fer wanted to know.

Hoskins took his turn shouting in Fer's ear and Roger stood back watching the different people, like people in some grotesque confessional, calling back and forth to their friends, or waving to prisoners standing back, hungrily waiting for a word with a friend or their families.

It was a fantastic sight, awful and absurd at once, part of an ironic scene. It was a part of the whole grotesquerie. It had to do with the grotesquerie of the insane juror, the singing of the Doxology by the mob intent on destruction, the teetering effigy of the corpse of the dead police chief. Horror that had laughter in it.

4

Filled with restlessness, Roger went back to see if he could do anything for Dewey. As he went along the street, he pondered on the fear every one had. In these days every one was afraid of every one else.

Dewey was alone for once with only Irma in the room and she went out when Roger came.

"I'm alayin' here, thinking what makes mob," Dewey said. He closed his eyes. There was mob. What was it? It was hate. How had it come? What made all these people hate? The mob had arms and legs and feet. It had guns. The mob hated the Union. The mob believed Fer and the Union had plotted to kill Humphries. It was as though the mob spirit was a contagion and filled first one person and then another.

He said out loud, "Who do you reckon made the mob? The preacher said the mob's a blind, ravin', witless thing."

"The mob doesn't think it's witless," said Roger. "They think that what they're doing is right. . . . Isn't there any way out of the meeting?" and he knew as he asked that there was not. For there was a feeling of fatality among the workers. They must hold the meeting. They would be forever at the mercy of the mob if they didn't.

Thursday there were more warnings in the paper. The shadow of mob grew long and dark. There was no person anywhere who was not touched by suspense.

Something murderous was coming out of this. Some awful calamity was to happen Saturday. It was like knowing by the clock when a catastrophe of nature was to occur. As though one could foretell earthquake. As though cyclone had a schedule. Only this was a cyclone of evil, and it was unclean.

Each side looked with horror upon their opponents. The comfortable people believed that the workers were going to march upon the mills. They had heard that under the shadow of night, guerillas and gunmen had been brought in.

In the courthouse an investigation of the kidnapping and flogging was being held. The story of the mob night was being told in homely words. Over and over again it was being told. It was as though the courthouse was the core and around it gathered the coming cyclone. Hate and fear stalked through the town.

Dewey was around again. The lacerations were still painful. He had a feeling as though hate were stalking him. People swooping past him in cars, ready to get him. It was as though the whole world was shadowed by a formless cloud born by panic and filled with fear.

He wished he could escape.

He wished he didn't have again to look upon the awful face of mob.

He wanted to go away.

There was no place to go to.

He had a feeling of utter hopelessness. He was trapped. This wasn't clean warfare. This wasn't fighting fair. This was walking up to something inhuman and mindless. Something which wished death to all the seventy of them who had been arrested. Something willing hate and death. The preacher had said, "Mob is pure hate. Mob is fear."

The shadow which had been over the barbecue had grown and grown. Now it was about to burst its hatred upon them.

5

Roger got up in the morning of Saturday with a feeling of something horrible about to happen. There was a hush over the town as though a storm was expected. He was to have met some of the newspaper men to go to the meeting. He had missed them, somehow.

Hoskins was the only one he could find. He didn't know where any one was. There was a car going from relief headquarters after a while. Roger wished that he could be with a large crowd of newspaper men, hardboiled and joking. He wished he didn't have to go. He wished it was over. It was something like a battle. You didn't know who would be dead by evening. Though it had elements of horror beyond any battle.

They drove along to Stonerton through the lovely August country, across the river. At the last minute the meeting place had been changed with an attempt to outwit the mob who would be there to receive them. They had planned to have the meeting in an empty lot, behind the Union headquarters which was now in Truitt's house. His house was on the same street as Landor's, and not far from the Thorns, Roger's old boarding house. The house was owned by Truitt. He was not a mill worker but had a taxicab. He had a son working in the mills. He, like Paul Landor, had received repeated anonymous threats but had paid no attention to them.

When Roger and Hoskins got there, there were a few people hanging around Truitt's. No one seemed to know anything. Truitt was away, and old man Truitt. They said a crowd had been there and had gone. Had the Union speakers been there? They didn't know. Had there been a big crowd? Some said it was, some said it wasn't.

Roger went down to Mrs. Thorn's a block away. She was crying. "A great crowd was yere. They choked the road. They was two thousand."

This again Roger knew was impossible. The feeling of frustration and emptiness grew and added to the feeling of horror.

They drove up to the old meeting ground where the mob had first met Dewey in East Stonerton, for the mills which divided the town were known by the points of the compass.

There was a holiday crowd going down to a swimming pool and a pleasure park, from whence came the noise of music. There was a crowd around a baseball field. Then suddenly there were a line of cars which ran six deep, and men with guns. They looked in every car as it passed. Roger and Hoskins passed a sort of speakers' stand in which stood Dick Durgan and the newspaper men. Roger waved to them. A little further and the driver managed to turn around.

Suddenly a cry arose. "Them's the organizers!"

"Them's the speakers!"

"Get'm! Get'm!"

Roger looked around. Not until Hoskins said a little bleakly, "They think we're the speakers," did he realize that the howl that arose was for them.

The word was passed down the line. Men held up guns in their hands. It seemed to Roger he was looking down a red yelping gullet, howling, "Get the speakers! Get them out!"

The driver stepped on the gas. The car sprang ahead but the cries went faster than they. Everywhere this hostile mass of howling men. Now a car slewed itself in front. Faces full of hate were inside the car. The police on motorcycles came up, smart, dapper-looking young men.

"You come along with us," they said, and at Hoskins' protest, "Oh, we know what kind of newspaper men you are. You come along."

The police rode them down to the jail, the mob stringing menacingly behind them. Soon the matter was straightened out. Hoskins and Roger showed their papers and mingled with the crowd which was waiting in hostile fashion around the jail for the supposed speakers.

6

Dewey got up Saturday with a feeling of execution. A death house feeling. He went as he had planned to the place in Tesner where Mamie Lewes and the other Union workers were to meet. They were getting a truck ready. They were all gay and a little excited as though the glitter of danger beckoned to them.

"What's them?" the truck driver said. "What you got?"

Two boys answered, "We got guns."

"You ain't agoin' to take guns!"

"We gotta right to defend ourselves."

The truck driver laughed a big booming laugh, reassuring to Dewey upon whom was the sickness of his flogging.

"We cain't git guns enough to defend ourselves. So best have none!"

"They wun't do nothin' to us," said Mamie Lewes. "Leave your guns to home, boys. They ain't agoin' to do nothin' to us on our truck."

"No, they wun't do nothin' to us." They were all gay and happy. They were innocent. They didn't know the obscenity of mob. Dewey tried to get into their world. Mamie Lewes' voice came out bright and strong:

"Come all ye scabs ef you want to year
The story of a mean millioneare.
Basil Schenk is that millioneare's name—"

The truck had stopped with a jolt as they got into Stonerton. Faces of mob again.

"Where youall think yo're agoin'?"

"We're agoin' to the speakin'."

"They ain't no speakin' to-day. You turn 'round dam' quick and git to hell back whar you come from!"

It was like a nightmare. Men with guns turning you back on a sunny roadway in broad daylight. Back somewhere a mob with a red throat yapping. Hundreds of people wanting to kill.

Dewey had the feeling of complete disaster. What had happened back there? What was going on at the meeting place? He was part of the will which had caused the meeting. Had he sent them out to be shot?

The truck was turned around now. Cars were chasing them. A curious feeling of lightness came over him. They had gone to the meeting. They didn't have to go any more.

What had happened back there? What had happened back in the crowd? Mamie Lewes looked at him. "We tried to hold it ennyway, Dewey. *'He cain't buy the Union with his money and frame!'* "

A car ran in front of the truck. There was a sound of crashing. The truck swerved.

There was a sharp report of a shot. Mamie Lewes screamed.

"Oh, Lawdy, they've hit me!"

There were more shots. Mamie Lewes fell in a heap.

"Mamie Lewes!" cried Dewey. "Mamie Lewes! She's daid! Mamie Lewes daid!"

People had gotten down from the truck. Men were chasing them and shooting.

He helped carry Mamie Lewes to a neighboring house. "It's over!" he thought. "It's over!"

Here was the victim that the mob demanded. They had shot the singin' woman to death. Blood was spreading over her bosom and over her dress.

One singing woman had been the victim of all the hate. The news of Mamie Lewes' death flew through the town. It came to the mob which blocked the road to the "speakin' place." It dissolved the knots of hate that watched for workers' cars. Clouds of fear and hate had grown big. Men had become mob.

Mob had killed the singin' woman. The news sped through people's homes. The news that the woman who made song ballits and sang them had been killed by a mob sped over the wires. All the world knew now about the life of one obscure mill worker. All the world knew how she worked to keep her children with her in her home.

The yard outside the farmhouse was filling up rapidly with people. Crowds came from nowhere. It didn't seem possible that people in Tesner should know so quickly that Mamie Lewes was shot dead.

The doctor came. The law came. Dewey sat there as though in a bad dream. He had known all along that there would be some incalculable tragedy on Saturday. Yet he had insisted that the meeting should be held. He had let Mamie Lewes go out in the face of the mob, Mamie Lewes who was so innocent that she didn't know what evil was.

He was here and she was dead. It seemed incredible that this should be so. He could not go. He couldn't leave her now. Suddenly he knew that he had loved her and that she had loved him. They hadn't been able to talk about it. There had only been that one moment in the cabin. She and her "song ballits" had been the very core of the strike to Dewey. Now she was dead.

What made mob? Who were mob?

Who had killed Mamie Lewes?

People were taking her away now; putting her in a coffin and taking her to the undertaking parlor. Dewey got up at last,—scarcely knowing what he did. He didn't know where he was going; his legs took him back to town; back to Landor's; back to the only place he had for a home. Fellows he knew stopped him on the street in front of the drug store. The bright lights in the drug store shone on their eager faces. One of the boys worked in a department store, the other fellow worked in a garage. Dewey was sure he had seen them on the edge of the mob the night they came for him. They said eagerly:

"I hear a woman was killed! I heard they shot the ballitt singer!"

"Yeah, I was thar when she died," Dewey answered mechanically.

"Who shot her, Dewey?" It was as though a light had exploded within him. Every one was guilty. Every one who thought mob, or hate was guilty.

"You all killed her!" he cried. "This town killed her!"

7

He walked along the street. He thought, "I am alive and she is dead." It seemed incomprehensible to him. His heels kept time to his thought which he repeated over and over. He remembered the few seconds long ago when he had had a grudging moment about her. When he had for a moment denied the love which was growing in him and had listened to the gossip of the mill people about Mamie Lewes being "none too keerful." And then he had cared for her. Caring for her had been part of the Union lately. They had both been too busy. Now she was dead.

Dimly, inside of Dewey's mind came the realization of what he had meant when he had cried in front of the drug store, "You all have killed her."

Who was mob? Every one was mob who hated the Union. The minister's wife sitting in her safe and secluded parlor, the young girls who talked contemptuously about mill hands, Mrs. Schenk away in her fine house in Richmond, the editors of the papers, the ministers who tried to "reason" with the poor, misguided people, the Governor of the State, so swift to call out troops, so slow to see that order was kept to-day. He had known that trouble was imminent. His representatives had said, "He did not like to abridge the rights of free speech." The community was responsible for Mamie Lewes' death. The whole community.

8

There was a speaking in Tesner. The speaking that the mob prevented on Saturday was held over the grave of Mamie Lewes. Roger and Hoskins, the reporters of all the great dailies, went to Mamie Lewes' funeral. It was to have been at ten. They went to the Union headquarters where a little knot of black crpe hung down. A small and meager knot of people were gathered. The funeral was poor. Like all the physical adjuncts of Mamie Lewes' life. Mamie Lewes who had never owned anything but who had had laughter and singing and chillren and love. A few Union people drifted around headquarters. Mamie Lewes was lying in state at her cousin's house. All the big metropolitan newspapers had sent their representatives. There had been hints that the mob was going to break up the funeral.

Roger was standing on the curb, waiting aimlessly when some boys drove up. They were young and their eyes held a fanatical gleam. Roger wondered whether they could be mob members. One of the boys asked him tensely, "Is it true these folks deny our Lord?"

Presently they drove away. If they were mob they were too scattered for action.

Finally the little funeral went up the muddy red roads to a deserted looking cemetery on the hillside. It had been drizzling. Now the rain had stopped. The day was gray and misty. People came in cars and lumbered through the splattering mud. Workers in twos and threes walked through the cotton fields that surrounded the cemetery. There was a red hole in the ground like a wound. Around the edge of the grave were Mamie Lewes' children. Only the eldest who had "heped so much" knew what was happening. The three younger ones were too small to understand clearly.

Then Dewey spoke, and Jolas, the head of the Union in Tesner, Lee Thomas. They all made Union speeches.

In the meantime there was always the noise of clicking cameras. Pictures of this small and far-off funeral of this obscure mill worker would go to workers all over the country, and all over the world.

Then one of the girls of the Tesner union sang Mamie Lewes' song, "How it grieves the heart of a mother!"

Her small voice, thin and uncertain, wavered into the stillness which was broken only by the insistent click of cameras.

The minister, who was a stranger to Mamie Lewes, said a few words and it was over.

24

1

THE LONG, LEAN solicitor arose and looked about the Lafayette County courthouse. The boys on trial watched attentively. Roger noticed the pose of Fer's head with its fine-cut profile and the wing of dark hair flung down over his brown cheek, not yet bleached by the months of confinement.

The public interest had flagged. Only the boys' nearest relatives were there. The press was as well represented as formerly for public interest had been kept alive by mob and terror. The public at large around Lafayette had heard most of the state's evidence and the workers had found it inconclusive while the comfortable people believed the boys to be murderers.

It was no use in trying to burn them in the chair. That was evident. There was evidently to be no legal lynching. The state, through the lean solicitor who was at every moment shaking some one's hand, was about to admit it.

"Your honor," said the solicitor, looking at his feet which were long and slim and elegantly shod, "the state will drop the death penalty against the defendants. The state will change the charge from murder in the first degree to murder in the second."

This had been hinted at in the papers for days. Since the trial had halted three weeks before, it had been evident that no jury could be found to electrocute these boys on the flimsy evidence which the state had to produce.

Dick Durgan of the Baltimore *Planet,* who had just come from an interview with the governor, prophesied that they would drop some of the cases. Hoskins objected:

"That would be to admit they'd rounded up these youngsters like a bunch of cattle, arresting everybody at the tent colony who was on the ground at the time of the shooting." The solicitor rose again.

"The case against five of the defendants will be dropped." He named Tetherow, Gilfillin, Cathcart, Truitt and Dan Marks. Now only one Southern mill worker was left, Wes Elliott, who throughout the strike had been known for his enthusiasm and fanaticism. On trial were the three Northern boys, two of whom, Hunt and Graham, had been down for only two weeks when the shooting occurred.

It was an admission of defeat for the mill owners, but it was not a victory for the defendants.

The released defendants went out quietly. They understood too well the meaning of this apparent retreat on the part of the state. They saw in it new tactics of the lawyers, an attempt to railroad the others to jail on a long term sentence. With the trial for the death penalty in North Carolina goes also the privilege of twelve peremptory challenges of jurors. In the first trial there were, with nine defendants, an enormous number of challenges.

With the death penalty removed only four challenges were possible and now with charges against five of the boys dropped, the number of challenges was small. It was immediately apparent to all sympathizers that the new jury would not be the young working class jury that they had had at first.

The whole atmosphere of the court had changed. The defendants all felt it. Roger went up to Fer as the court was dismissed, as it briefly was when the lawyers for the defense withdrew to discuss the proposal made by the solicitor.

Fer, who looked especially clear and pale, said a little flatly:

"Well, I guess here's where they get us. This'll satisfy everybody. No one's going to cry if a few of the Northern organizers get shoved into jail for life."

And that was it. That sense that "nobody cares now" was over the proceedings and intensified the general discouragement. It was a clever move on the part of the state. Deprived of the electric chair, they changed the trial from a major issue, a second Sacco-Vanzetti, into one where "the Northern agitators" were going to get their just deserts.

2

Moreover, there was reason to fear for the safety of the released boys. The mob had threatened that if the state did not convict the defendants, it would take a hand. They had adopted a slogan, "If we can't drive 'em out, we'll shoot 'em out." They stated openly that they meant to drive out every union organizer in the south.

The mob was under way before the first trial was over. They had gone on from terror to terror. Three men had been kidnapped and beaten. Mamie Lewes had been killed. But even since her death there had been new outrages. A young fellow in Rock Mountain, a town ten miles south of Tesner, had been taken out of his bed at night by masked men, carried into the woods and beaten. A shout of disgust had gone up all over the country. The fate of Mamie Lewes had aroused sympathy everywhere. The most liberal elements of the state were loud in protest and clamored for the conviction of her murderers. And now with the red earth of her grave not yet sodded over another flogging had occurred.

Terror had stalked the countryside. There had been organized, regimented, directed violence. Unleashed mob violence. Now to this was added the terror that walks by night.

A union boy, an organizer named Norris, was shot through the arm and told to keep his mouth shut about it. Robert Duncan only learned this by chance. The boy's family was sullen and would not talk to the Northern mill worker. They were afraid.

People knocked on the windows of union members at night. Women were waylaid in dark places by unknown individuals and warned to "tell their men to leave the union if they didn't want nothin' to happen to them."

Terror like a slow underground fire was crawling throughout the mill hill. Terror walked throughout the tent colony. It was decided now to disband what remained of it.

3

During the last days of the trial a sense of doom pursued Roger and Hoskins. The new jury was old, fundamentalist, a number of them, hard shelled, hard visaged, middle-aged farmers. That the boys were radicals, the fact that they were Northerners, the fact that they had wanted a union even, the fact that they "had no religion" would all be against them. They were men who were repressed, but used to the emotional release of conversion, Southerners who were accessible to flowery appeal. The long, clever solicitor knew his people.

Three pictures stood out clearly in Roger's mind. One was the picture of Graham's little wife Ruth, her sleek, clipped, gallant little profile, a boyish head, unconsciously swearing away her husband's liberty as she confessed she did not believe in God. She had been at headquarters that night and testified that neither her husband nor Fer had had anything to do with the shooting.

She gave a clear picture of what had happened among the leaders up in the wooden shack of the strike headquarters while the shooting was going on. Fer had been going over some accounts. Irma, with Doris, had been talking idly together, going over the details of the day, of the throwing of the vegetables, a man found with a pistol, the breaking up of the picket line. Then had come one shot, then another shot, and some one said, "What's that?" and some one had said, "Put out the light," and then came a fusillade of shots and Fer said:

"It's the Committee of One Hundred. They're after us."

And they lay down on the floor of the little darkened headquarters to be out of the way of flying bullets.

She evoked again the confusion and surprise and the terror of that night. Unpremeditated, unsought, unexpected, calamity had descended on the tent colony on the eve of what they had hoped would be another victory for them in the mill.

4

But because she didn't believe in God, the jury disregarded her testimony. Because, if she did not believe in God, her oath was valueless. Apparently only those who thought that God was going to punish those who told a lie with fire and brimstone, could be relied upon to tell the truth.

Even the impartial, young, ascetic judge believed this,—believed that a person who did not believe in God could not tell the truth.

The Northern reporters, probably not one of them with more orthodox religion than the defendant,—unorthodox Jew, a Catholic who hadn't heard mass in fifteen years, a young man brought up outside religious training, listened with amazement.

"It's a grand anachronism," Hoskins whispered to Roger. "The modern court room and this medieval concept."

There was the picture of Fer through his long day of testimony, patient, frank, sincere, clear and lucid in all his answers. Roger remembered him always as he saw him there in profile in the witness chair, his fine aquiline features, his face shadowed a little and blurry. Yet he had a great gallantry of bearing. He was a touching and sincere person, shut away from any touch of compassion of this especial jury who hated everything this young leader had done, who hated that he should have come to their "Southland," who really believed that he and his companions were a form of anti-Christ.

Throughout the long examination, Roger's hopes slid gradually downward. Fer's testimony should have liberated him. Roger knew it would not.

This jury was deaf to anything but the voice of its own prejudices.

Inseparable from the picture of Fer was the picture of Lissa. Lissa with her beautiful straight brows, her untouched youth, and her earnestness. The emotion of her concentration gave her true beauty as hour after hour she listened. She could not have told that hopelessness was creeping through her in a paralyzing fashion. But she knew, as Roger, as every one whose sympathy was with these unfortunate boys, that their cause was already lost.

They scarcely needed the grotesquerie of the last day. The appeal made by the lawyers for the defense was scholarly and accurate. It lacked some essential fire. Old Burdette's fury, for instance,—old Burdette's sarcasm and lashing, the swift venom of his tongue. The jury would have understood that.

What they did understand was the melodrama staged for them by the solicitor. He lay on the floor, imitating the dead man. He told how the innocent blood had flowed at the hands of these fiends who had plotted this murder. Meantime the widow sobbed aloud. He ended by kneeling down beside her, grasping her hand and praying God to guide the hearts of the jurymen aright, to convict the unspeakable fiends who had slain her husband.

It was a sensational ending to a sensational trial, a juicy story for the newspaper men to send over the wires, as inconceivable an ending as had been the beginning, the waxen image of the dead man which jiggled into court. The solicitor had done well. He had spoken a language the hard-faced farmers understood.

Of the days of the defense, and of the summing up, Roger remembered only blackness. It was all over except suspense. They had lost. There was nothing now but to wait for the inevitable verdict, the inevitable sentence. The hours crawled by. The days crawled by. There was Fer's clear, anxious face, and behind him Lissa's face. The small handful in the court room, of interested people. It was the monotonous boredom of the death watch. Yet time crawls and goes fast all at once.

The verdict of guilty was brought in. They were guilty of conspiring, planning, plotting together to kill Richard Humphries. Again there was the haunting sense of grotesquerie that these youngsters could have made such a plot. It had all the distortion of nightmare to the two reporters who knew Fer's mind so well. It was as grotesque as the mob which sang the Doxology, and like the mob, it would have been ridiculous, a thing to laugh at, if it had not been real, if it had not carried the sting, the sentence of twenty years.

The kind, unfailingly courteous, patient judge, the just judge, handed down the shattering sentence of twenty years for all but Wes Elliott. Wes Elliott received ten. They had known it was coming. They had known every day that actual doom was near, but they hadn't quite believed it. The sentence fell crushingly upon the condemned boys and their sympathizers alike.

25

1

FER WAS TO BE let out on bail. Bail was so high that the other boys had to stay in jail for a while during the time that the bail was being collected. The authorities demanded cash bail. They would not take property.

In the early morning people began assembling around the court-house. Workers, men and women, came in trucks and in every kind of conveyance. Old men and young and the children came. The streets were lined with quiet people from dawn on.

All of Fer's friends had been afraid of what might happen when he got out of jail, afraid there might be a mob ready for violence. It was as if these fears had been echoed in every one of his sympathizers. Every mill worker who believed he had fought for the Union; the hill preachers like Quinn and Williams; Union members and non-Union; came strikers and people from mills where there had never been a strike; as though to leave no place for a mob they came and waited quietly for Fer to appear.

It was a strange demonstration, this flowing into Lafayette of mill workers who wanted to greet Fer. To them Fer was the symbol of their fight for liberty. He had fought against their cruel hours, he had fought against their under pay and their poverty. And now he, too, was enslaved and imprisoned. It was as though this whole community had streamed out to say:

"Fer, we know you never shot Humphries and you never planned to shoot him. We know they framed you because you fought for us."

Waiting close to the door for Fer to come out was Burdette with

Hoskins and Roger. Nearby was a group of local reporters. The reporters of all the big metropolitan papers had gone as soon as the verdict was given.

"Where will Fer go first?" asked Roger.

"He ought to go North. I plan to drive him to some station where he can get on a train without being recognized." Burdette spoke with decision.

"Duncan said the Union here wanted him to speak to them once."

"They must be crazy," said Burdette shortly. "He can't remain around here."

And then Fer appeared and a great shout like a wave went up from the people and even from the side streets where they couldn't see him.

The workers near the door, Dewey Bryson, Del Evans, who had always been his bodyguard, and the Trent boys, lifted him over the heads of the crowd into a waiting truck.

The old lawyer ruffled like an angry bird. "They've taken leave of their senses," he repeated. "He mustn't speak here." He fought his way through the crowd to the truck.

But Fer's clear voice, which was so effortless and carried so well, came to them all.

"I'm mighty glad to see you all and to be out," he said. "You've done a fine thing to welcome me." He said little more. Burdette flagged his attention.

"Tell 'em to go on home," he told Fer. "Tell Dewey to speak to 'em. You'll have trouble else."

So Dewey made a brief speech, and the crowd, peaceful and satisfied at a glimpse of Fer, began to seep away.

2

Nothing had happened and a great deal. A group of the Union boys followed Fer to the room that had been engaged for him.

Del Evans said, "We've got 'em on the go this time sure."

"They are all fixed over to Basil Schenk's to come out."

"When Mamie Lewes wuz shot, we all tuk an oath we'd not rest till we'd got 'em out ag'in."

"Now they know for sure they framed you, they'll come out all the more."

"They was awful bitter feeling all through the mills here when the mob shot Mamie Lewes. There was awful bitterness about all the mobbing. So we ben aworkin' night and day, inside the mills and outside."

"We ben havin' small meetin's in homes of folks we could trust.

Sence five weeks ago when Mamie Lewes was killed, there hasn't ben a night when they hasn't ben meetin's held through the mill hill."

"The women's ben takin' a part. Mis' Cuthbert and some of the Trent wives ha' ben organizing right smart amongst the women. We sent you all the word we could, but this last week things have ben coming to a head."

Fer spoke at last.

"When do you think they'll come out?" he asked.

"We're planning it fer Monday night when the shift's changed. We're planning to walk the plant out and let no one come back in."

"But if you're there, Fer, they'll be sure to come out. The sight of you would clinch everything."

"We'll hev you guarded night and day. They won't no mobsters git you, nor no lynchers."

Roger knocked on the door. "Fer," he said, "Burdette's car is ready. He thinks you ought to start."

"I'm not going with him," said Fer.

"What do you mean?"

"I can't go, Roger. There's something the boys want me to stay over for."

"Where are you going?" Roger asked sharply.

"Well, I guess after nightfall I'll be going into Stonerton to the old mill hill."

"You can't," Roger cried. "You can't do it! You're crazy, Fer!"

The big mill boys sat silent and waiting. They looked at Roger without hostility because they knew he had no power with Fer.

"Do you know what you're doing?" Roger cried.

"Yeah," Fer said quietly and with the air of a person profoundly weary. "Yeah, I know what I'm doing. But you see, Roger, I got to."

The young Trents lived in a house on the side of the mill hill which was owned by Trent's brother-in-law. It was larger than the houses on the mill hill and had two extra rooms. The house was not conspicuous. It had shrubbery in front of it and stood off by itself a little. It had therefore been used lately as one of the places for Union meetings. All the shades would be drawn, not a glimmer of light would appear on the outside, yet at different times, ten or eleven men would drift in by the back door.

It was here that Fer stayed over Sunday. Only a few people who Fer needed to see or whom he knew best were allowed to come. It was not supposed to be generally known that he was here. The press had given it out that he had gone North after his release. Burdette had made the statement definitely and had washed his hands of the whole affair.

3

It was impossible to keep news like that still. The rumor of his presence sped through the mill village. People whispered to one another:

"Fer's here!"

"Where's he at?"

"Dunno. They say he's here."

It was as if his presence were the light, and flickered and rippled through the community. But it was light which was uncertain. No one was sure but those who had seen him and who had held their tongues.

"Is there any one you want to see, Fer?" Del Evans asked him.

"Yeah, I wanta see Lissa Thorn. She came every day to the trial."

Lissa sped across town from her house. She streamed along so fast, so ardently, that people whom she knew cried:

"Where bound, Lissa?"

She wanted to cry back, "To Wilcox's! To Fer! He sent for me!" It simply seemed unbelievable that Fer had sent for her.

It seemed odd to Fer himself, who was engaged all day long with plans of the walkout, planning, advising, listening, and then suddenly sending for Lissa in much the spirit that a man may leave a hot conference room for a breath of clear air. It was as if Fer said suddenly:

"Hang it all, I've been in jail for months. I haven't spoken except through bars or in the court room, to a girl. I haven't got a girl. But just for a minute I want to speak to some one young and lovely. Just for ten minutes in the midst of this responsibility which has rolled over me."

The boys, too, wondered at Fer's sending for Lissa.

"I didn't know that Fer set store by Lissa Thorn."

"No, me nuther."

"He must though, to send fer her now."

They left them alone.

"Hello, Fer," said Lissa. "I'm glad you're out."

"I'm glad to be out. It was nice of you to come, Lissa. I wanted to see you."

She flushed. "I was right glad to come. I'm right glad you do want to see me."

"I saw you all the time in the courthouse."

"I got there every day, somehow. I never knew you noticed me."

Such unimportant things were all they had to say to each other.

"I hear you been workin' with the women."

"Yes, me and Mis Trent and a lot of others has ben workin' right through the houses in the mill hill. They are all ready, Fer."

"Yes, seems like this time it's true."

4

The walkout had been carefully planned. The workers individually had been gotten back to work by promises of the management which had not been fulfilled. It had been spread, through the foremen, that old employees would not be discriminated against for Union activities, since they did not recognize a union. These unofficial promises had not been kept. There was discrimination. Ma Gilfillin and Daisy West could get no work. Nor could Jolas or Binney nor any other of the Jolas girls.

The plan was for the outgoing shift to strike. A strong picket line was to be formed by the strikers on the incoming shift. The outgoing strikers and the picket line were to prevent the scabs from entering the mill. The plan had been carefully guarded. But it was impossible to guard a plan as widespread and which affects hundreds of people.

The new sheriff, Ike Cooney, had deputized a score of men, the foremen of the mill, mill workers loyal to the management, and others. Before closing time in the mill, the word had spread from room to room. The foremen patrolled nervously. It was no use. The moment had come, the day had arrived. The day that had been planned for and prayed for was here.

The men and women rose up with a shout from their work, left their looms and spindles, and called through the mills:

"Strike! Strike! Strike!" Some one started the cry,

"Fer's outside! Fer's here!" and from the mill windows went out the cry, "Fer! Fer! Fer!" A big shout.

It was taken up by the crowd gathering outside. The whole paling heaven was filled with the sound of Fer's name. Was he actually in the crowd at the moment? It made no difference: He was there. What he stood for was there.

"Union!" came the next cry. "Union! Union!" from the hundred-throated crowd.

A tremendous excitement shook the people inside. The foremen rushed around, placating, begging, and were brushed aside unregarded. The strike now was in spate. The men and women were rushing out of the mills. The picket line was swinging up. Sheriff Cooney said:

"Keep open this yere gateway! I cain't hev you pluggin' up this yere gateway."

A voice cried insolently, "Shurf sez, 'You all leave a line fer the scabs to march in!' "

At that, another cry went up.

"Woof! Woof! Woof!" the bark, the cry, that was the voice of an animal whose derision was human. A gay, awful, terrifying noise it came,

"Woof! Woof! Woof!" Down the street, others woofed back.

Now the truck loaded with scabs had driven up. People started to go toward the mill. It was the showdown. Who had strength, the strike or the sheriff?

The woofing rose to a roar. A stone cracked against the glass of the mill.

"I don't want no trouble! Keep this open," the sheriff called.

Another stone flew. Fer's voice rang out, "Keep 'em out of the mills!"

"There's Fer! Fer! Fer!" The crowd took up the name and again Fer's name filled the heavens. And suddenly there was a knot of men swaying together.

5

There was a pistol shot. A man threw his arms in the air, swung around and fell on his face.

There was a fusillade. Some one cried:

"Fer's hit! Fer's hit!"

Jolas, with his stick in the air, advanced toward the sheriff. Two deputies arrested him. The air was cut as with a knife with a high, sharp scream. It was Binney.

"They shot him ! They shot my father!"

A tear gas bomb exploded close between the strikers and the deputies. Now the shooting seemed to come from all sides. The strikers were fleeing in all directions. Young Cuthbert, running with his hands before his eyes, felt something strike him like a blow. He fell unconscious on the ground. A voice said,

"Fer God's sake stop shooting! There's enough done now!" People said it was the sheriff's voice. "There's enough dead now!"

The strikers were fleeing in all directions. The tear gas had cleared off. Everywhere the place was a shambles. Slightly wounded men were getting out of the way. But on the ground there were thirty wounded. How many dead, no one knew.

Fer, with a bullet through his heart, lay dead, his head pillowed on Del Evans' knee. Del Evans kept repeating in a half whisper, as though he could not believe his own words or his own senses,

"Fer's dead. They shot Fer an' he's dead."

The ambulances began to arrive. The scenes around the hospital were like those after a battle. People streamed up to the hospital gate, most of them to be turned back. They milled around, weeping and crying. Frightful details began to seep through the crowd.

Old Jolas, so gentle, so well beloved, had been thrown on the operating table, his handcuffs still on him. He had never regained consciousness. He had died in his handcuffs. The rumor persisted that he had been shot after he was handcuffed. Dewey Bryson said he saw him through the smoke, his old head bloody and wobbly as they beat him after they handcuffed him.

Binney sat outside, her thin little pointed face between her narrow hands, sobs shaking her shoulders perpetually. They could not get her to go away. She sat outside, as though on watch, sobbing her life away.

Young Lucy Trent had gotten inside the hospital. Trent was wounded to death. There was no hope for him from the first. In another room, Cuthbert was bleeding his life away from a frightful stomach wound, his mother sitting beside him.

Del Evans' father was hit. They didn't expect him to live the night.

6

The reporters flowed back into town. By night every one was there. The rumors had sped that Fer had not gone North, that he was still South. But the secret of the walkout had been kept. Only one of the local men, Otis Bingham, had seen the shooting. He had been down on the picket line when suddenly the sheriff and the deputies had fired. He was completely taken out of the reporters' usual hard-boiled pose. What he had to say was that the attack had been utterly unprovoked, none of the picketers or strikers had had guns, not a shot had been fired by the mill workers.

Fer was to be brought to the Thorns' house. It is the law that a body must be claimed by relatives. They had been afraid that an effort would be made on the part of the mill to prevent Fer being buried with the rest. Lissa, weeping, and dressed in black, accompanied by her mother, claimed Fer. They were to have been married, she said. No one questioned it, though all the people nearest Fer knew this was not so. Though every one, too, knew that Lissa was the only one he had asked to see on that Sunday outside of those who had union business with him.

By afternoon the streets of the town were absolutely quiet. Every one was indoors. Little knots of people in the mill hill only talked together. The governor had again ordered the militia and it had arrived in the afternoon. Up in the hospital were still groups of anxious relatives visiting or making inquiries. Dick Durgan, Roger and Hoskins and the other reporters marched in and were taken to one of the wards of the more lightly wounded.

Three very young boys lay with bandages around their heads and arms. They had not been strikers, they had merely been bystanders, and for that reason the hospital authorities let the newspaper men talk to them. From them came the most damaging of all the stories. They had no ax to grind, no reason for exaggeration. They were just coming along and stopped to watch.

"Shurf,—he giv order to fire."

"I seen the pistol smokin' in his hand. I seen them other deputies crack down. People were runnin' right and lef'."

"Did they fight back?"

"No one fit back. Every one jes' run."

"They fired right into the crowd. No one hadn't done nothing to 'm."

"Was the crowd rioting?"

"No, sir, they was not riotin' at all. Everything was quiet but they was woofin' like they al'ays done on the picket line."

"And we started for to run and git hit, too."

"They say Del Evans' father was shot so close to that it burned his clo's."

There had been no such slaughter in a labor encounter in years.

26

1

IN THE NIGHT Dan Trent died. Roger went early to the older Trent's. Old man Trent was out. Old man Trent had been peace officer for many years. He knew every one of the young people in the mill. He had always urged among them moderation and law-abiding methods, but he had upheld the strike. Mrs. Trent was there alone. Two or three of the grandchildren were playing unconcernedly in one corner of the kitchen. A fire was burning on the hearth. The room was swept and clean. Mrs. Trent had been getting up early to prepare for the visit of death.

"I want for him to be brought here. He was jest boardin' down to Wilcox's. It's right and fittin' he should be brought back home. He ain't been gone more'n a year. He ain't been ma'ied long. He's the youngest. He's the baby. I want him to be brought back."

She was a little woman, contained, iron in her grasp on herself, and she spoke quietly. Then her voice rose, still contained, but terrible in its intensity.

"Ef you want to know how my Rob died, you go down to see his brother Jim. Jim saw 'em shoot Rob. I seen him die. I was with him up to the las'. He was aholding my hand to the last. Jim'll tell you how they killed the others. He seen 'em hit old man Jolas with a blackjack after they had him handcuffed."

Roger went to the older Trent's. Jim Trent was one of the few mill workers who owned their own homes. The Trents as a family were better off. They were dark, energetic men, clever and high tempered. Jim Trent was in his back yard. Near him his young brother Joe and a group of neighbors surrounded him. Tears were sliding down his face and he didn't know that he was crying. From the back yard you could look across the mountains. The red road which ran past the house was quiet. There was an unnatural quiet on the mill hill. In contrast with the calm of the day and this beautiful and peaceful landscape, was this little knot of grief in Jim Trent's back yard.

"They blinded him with gas first. He was out there on the picket line. Shurf, he tol' us to disperse and then he threw gas, and Robert, he put his hands up to his eyes and then I heard a shot and I couldn't see who fired it. Rob, he fell into my arms. 'I'm done fer, I'm shot,' he sez to me. There wasn't no chance fer 'm from the first. He jes' bled his life away."

"Did he suffer much, Jim? Did they tek good keer of 'm?"

"I reckon they done what they could. The blood soaked through everythin'. They couldn't stanch him."

"Seem's if Lucy Trent knew all the time. She's ben scared ever sence the strike come. Seems Lucy was warned."

"They wasn't no chance for Rob ever," Jim replied.

2

Lights were shining in the mill village east of old Stonerton. Folk were waiting on the dead. Folks in cars going on a strange round of visits. A steady trickle of visitors going "visitin'." To the Thorn's, to Evans', to Jolas', to young Robert Trent. Three men lay dead with gaping wounds in their backs. Some were shot so close to that the doctors testified that their clothing was burnt and the skin blackened.

All the mill hill was visiting to men shot down by Sheriff Isaac Cooney and his deputies as they dispersed the picket line in front of the Basil Schenk Manufacturing Company. There were two more mortally wounded, fifteen others received slighter wounds that necessitated them being taken to the hospital, and a half score others with smaller wounds. People around East Stonerton were saying quietly:

"I'd hate to be in the sheriff's shoes."

Duncan had asked Roger to go "visitin' the dead." Dewey Bryson drove. Del Evans and Poddy Smithson were with them. They plunged in darkness down sheer hills. Roger could not tell where they were going. He could not recognize the streets down which Dewey drove precipitously.

They went to the Trents. The room was full of quiet visitors and watchers. People came in quietly and went out. Women sat near the fire with their heads in their hands and the stream of visitors passed quietly before the coffin. They were talking in low voices together in

another room. This was no ordinary funeral. This was no ordinary
mourning. This was murder. Mass murder in cold blood of many people.
Their only fault was that they had gone on strike in a demand for
slightly better conditions. For this they were lying dead and the mill
village was visiting.

"It's a sorry day," some one said quietly.

"We haven't seen the end of this," came the answer.

There were no threats of vengeance. There was an ominous quiet.
One tall old man, a friend of old man Trent, said significantly:

"Rob's got three brothers livin'."

They were all there, Jim, Joe and Luther.

Roger and the boys with him said good-by to the Trent boys and
to old Mrs. Trent. Her tanned and wrinkled face kept its composure.
No tears for her, but somewhere out of sight, Lucy Trent was crying.
Lucy Trent did not know there was a visitin'. All she knew was that
her young husband was dead.

The car wound dark corners and scaled rutted perpendicular hills.
Before Evans' house the road was so steep that they had to block the
wheels of the car. There was a pile of homemade wreaths of dahlias
on the porch. Inside in one room lay murdered Sam Evans. They called
him "old man Evans." He was only fifty-six. He had worked all his
life in the mills. For eighteen years he had worked for the Basil Schenk
Manufacturing Company. Now the sheriff had killed him.

Men came and men went before him. There were all the members
of his lodge coming and going. They looked at the quiet murdered face
and recalled how he believed in the union. They recalled too how he
was always a great one to laugh. Even now in death there were fine
humorous lines around his well drawn mouth which was always so
ready to smile. He had worked all his life long. He had raised sons
and daughters to work. He was a good friend and a good neighbor.
People loved him. Love and affection and children were all that old
man Evans had accumulated in his life. He owned nothing. A lifetime
of toil had gotten him a scant daily living and now they had murdered
him.

From the other room, the "warm-room," came the keening of Mrs.
Evans, terrible and monotonous. She had gone through the suspense
dazed and had broken at last. Roger had gone with some of the others
into the warm-room where a fire was burning on the hearth. Mrs.
Evans had been sitting between two of her friends, staring ahead of
her. Suddenly her head jerked back, her long bony hands were clasped
before her face, the cords of her neck stood out, and high, high notes

of grief, the highest keening note of the bereaved of the mountains, cut through the silence. People murmured sympathetically:

"It's good she broke."

"Yes, it's good she can cry. Better for her to cry, poor thing, than to set alookin' lak she's done ever sence Sam Evans passed. She sat by him two days and two nights and she never moved, and she didn't speak nor eat."

"She sot there til he'd passed."

The visitors came, the visitors went, a steady trickle of quiet fury. None of them would forget the sound of Mrs. Evans' crying. Their eyes promised that she should not grieve in vain.

3

There were no tears for Jolas. There in the warm-room, people were asleep. Binney and her two sisters and her married sister's child all asleep in one bed. Only two weeks before, Binney's married sister had come home with her little girl. Her man had gone. There lay Victor Jolas' daughters, worn out with grief.

Visitors retold the story of Jolas' death in whispers.

"They beat him after he was shot and handcuffed. He was handcuffed when he come to the operating table."

"Shurf sez he threatened him with a stick."

Victor Jolas was always lame with rheumatism and walked with a heavy stick.

And they wound up all this with:

"He was handcuffed when they took 'm on the operatin' table."

"Yes, he died handcuffed."

Death had opened all the doors in Victor Jolas' house. There were no proud reservations about his poverty to-night. They had nothing, for Jolas had been infirm and earned little. The girls were still young. The only grown one had had a baby.

Any one who wanted could see them crowded together, for the moment mercifully unconscious in sleep. Binney's pointed face, sharper than ever, looking crumpled on the bed, smaller than ever.

4

Thorns' next.

A great crowd at Thorn's. A great passing and repassing of people. People coming on foot to look once again on Fer. People coming in cars. Great piles of homemade wreaths of fall flowers. Piles of wreaths about Fer's coffin. Waiting with Fer were all the principal men and women of the Union. All around the room they sat quietly on chairs, waiting with the dead. They would be there all night, some would always be awake, waiting. At midnight new watchers would come to wait, to have the honor of waiting on the dead.

Beside Fer, Lissa sat, looking taller and older in a black dress, her dark, stubborn eyebrows a contrast with the childish contours of her face, her deep full voice, always contrasting with her youth. The voice of a mature woman speaking through a child's lips.

For her there was some solace in this masquerade. For her it was almost reality, the only reality her love for Fer had ever known. For the moment in the eyes of the mill hill, she belonged to Fer as she would have chosen to belong to him.

The Thorns had not suggested the subterfuge. Evans and Dewey and other leaders in the Union had thought of it. Now all the mill hill walked through the Thorns' neat rooms, sat a moment in the warm-room, where Mrs. Thorn, also in black, sat by the fire.

Roger stood looking at Fer a long time. Already he seemed remote and unreal. He had the waxen look of death that people confuse with peace. Lissa said in a low voice:

"Fer always sensed this was going to happen."

"Yes," said Roger, "I think he always did know."

"Dewey says that when the fellows told him about the walkout and how they wanted him to come, he looked strange at them."

"He didn't hesitate," said Roger.

"Fer, he knew. It was bound to come one way or another. He always knew. He was like that, he knew he was going to go."

There came to Roger a curious knowledge that this was true. That coming down from the North, Fer had known. That in the early days of the strike Fer had known, and that longingly he had turned his eyes away from his fate, to the North.

"I wisht I was North. I wish I was North where I know the folks."

Roger could remember the longing in his tone. But he had never thought of going North. He had gone on patiently on all the long path which led directly to this.

"Where's Irma now?" Lissa asked.

"Irma and Doris are both North collecting funds," Roger answered. It was strange that Irma wasn't here. Irma would have walked unfaltering into the fire. She would even have gotten a solemn exultation out of it. Fer had gotten no exultation, no feeling of the martyr's crown. Being killed with him was part of the day's work. You got killed if you had to.

Roger stood by Lissa. The mill village passed by the coffin gravely, one after another taking leave of the dead boy. There was a sound of wheels, a creak of brakes. More of the ceaseless line of friends had come. Every one in the mill village was "waitin' with the dead," was "visitin' " to-night.

27

_____

1

ON THE DAY of the funeral, eye witnesses were telling what happened at the shooting in the hearing held before Judge Sheldon. The courthouse of East Stonerton, with its two high pillars and its high flight of steps, was packed with mill workers, a solid roomful of American working people. Almost all of them were relatives, or at least friends of the dead men, and of these now lying wounded to death in the hospital. As Roger went in he saw Del Evans and Dewey.

"We came from the hospital," they said. "Cuthbert died this morning."

"There won't be time for him now to be buried with the others. It's too bad."

Roger had been to the hospital and had been admitted with Cuthbert's relatives. He was not conscious. An unusually handsome boy, his dark hair tossed back from his young forehead, a little mole on his neck and his cheek. He had always worked twelve hours a day, so he had given twelve hours a day to the Union.

Mrs. Cuthbert, sitting beside him, looked very young to be his mother. She sat there, composed, waiting to be of some service to him, keeping her grief off as long as he should be alive. She herself seemed removed from life. The intensity of her calm had something of the religious in it, as though she were being upheld by some "supernatural power." Now that life had gone out too. The only man Mrs. Cuthbert had to depend on had been shot to death.

Five men were dead and another was to die. Judge Sheldon, middle-aged, rather elegant, heavy-lidded, heavy eyebrows, indolent, asked questions. A fiery red-headed little solicitor asked questions like a popgun. The mill lawyers were able and keen. Rappalye, the bitterest cross-questioner of the North Carolina bar, slender, a gentleman, drooping mustaches, fanatical, deep-set eyes, heckled the witnesses unmercifully. Like a blade, his questions pierced him through and through.

Already Otis Bingham had testified that he had seen the sheriff and his deputies fire at the backs of the scattering mill workers who, blinded with tear gas, were trying to escape.

"I saw Sheriff Isaac Cooney hold Jolas with his left arm and fire a pistol point-blank into his body," a striker named Russell testified. He was a short, sandy-haired man with broad shoulders and long arms hanging down. He stood on both feet and looked with clear blue eyes at the lawyer.

The vicious cross-questioning did not shake him. By voice, by rumor, by innuendo, Rappalye, swift as a snake, attempted to undermine him.

Roger had never seen such brilliant, such inhuman efforts to undermine the integrity of a human spirit. There was no attempt to get at the truth. It was an attempt to browbeat, confuse, a skilled bullier playing his game magnificently against an unlearned mill hand.

Russell's examination was a triumph of a simple man armed with truth. Sure-footed, he walked through all the pitfalls and traps placed for him. Clearly he stated and restated the truth as he saw it.

"Didn't Minish shoot Jolas and didn't you pick up the gun which was used?"

"No, sir! *Cooney killed Jolas!* I was about eight feet away. It was like this."

In the midst of complete silence, Russell pointed his finger at the officers who had fired into the unarmed crowd. The people in the court room craned their necks forward.

"Cooney fired. I saw 'm. Nary shot was fired by the strikers. When Cooney quit his hold of Jolas, the man fell. The sheriff then begun shootin' at the strikers who were all runnin' away."

The workers all around were whispering together.

"Shore we didn't hev no guns! We ain't from the first ever packed a gun on the picket line."

It was established that the strikers had been entirely unarmed when the shooting occurred. Walter Minish testified next that the sheriff held and shot Victor Jolas. Minish was a long man, with big features, rough-hewn. He rose to his feet and pointing his finger at the sheriff, cried out with intense conviction:

"There is the man who shot our people!"

The sheriff all through the testimony sat back at ease. He was a burly man with a red face and a heavy jowl. Sitting on either side of him were some of the other arrested sheriffs, Wally Stoop and Abe Bland. The sheriff spoke to them from time to time, smiling, cupping his big thick hand before his thick mouth. Then he would sit back, lolling at ease, unconcerned. His manner indicated that nothing was going to happen to an officer of the law who had so nobly discharged his duty. He should worry. Nothing ever happened to sheriffs. Nothing did happen to him.

When the trial came he was released by the judge as being an officer of the law who had a right to employ whatever force seemed necessary to him in case of disorder.

When Lonny Coles was on the stand and testified in the face of all the virulent cross-questioning that he had heard the sheriff cry, "Shoot 'em down, boys!" Sheriff Isaac Cooney smiled. Was it security, Roger wondered, or stupidity, or bravado?

All the principal strikers were now arrested on riot charges and revolution against the state of North Carolina. Dewey Bryson, Del Evans, all the Trents, all the Cuthberts and Cathcarts. They were released upon their own recognizance.

2

The questioning went on ceaselessly. It went on the day of the funeral and it went on during the next days. Evidence piled up. The whole of Saturday morning was taken up by the quiet, assured testimony of Ned Stoll. The lawyers for the defense barked at him, bullied him, tried to confuse him. This was not possible. Quietly, positively, without drama, he told what he saw. He saw Cooney and the deputies standing at the mill gate. He saw the sheriff fire a tear gas bomb. That was the signal for trouble. Everything had been quiet. Sam Evans had said:

"Shurf, don't throw that there stuff in my eyes!"

Jolas raised his arm—the stick he always carried on account of his rheumatism, as though to protect his eyes. The sheriff collared Jolas and a deputy, Wally Stoop, squirted tear gas in his eyes.

By Saturday reporters and representatives of magazines had come from everywhere. The long cross-questioning was exhausting, the bullying of the clever lawyers became intolerable.

Ed Hoskins and Roger and one of the magazine writers went out into the lobby. Behind the court was a back way through the building so they could avoid climbing through the crowd.

"Do you think they'll let these men off?" Fallowes, the magazine writer, asked. "After they've given the other men twenty years?"

"Sure they'll get off. No sheriff's going to be convicted in this."

Curiously, there was no testimony as to who shot Ferdinand Deane.

He was standing at a little distance from the sheriff and the deputies, a little to one side. Lissa had been not far off. There was tear gas and Fer said:

"I guess I'm hit." Quite quietly he fell.

Dewey held his head and tried to lift him but already he was dead. There was nothing to show whether it was a chance shot like the shots which had wounded so many, or whether some one had taken deliberate aim. He had been outside of the center of the skirmish in which Evans and Victor Jolas had been killed.

3

A little man, very nattily dressed, was standing mopping his bald head. His face was almost purple. His watch chain stretched out over his round stomach. He had tiny and beautifully shod feet, broad shoulders for his height and a big head. An absurd, pompous little figure. He approached the magazine writer.

"You're Mr. Fallowes," he said. "You're from the North. I expect you must want to hear both sides of the case. I'm Mr. Schenk. I can prove to you that these people brought this upon themselves. Their leaders are to blame. I know you want to hear both sides of the case. I know you want to be fair. If you're fair, you want to blame the leaders. This Duncan gave an interview to the papers two weeks ago that there was going to be trouble. They've been trying to bully me, sir, to take back people disruptive to the industry, trouble makers."

"You've had no discussion with the Union, have you?"

"There is no Union!" he cried. "There is no such thing as a Union. It's a lot of anarchists and trouble makers leading people around by the nose. Why, the Basil Schenk Manufacturing Company has built up the prosperity of this town! We enlarged and made over this plant twelve years ago, employing twice as much labor as we did before and we organized to manufacture automobile fabrics. Never would have had any trouble. And now this! If you're fair you understand they have themselves to blame. You can go far and wide and you'll find the Basil Schenk Manufacturing Company measures up in wages and conditions with any other place. They don't have to work here if it's not so. It stands to reason they don't have to work here if it's not so. Everything was going on well till this convicted murderer Deane got out of jail." His face grew a darker and darker purple and he mopped it continually. His hands quivered but he stood plumb on his two little feet and built up about him an impregnable defense.

It was all clear to him why five men were dead and another dying, and why there were so many wounded.

"The sheriff and the deputies only did their duty," he kept repeating. "If you want to be fair, if you want to be fair, you'll understand that. I want to talk it over at length with you. I want to tell you the things that have been done in this community by unprincipled outsiders."

He had not spoken a word of regret for the deaths of the men and for their families. He saw one thing.

"He's the spokesman for all the comfortable people in Stonerton," Hoskins said. "Every one on the prosperous side will believe Basil Schenk. They may say that they're sorry for the deaths of these murdered men, but banked solid behind him will be every storekeeper, every business man, every one this side of the mill hill and their friends. The public opinion that counts, the public opinion that has money, that controls newspapers, churches, schools, business organizations, will all believe exactly as Basil Schenk does. 'They brought it on themselves.'"

28

1

THE GRAY CASKETS of the murdered men stood end on end in a long line. They were heaped with fall flowers, white dahlias and red. There were homemade wreaths, picked from people's fall gardens. People who had no gardens made paper wreaths.

It was a long line of death. Here was Ferdinand Deane. He worked in the mills when he was a boy. He had joined the Union early. He believed in solidarity and tried to organize the workers in the textile industry into unions. He was twenty-nine. This was his life history.

Next, Victor Jolas, sixty-seven. He had worked sixty years in the mill. He had seen the great spread of prosperity in Piedmont. He had raised a family, seen part of it die and part of it scatter. His share in the prosperity had been death.

There was Sam Evans, an old man at fifty-six. His story was like Jolas'. He was more fortunate. He had had strong sons round about him.

Young Trent, twenty-three, just married, handsome, gay, beginning things, beginning life with hope and happiness. As yet he had everything. He had youth, gayety and love.

Four open coffins stretched end on end. All were gray and all were piled with flowers and wreaths. Up in the hospital Cuthbert lay dead too. Cuthbert was eighteen. This was the price paid for unionism. This was the end of the long struggle. Death by shooting at the hands of the law.

2

The open coffins stood before the speaking stand in the grounds of the second tent colony where the workers had listened to the speaking at their meetings and at the barbecue. Well, there was to be a speaking to-day too. Painted on the stand was "Textile Workers Union of America" in high red letters. There were Union flags. There was no American flag. They had had American flags at other meetings.

Randolph Gaylord, down from the North for the funeral, had said, "What the hell do we want of an American flag to-day?" They had been meeting in Jim Trent's house, half-dozen Union men charged with the details of the funeral.

"No," said Del Evans, "I guess we'll do without the American flag this time."

The others had nodded silently. An American flag seemed an irony to the strikers with all the roads to the mill patrolled with soldiers. With their friends and relatives lying there dead, shot in the back by the sheriff who represented law and whom they had helped elect to office.

In front of the speaking stand, behind the coffins, the hill stretched upward gently. Pine trees shaded it. A natural stage, and a natural amphitheater was formed here. A red road ran not far below the speaking stand. Usually a quiet and deserted place, now choked with motors and trucks, which had brought people, from far and near, to the burying. Facing the speaking stand from the hillside one could look off to not far distant hills.

Behind the flower-heaped coffins, a line of fifty people sat on chairs, men and women and children. They were dressed heavily in black, a deep border of black beyond the coffins. These were the relatives of the murdered men, their sisters, mothers, children, wives and kinfolks. They sat there, some of them dry-eyed, some of them weeping. Up the shaded hillside were over a thousand people, an audience of work-worn faces. They came there dressed in what poor best they had. There they were, spread out before one, quiet as though they were going to have their pictures taken, the docile, one hundred per cent American workers. They were now paying the price of having dared to rebel against the stretch-out, the day of twelve hours and twenty minutes, and an average weekly wage of twelve dollars.

3

Their dead lay stretched there in a long line, as a warning to them, what happened to American workers when they are no longer "loyal and docile."

The flower girls were around the coffin, bringing wreaths. They were dressed in white cotton dresses and had wide cotton bands on their sleeves, "Union Workers" in red letters on the band. They gathered near the speaking stand and their thin voices which were both piercing and uncertain, rang out in "Nearer, My God, to Thee." A thin, fine noise of weeping came from the line of black-clad, mourning women, a high keening of grief. They had been quiet a long time. The quiet weeping became unrestrained. The high keening grew loud. The whole audience rocked. A terrible protest of grief echoed from the quiet hillside. For a minute the little thread of singing mingled with the sound of the weeping men and women.

Duncan from the speaking stand made a gesture to the girls. The singing paused. Grief like a wind blew through the audience. The mourners became quieter. The singing girls struck up a Union song, one of Mamie Lewes' songs. It gave them a minute to get hold of themselves. But the black line was never quite quiet. You could see Mrs. Evans, blinded with tears, shaking with sobs, uncontrolled. There was Binney, her little peaked face pale, her eyes showing out large, deep shadows under them. Sleep hadn't restored her. Her eyes looked out frightened as though looking at some horror in which she couldn't believe. Young Lucy Trent crying too, with a high keening noise, the ritual cry of simple people in the face of death. A strange funeral, more a demonstration than a funeral. There were several preachers that spoke and many Union people.

Funeral speeches. Brother Williams, the bearded itinerant preacher from the hills, visiting Northern clergymen sympathetic to labor, who had hurried here to bring the sympathy of their organizations, Union people from the North, and those of Stonerton, all speaking on one platform.

There was one local preacher. One small church in East Stonerton did not stand on mill ground and without mill owners' money was meagerly supported by its own parishioners. He was the single clergyman of the South who was upon the speaking stand. He was there to bury the dead.

It was a strange funeral. The words that people spoke were no longer meaningless words in this audience. It was as though the consciousness of this audience had been flayed with grief and horror. Each word that was spoken made an echo among the people, as though in answer they made a silent promise:

"These men shall not have died in vain."

This was the keynote in which all spoke. What else could they say? They had died for the Union as surely as men on the battlefield give their lives for the country. For that moment the Union was the country of all these people present. They belonged to no other.

It was as though the use of gunfire had shot a hole into peoples' consciousness. This funeral on a distant hillside in North Carolina was not isolated. It was as though there were also present all the textile workers of Piedmont and of all the South. Who was there to-day among the textile workers of the South who was not talking of these dead men? Where were the people who were not also mourning for their murdered brothers?

4

The people did not listen perfunctorily, but with a terrible intensity as though they and the speaker and the dead men and the Union were one thing. They were filled full with an emotion which swept them out into the world of workers, struggling like themselves for freedom. It seemed to Roger that there was another audience present here beside this which he could see, an invisible host of the other workers in America who were thinking to-day of these murdered people, and beyond that, workers in other countries who, too, had suffered and had also seen their dead, too, were here, a mighty army of them.

A strange thing happened on this hillside. Unspoken promises were made beside these open coffins, pledges to build for the dead men a Union. There were also unspoken pledges never to forget—unspoken promises of vengeance. Murdered by the mill owners, murdered by the officers of the state, they would never be forgotten by the mill workers of the South. There was but one monument to build for them, a victorious Union.

Brother Williams, the bearded preacher from the hills, prayed. He knelt down on the speaking stand, stretched out his arms like a cross, closed his eyes tightly and lifted his face to heaven.

The emotion mounted and mounted until this fantastic thought invaded Roger that they were there partaking of a sacrament of vengeance. But a vengeance not of gunshot for gunshot, but the right and dignity of human life against the crushing power of money.

"Oh," Preacher Williams said, "our dead lie here before us. Oh Lord, look down on these murdered brothers." His voice rose and fell. What mattered what he said. He spoke now in the language of their emotions. He unleashed the emotions which had been gathering and gathering in that large audience.

They answered him, "Yes, brother," "True, brother," the women and men before the coffins bowed over again in weeping. Grief blew over the audience like a strong wind.

5

Now there was a stir among the people. A little lane opened and a woman and another woman in black came walking slowly, supporting herself on the arm of some friend. She moved like a person barely able to walk. And yet, like some one walking in his sleep, as though she was surrounded by a sense of unreality.

It was Cuthbert's mother. He had died that morning early and now she was here as though in spirit they were burying him too with his comrades. A chair was brought for her and she sank slowly into it and looked straight ahead of her as though, like Binney, in amazement at what she saw. Her coming sharpened and concentrated the grief of those who stood so shaken in the presence of their dead.

The speaking was over. The girls with the brassards gathered now together before the speaking stand to sing. The audience joined in the hymns. They sang a long time. At last the hymn singing was finished too. The entire company of a thousand people then filed slowly, one by one, before the dead. Every man and woman and every child looked into the faces of their four murdered fellow workers. A slow trickle began from the middle of the assembled people. The rest stood quietly waiting their turn. Slowly, unendingly, they filed past the dead. There was no sound at all, as slowly, slowly, they walked past, each person looking at each one of the dead men's faces.

Amid dead silence, Binney walked before the coffins. She paused at each one to touch each forehead lightly. She bent over her father and kissed him. Quietly, composedly, still walking like some one in a dream, she went on.

But Lucy Trent lost all knowledge of herself. She had sat for two days beside her dying husband without a tear. Now she wept aloud her grief before the assembled workers of the mill village and they wept with her. At last people went slowly away in little groups.

"We haven't seen the last of this," men said gravely to one another.

6

The red holes in the ground had been filled up. Mounds of red earth were heaped over the dead. People in black around the graves. The sound of weeping as the last works were said over each man in turn. Almost the whole assembly filled the cemetery of East Stonerton. Now it was over.

Fer had not been buried with the others. His old father from the North had come down for the funeral service. He would be buried in a New England cemetery among the people he had been brought up with. Fer's father had stayed at the Thorns', and treated Lissa as though she had been his daughter. They liked each other.

Roger, Del Evans and Dewey Bryson walked silently away together. Dewey spoke:

"I wish Fer could have stayed yere with us instead o' bein' bu'ied in the No'th. He was a great man. We Southern textile workers oughta give him a great monument."

Del Evans said, "Yeah, he was a great man."

They had been Fer's bodyguards in the early days and slept in the room with him night after night to guard him.

Already the enormous arc of events had lifted Ferdinand Deane into the place of a great hero. And he had not been a hero. Roger and Del and Dewey Bryson knew that Fer, who had lived and fought for unionism and been killed for unionism, was a boy much like themselves. Now, Roger reflected, Fer was already a legend. The memory of him was already being obliterated.

He wasn't yet buried and already they had forgotten the living, breathing Fer, with his faults and uncertainties, with his kindness. He was a great man already, a hero. Not even in Irma's mind would he remain real! Not even in Roger's mind. They would talk about him and idealize him and, therefore wipe out and create in his place an unreal hero, a composite of all virtues which he had not possessed.

Roger's heart was twisted within him with sudden grief. What had been the use of it all? Was there any use in people's striving, was there any use in fighting the great machine of wealth?

Seven lives sacrificed, others possibly dying. Women and children thrown out of their homes. What had been the good? These people who had fought, had they gotten anything?

The managements had announced a shorter day, a little larger pay check. It didn't seem worth it. All this pain, all this grief, all this effort which had led only to death.

Dewey said, "We'll be goin' right on from yere now to build the Textile Union."

"Yes," said Del, "we're agoin' to bring solidarity to the whole South. We cain't lose no time. We gotta make a Union."

"Yeah, so's they all, an' Mamie Lewes too, won't have died fer nothin'. We jes' gotta go on."

Yes, thought Roger, that's the answer. "We jes' gotta go on." We can't help ourselves. They are a part of a flowing stream of workers. They had no choice in the matter. They had to go on.

And he had to go on, too. He had lost his own class; he could never belong in their class of the workers. He was without country now, and yet wherever they went, whatever their destination might be, he had to go with them.

THE END